ACKNOWLEDGMENTS

Dear Race Fan,

What a year in racing 1995 brought us! In February, who would have expected the triumvirate of driver Jeff Gordon, crew chief Ray Evernham and owner Rick Hendrick to band together and lead the rest of the competition by 309 points as early as the MBNA 500 at Dover and then hang on to win the NASCAR Winston Cup championship in only their third year together? Everyone knew Gordon would be strong, but to watch the 24-year-old driver claim the crown as the youngest champion in the modern era was an event for the ages! And who could forget the drama of Dale Earnhardt's late-season charge as he attempted to catch Gordon and claim another championship — which would have been his record-breaking eighth?

As always, the folks at NASCAR have done an excellent job and provided us with another tremendous, action-packed season. We would especially like to thank Mr. Bill France, Mr. Jim France, Mr. Brian France, Mr. Bill Seaborn, Mr. Paul Schaefer and Mr. Kevin Triplett. Neither this book nor the great door-to-door racing we enjoy every weekend would be possible without them.

Also deserving our thanks and appreciation are all the members of the NASCAR Winston Cup team at the R.J. Reynolds Tobacco Company. Special thanks go to Mr. T. Wayne Robertson, Mr. Jeff Byrd, Mr. Greg Littrell, Mr. John Powell, Mr. Larry Prillaman, Mr. Steve Tucker, Mr. Curtis Gray, Mr. Chris Powell, Mr. Dennis Dawson and Mr. Randy Chapel.

Mr. Bob Kelly did another fantastic job recounting all the events of the season for your enjoyment. The beautiful photography in this book is the work of a very accomplished group of photographers. Mr. Don Grassmann, Mr. Ernest Masche and Mr. David Chobat, we thank you.

But our greatest appreciation and gratitude is reserved for YOU, the NASCAR Winston Cup racing fans. You are the reason for NASCAR racing's phenomenal success; this book would not have been possible without you.

Thanks for your support. Please enjoy.

• • • • • • •

NASCAR Winston Cup '95 Staff:
Publisher, Ivan Mothershead; *Associate Publisher*, Charlie Keiger; *Controller*, Lewis Patton;
Senior Editor, Bob Kelly; *Managing Editor*, Amy Vail; *Associate Editors*: Jeff Huneycutt,
Betty Alfred Mackinson and Ward Woodbury; *Art Director*, Brett Shippy;
Layout & Design: Mike McBride and Paul Bond; *Administrative Staff*: Henry Boardman,
Mark Cantey, Mary Cartee, Mary Costner and Carla Greene.

FOREWORD

"There could have been no better year to mark the 25th anniversary of R.J. Reynolds' association with NASCAR and the NASCAR Winston Cup Series. The company's Winston brand and its promotional programs have been instrumental in the success and growth of the series over the past quarter-century ..."

For many reasons, the 1995 NASCAR Winston Cup season will be remembered as one of the finest years of competition in the history of our sport. The year-long battle for the championship was a classic — the firmly established championship team of Richard Childress and Dale Earnhardt battled a group of enthusiastic youngsters fielded by Rick Hendrick for Jeff Gordon tooth and nail. The struggle raged until the final stages of the season and, indeed, the final race of the year, when the title was at last decided.

We also saw the emergence of a new group of stars: Gordon led a pack that included Ward and Jeff Burton and Bobby Labonte. Both Bobby and Ward visited victory lane this season for the first time.

This year's battle for the MAXX Rookie of the Year championship was yet another struggle between two worthy contenders that went down to the wire. Both Robert Pressley and Ricky Craven will undoubtedly be part of the NASCAR Winston Cup scene for years to come.

Right from the beginning of the season, when Sterling Marlin took Kodak and the Morgan-McClure team to the Daytona 500 winner's circle for the second-straight time, it was clear that the team had become one of the best in the business. Throughout the season, Sterling's consistent finishes made him a contender for the championship.

And Sterling wasn't the only driver making his fans proud. Hundreds of thousands of Petty Enterprises fans had reason to cheer with the performance of the STP Pontiac in 1995, during which Bobby Hamilton rapidly became one of the fastest drivers on the circuit.

Dale Earnhardt's triumph at Indianapolis Motor Speedway and Ernie Irvan's successful return to the sport at North Wilkesboro only added to the excitement of one of the best years in the history of the sport.

There could have been no better year to mark the 25th anniversary of R.J. Reynolds' association with NASCAR and the NASCAR Winston Cup Series. The company's Winston brand and its promotional programs have been instrumental in the success and growth of the series over the past quarter-century, and we are proud to have been associated with Reynolds and its personnel. They have always been a credit to our sport.

One of the most important factors in the success of the 1995 season is directly attributable to you, the fan. Tracks have continued to expand, and you, by being part of the race weekend crowd, are responsible. Your enthusiasm for and support of the sport we all love continues to amaze the sports world and make NASCAR Winston Cup racing the fastest-growing sport in the world. As always, we thank you; we hope you enjoy this book as it brings back memories of a great season of competition.

Bill France
President
National Association for Stock Car Auto Racing

TABLE OF CONTENTS

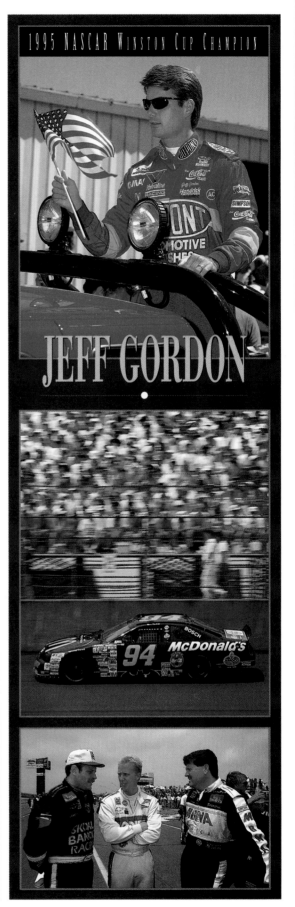

1995 NASCAR WINSTON CUP CHAMPION

JEFF GORDON

PREFACE

••••••

The 1995 NASCAR Winston Cup season marks the silver anniversary of R.J. Reynolds Tobacco Company's association with the world's premier form of stock car racing. And as has often been the case throughout their 25-year partnership, the start of another NASCAR Winston Cup season marked new beginnings for many of the teams which would contest the year-long battle for the championship.

The months between the November '94 season finale at Atlanta and the February 1995 lid-lifter at Daytona's 2.5-mile superspeedway became one of the busiest "off-seasons" in the history of the sport. No fewer than 18 drivers changed seats!

And the drivers weren't the only ones playing musical chairs. More than a half-dozen crew chiefs moved their tool boxes from one shop to another, at least six major car sponsors changed teams, six new car sponsors joined the series, four new teams prepared for competition and innumerable crew members changed uniforms.

As the teams assembled for preseason testing sessions, more than a half-dozen "new" faces began familiarizing themselves with their teams and cars as they prepared to campaign for the MAXX Rookie of the Year title.

Among the veterans, one of the biggest changes involved former NASCAR Winston Cup champion Bill Elliott. Elliott left his ride in Junior Johnson's famed "11" Ford to form his own team with his brothers Ernie and Dan and businessman Charles Hardy. When Elliott returned to his hometown of Dawsonville, Ga., he brought the McDonald's sponsorship from Junior's other ("27") car with him, and the new Ford team also welcomed additional sponsorship from Coca-Cola and Reese's candy. (Reese's moved to Elliott's red Ford from Jack Roush's Mark Martin-driven Thunderbird.)

Jimmy Spencer, the winner of two '94 races in the Johnson-owned McDonald's Ford, moved to the Travis Carter-owned Ford team. RJR's Camel brand remained the primary sponsor for the Smokin' Joe's team after Hut Stricklin vacated the purple and yellow Fords at the conclusion of '94. Travis also persuaded Cecil Gordon to leave the '94 championship-winning Richard Childress team and join the Camel Ford effort as shop foreman.

Budweiser, long a sponsor of Johnson's Fords, moved its colors to a Hendrick Motorsport effort for the '95 season; Bud would now sponsor Missourian Ken Schrader.

That left Johnson with two teams, no drivers and no sponsors, but it didn't take Junior long to fill in the blanks. He signed Brett Bodine to drive the "11" car and welcomed North Wilkesboro-based Lowe's home improvement stores as the major sponsor for that team. In short order, the red Budweiser paint was covered with the blue, yellow and red paint scheme of Lowe's. As for the "27" car, Hooters Restaurants agreed to replace the red and gold McDonald's colors with its own orange, blue and white paint. Loy Allen became Johnson's second driver.

Since Budweiser was now sponsoring Schrader's Chevrolets, the green and white Kodiak colors traveled to Larry Hedrick's team. The hood of the "41" car had become available when Meineke Mufflers decided to take its yellow and black colors to the Gary and Carolyn Bechtel-owned Diamond Ridge team. Hedrick also was delighted to welcome rookie contender Ricky Craven — recently graduated from the NASCAR Busch Series, Grand National ranks — as his new driver after Joe Nemechek departed at the conclusion of the '94 season. Nemechek formed his own team and signed Burger King as his sponsor for the full '95 season.

Since both Brett Bodine and crew chief Donnie Richeson had left the team (Richeson moved his tool box to the Stavola Brothers team to work with 1994 MAXX Rookie of the Year Jeff Burton), drag racing superstar and NASCAR Winston Cup team owner Kenny Bernstein had a green Quaker State Ford to fill. He immediately surprised many by signing 14-time World of Outlaws champion Steve Kinser as his driver. He then signed Rick Renn as his crew chief. (Renn had worked with Ricky Craven's NASCAR Busch Series team in 1994.)

Dale Earnhardt (signature)

(Opposite Page) In hopes of
repeating his '88 history, Bill
Elliott reunited with brothers
Ernie and Dan at the close of the
'94 season to field his own team
from his hometown of
Dawsonville, Ga. Elliott took
McDonald's sponsorship with
him when he left Junior Johnson's
effort and welcomed additional
sponsors Coca-Cola and Reese's
prior to embarking on the 1995
journey in his No. 94.

Seven-time champion Dale
Earnhardt may be hiding out in
his brand-new Monte Carlo in
search of a little peace and quiet,
but he hides from no one on the
track. In fact, Dale had already
made his goals for the 1995 season abundantly clear. First on the
list was a record-breaking eighth
championship, closely followed by
another goal near and dear to his
heart: winning the Daytona 500.

The A.G. Dillard Hardee's team and driver Ward Burton struggled in their freshman season on the NASCAR Winston Cup circuit after moving up from a successful Busch Series campaign in '93. But with an invaluable year of experience under their belts, all had high hopes for '95.

Bobby Labonte was prepared to start the '95 season behind the wheel of the Interstate Batteries Chevrolet. He would work with crew chief Jimmy Makar and car owner Joe Gibbs. Labonte had transferred from Bill Davis' Pontiacs and was replaced by rookie contender Randy LaJoie, who had competed in a few races in 1994 in Dick Moroso's Fina Ford. Labonte, a native Texan, was delighted by General Motors' demonstration of faith in him; GM was determined to keep him in the family and was more than happy to help him move from the Pontiacs to the Gibbs-owned Chevrolets.

The Interstate Batteries position had become available when Dale Jarrett moved from the green and black Chevrolets to the Texaco Havoline Fords owned by Robert Yates. Jarrett would act as an interim replacement for the recovering Ernie Irvan. Although he knew that he might drive for Yates for just one year, he took the ride in the Ford anyway. He felt he could win races and challenge for the championship in a car that, over the past few years, had proven to be one of the fastest and most reliable on the NASCAR Winston Cup tour. Jarrett's understanding with Yates was that when Ernie was ready to return to action, Irvan would re-assume his role as the team's primary driver.

Dick Trickle replaced Lake Speed as the driver for the Ford Quality Care Thunderbirds owned by Bud Moore.

The Moore ride had become available after Speed decided to "go a different direction" at the conclusion of '94. Moore was quick to entice Trickle to slide through the window of the tri-tone blue Fords.

Speed, meanwhile, became the driver and general manager for Harry Melling's Fords. Following the '94 New York NASCAR Winston Cup Awards Banquet, Speed and Melling welcomed Hormel Foods (its Spam product in particular) as the new sponsor of the famed No. 9 Fords.

Trickle's departure from the Active Trucking team left the Chevrolets open, but car owner Dean Myers and crew chief Mike Hillman quickly nominated '94 NASCAR Winston West Champion Mike Chase as the team's new driver.

When Wally Dallenbach exited the seat of the STP Pontiac two-thirds of the way through '94, John Andretti had come on board to finish the season. At the conclusion of the '94 season, Richard Petty named Bobby Hamilton as his new Pontiac driver. Hamilton moved to the legendary red and blue "43" car from the Dick Brooks/Felix Sabates-owned Kendall Pontiac. Hamilton was overjoyed by the opportunities the transfer presented and looked forward to continuing the progress the team had made in the final third of the previous season.

Hamilton's jump left the Kendall Pontiac seat open, but not for long. Almost immediately, Brooks announced that

Greg Sacks would be his '95 driver. Sacks moved to the "40" car from his USAir/Jasper Engines Ford, creating another vacancy. But once again, it took only a few days for car owners D.K. Ulrich and Doug Bawel to name rookie Davy Jones as the driver for the re-numbered "77" Ford.

John Andretti, meanwhile, who had begun the '94 season with Billy Hagan's team and ended it with some promising runs in the Petty Enterprises Pontiacs, chose to join a newly formed team for the '95 season. Former worldwide Ford Motorsports boss Michael Kranefuss and Indy car impresario and Lola car importer Carl Haas had joined forces, brought NASCAR Winston Cup champion crew chief Tim Brewer into the fold, signed Kmart and Little Caesar's Pizza as sponsors for the Ford team and signed Andretti as the driver for the red and white Thunderbirds.

Phil Parsons was named the driver for TriStar Motorsports (No. 19), where Loy Allen and Hooters had spent the '94 season. And longtime independent driver Jimmy Means signed ARCA driver Gary Bradberry as his full-time pilot. During the '94 season, several drivers had taken a turn behind the wheel of Means' Ford, but Bradberry's performance in the November Atlanta race had inspired Means to hire Bradberry on a more permanent basis. Means planned to have Bradberry run for the MAXX rookie title. In addition, Alltel Mobile signed on as the '95 season sponsor.

But wait, we aren't quite finished!

Kenny Wallace, who had done an excellent job while filling in for the injured Ernie Irvan in late '94, stepped up to the NASCAR Winston Cup level full-time with the help of his car owner, Fil Martucci. Kenny also planned to continue competing in the NASCAR Busch Series, Grand National Division, with his FilMar Fords. The black Martucci Fords would carry the familiar TIC Financial colors in NASCAR Winston Cup competition and be decked out in Miller's Red Dog beer colors in the NASCAR Busch Series.

After Harry Gant's retirement, the Leo Jackson-owned Skoal Chevrolets were turned over to Robert Pressley. Pressley would join Kinser, Craven, Bradberry, Jones and LaJoie in what was expected to be one of the best MAXX rookie battles in recent memory.

With Meineke on board as his team's sponsor, Alabama native Steve Grissom couldn't wait for the season to start. Not only would he be competitive in the Bechtel-owned cars, but the team would be reliable thanks to the signing of Buddy Parrott as the new general manager and crew chief. When Parrott's decision to leave the powerful Penske South team and driver Rusty Wallace was announced late in the '94 season, many of his fellow crew members were astonished, to say the least.

Parrott's departure left team owners Roger Penske, Don Miller and Wallace looking for a crew chief for the Miller Fords. After a careful search, the triumvirate chose Robin Pemberton as Buddy's replacement. Pemberton moved to the immaculate Penske South shop from the Liberty-based Roush effort that fields Family Channel Fords for Ted Musgrave.

Stepping up to take Pemberton's spot on the Roush team was Howard Comstock, who had been Musgrave's crew chief early in '94 before Pemberton joined the team from Kyle Petty's Pontiac effort.

Petty himself was champing at the bit to get the '95 season started. The black, neon-yellow and lime-green Mello Yello colors had vanished from the Felix Sabates-owned Pontiac, and Petty couldn't wait to unveil his new blue and red lightning-bolt paint scheme for the new season. Coors, after an absence of several years from NASCAR Winston Cup racing, had returned with the Coors Light brand, and Kyle was the Golden, Colo., brewery's new driver and spokesperson.

The circle was nearly complete.

MBNA Bank replaced Maxwell House Coffee as the sponsor for Bill Davis' Pontiacs and driver LaJoie. Cale Yarborough's team would carry new colors as well: RCA replaced Fingerhut's mail-order catalogs as the team's primary sponsor. Yarborough was also joined by Steve May, who would act as the new crew chief for the Fords driven by Jeremy Mayfield.

As the teams began final preparations for the season-opening Daytona 500, many questions circulated through the garage area regarding the huge number of changes that had occurred since the checkered flag had fallen on the final '94 race at Atlanta Motor Speedway.

But at least two questions were on everyone's lips: Could Dale Earnhardt win his eighth NASCAR Winston Cup title in '95? And how would the spanking-new Chevrolet Monte Carlos — returning to the battle after Chevrolet's Lumina model had carried the Bowtie banner to NASCAR's Manufacturer's Championship four times in its six years of competition — fare?

At the conclusion of the 1994 season, Hut Stricklin vacated his seat in the Smokin' Joe's Ford in search of a better opportunity. The 1995 season would provide not one, but a couple of those, as Hut moved from team advisor to driver of Kenny Bernstein's Quaker State Ford.

1995 NASCAR WINSTON CUP CHAMPION

In January, very few people, myself included, thought that I would be the one writing the Champion's portion of the 1995 NASCAR Winston Cup book.

But now, with the season complete, I am the one fortunate enough to have compiled more points than any other and have the chance to talk about the season that brought myself, Hendrick Motorsports and the team the NASCAR Winston Cup title.

One of the reasons why the championship is so special is that it's everyone's first, including Hendrick Motorsports' first since its inception in 1985. But it's also special because few expected us to win the title this year — least of all ourselves!

Last year, we won two races and a pole, and when we sat down in January of this year to make a list of goals for the DuPont team, we merely wanted to improve on what we had accomplished during 1994. Nowadays, if you win a single race during the season, you have accomplished a great deal. When you stop and think about it, that statement really rings true — all you have to do is look at the final rundown of the teams competing this year and see that many of the biggest teams and favorite drivers failed to win a single race for one reason or another.

So because of the level of competition in the sport right now, to win any race on the schedule is a huge accomplishment for a team. Since we had won two races in 1994, our goal was to win three this season. We also wanted to win a Busch pole so we would be eligible to compete in the Busch Clash. We thought those were realistic goals for our team, but on the "wish list," we wrote down five race victories and more than one pole. We hoped to find enough consistency within the team to enable us to finish in the top 10 in the point standings, so in that column on the "wish list," we wrote down a top-five position in the final standings.

For a team as young as ours was at the beginning of the season, we felt that the goals were realistic, and that with a little luck, we might also meet the goals on the "wish list."

Little did we know what was in store for us!

One of the biggest question marks we had as we entered the season was the new Chevrolet Monte Carlo. We were all pleased that we had a new car to work with. Our early testing with the car in Texas showed that it was really fast. But we didn't really have anything to compare it to, so when we went to Daytona in February, we really didn't know what to expect.

As it turned out, the Monte Carlo was a great surprise to everyone! It was good on every type of track — from the biggest superspeedways to the tightest short tracks to the most twisty of road courses. It was better than what any of the Chevrolet teams had expected, and it proved to be a major asset to all the teams as the season went on.

At Daytona, right out of the box, our team was clicking. We had a car capable of challenging for the victory, but the problem on pit road — when the car fell off the jack — disturbed the aerodynamics. The following race at Rockingham, though, really set the tone for our team for the remainder of the season. Instead of getting down on each other for the Daytona problem, we instead learned from the mistake and propped each other back up. We won the pole and then dominated the race to score our first win of the season — a great way to come back from the Daytona mistake.

At Richmond, we had a problem with the fuel pump, but we came right back the following week by winning at Atlanta. At Darlington, although we had one of the best cars in the field, we ended up having problems. Once again, we came right back the following race at Bristol and won our first short-track race!

We couldn't help but look at each other and wonder what

JEFF GORDON WOULD LIKE TO THANK ALL OF THE FOLLOWING:

John and Carol Bickford (Jeff's Parents), Lee and Todd Osborne (1st Sprint Car Builders), Bob and Janice East (Sprint, Midget & Silver Crown Builders), Dave Calderwood, Terry Winterbotham (Sprint Car Owner), Butch, Janie and Chris Smith, Rollie Helmling (Midget Car Owner), Dave Heitmeyer, Fred Ede Jr. & Sr. (Silver Crown Owners), Larry Nuber, Jack Hewitt, Brad Doty, Cary Agajanian, MPD Racing Products, Hugh Connerty (1st Busch Car Owner), Bill Davis & The Baby Ruth Team, Rick and Linda Hendrick, Ray, Mary and Ray J. Evernham, Ken Schrader, Terry Labonte, Hendrick 5 & 25 Car Teams, Ken Barbee & Motorsport Traditions Ltd., Ron Miller & Staff of Performance PR Plus, Employees of Jeff Gordon Inc., Max Helton & Staff of Motor Racing Outreach, **Rainbow Warriors & entire 24 Team:**

Ray Evernham	Crew Chief	Patrick Donahue	Tire Specialist
Mike Belden	Gas Man	Edward Guzzo	Chief Mechanic
Darren Jolly	Tire Carrier	Phil Hammer	Suspension Specialist
Chad Knaus	Rear Tire Changer	Morey Herendeen	Paint and Body
Michael Landis	Tire Carrier	Doug Jackson	Cylinder Heads
Barry Muse	Jackman	Steve Mann	Mechanic
Andy Papathanssiou	Catch Can	Eddie Nawrooki	Paint and Body
Mike Trower	Front Tire Changer	Tim Smith	Left-side Tire Changer
Dave Tatman	Spotter	Gary Wall	Scorer
Charlie Siegars	Engine Builder	Brian Whitesell	Team Engineer
Peter Bingle	Head Fabricator	Pete Yankopoulos	Paint and Body
Bill Deese	Fabricator		

In a virtual repeat of 1980 history, upstart Jeff Gordon stole the title from veteran Dale Earnhardt by taking it "one race at a time." And speaking of history ... When NASCAR and RJR joined forces in 1970, their 1995 champion, Jeff Gordon (here posing with the Winston Cup and wife Brooke), had not yet been born.

Rather than recruit a cast of "all-stars," Jeff's crew members were chosen, to a large extent, based on their desire to work and, more important-ly, win. Their "Refuse to Lose" attitude translated into success on the race track, and they were rewarded with the highest honor in the world of stock car racing: the NASCAR Winston Cup championship.

was going on! Six races, three victories and chances to win in the other events! Things were really clicking, and some-times, it seems that when you get on a roll like that, every-thing you do is right. That's the way the season started.

Looking back, I think that 22nd-place finish at Daytona was pivotal because we fell out of the spotlight for the first few races of the season. It gave the team a chance to jell. We had won some poles and some races — in fact, had accomplished our goals for the season already! But still, no one looked at us as contenders for a championship. Most everyone felt that our team, although competitive, was too young to survive the year-long battle for the title.

We weren't thinking about a championship at that point, either. We were concentrating on trying to win each time we went out on the track, and if we couldn't win that day, we wanted to get the best finish possible and be con-tent with it, knowing full well that we couldn't win every race.

After the Winston Select 500 at Talladega, we were tied for the point lead with Dale Earnhardt, but because we had won more races than Dale had at that point in the sea-son, we won the $100,000 bonus from R.J. Reynolds, given to the point leader after the first third of the season. Had Dale finished a single position higher in any of the races in the first third of the season, or had we finished a single position lower, he would have received Winston's check.

It was at that point that the first thoughts of a champi-onship began creeping into our minds. None of us talked about it with anyone because we knew there was a huge amount of racing left in the season. No one wanted to begin building expectations that we couldn't live up to.

We won The Winston Select — the first time a Hendrick Motorsports car had won that event — and it was a very special occasion for all of us. The way we won it — with a thinking move on the driver's part, rather than the driver trying to force the issue and cause a wreck — made the entire team begin thinking a title might be won.

A run of top-10 finishes began at the first Michigan race. After we won the Pepsi 400 at Daytona by beating Earnhardt in a one-lap shootout, we went to New Hampshire. We crashed in qualifying but went to a strong victory on the one-mile track. The win gave us the out-right point lead for the first time in the season and enabled us to win Gatorade's $50,000 award for the half-season point leader. It also seemed to crystallize the point race for us. When we left the New Hampshire mountains, we found ourselves really beginning to believe that we were a championship-contending team and that, given some breaks, we could be in the hunt at the end of the year.

The second half of the season was upon us, but unlike past years, this time, we ran really well. We kept surpris-ing ourselves with finishes, and sometimes, we really couldn't explain it. We'd have a 15th-place car and finish eighth, or a 10th-place car and finish third. Looking back, those were great accomplishments, and those were the finishes that eventually added up to a championship.

We knew that Earnhardt and the Richard Childress team were going to wind up and come at us with everything they had during the stretch run to the title. Everyone knew it.

And they did.

For us, Darlington and Dover turned out to be the races that stemmed the Earnhardt tide.

I've not been around NASCAR Winston Cup racing long enough to know all the tradition of the Mountain Dew Southern 500. I do know one thing, however. To win at Darlington is a huge accomplishment for any driver. To win the Southern 500 is even more special. We had a car that had survived a spin-out and a flat tire and wasn't the best-handling car on the track. Yet we were around at the end with a chance to win, and we were able to capitalize on it. That Southern 500 victory was one of the biggest I've ever had, and to have it come by beating Earnhardt under the pressure of the point battle made it even more special.

One thing about Darlington is that it's a true driver's track. You are never going to get your car perfect for both ends of the race track. If your car is great at one end, it won't be great at the other. So a driver has to find a way to make the car work the best he can and keep up with track changes by communicating with his crew throughout the afternoon. It is a great challenge, and that's why a victory at the track is so precious. All you have to do is look in the Darlington record book and see who has won there in the past ... you won't find very many surprises.

The victory at Dover in September was just as important to us, but for different reasons. We've been trying to win at Dover for the last three years because that's the "home" track for DuPont; its headquarters are located just an hour up the road. We had failed to get the job done in the past, but this time we did it in great style. We led 400 of the 500 laps and won in front of all the DuPont executives, including Ed Woolard Jr., the president of the company. He's retiring this year, so it was wonderful for all of us to give him a victory at his "home" track and help pay him and the company back for their unflagging support of our team for the past three years. The DuPont people simply have been great to work with, and I know we're all looking forward to working with them for years to come!

That Dover win was also extremely important to the team because it proved to us that we could win even in the middle of the title chase. We knew then, when we left Dover, that our team truly had become a championship-caliber team. It was our seventh win of the season, and to post wins at Darlington and Dover in September was a great confidence-builder at a time when we needed it.

Ray Evernham and Jeff Gordon teamed up for Jeff's first effort in a stock car, and they've been working together ever since. The two have also become extremely close off the track, and their friendship has only contributed to the team's success.

After we fought our way to third place at North Wilkesboro and had a more than 300-point lead on Earnhardt, a lot of people were saying that the championship was in the bag. I wasn't one of them. I knew that point leads could disappear just as fast as they had been gained, and no one on our team was sitting around, resting on his laurels. We knew that we had to remain focused and give our best effort because anything less than that would keep us from the title.

At Charlotte and Rockingham, we had problems. It was a good thing that the team members hadn't been passing the time by picking out the colors of their ties and cummerbunds for New York! The points we lost at those two races proved that the championship is never won until it is truly locked away.

At Phoenix, we ran a smart race and did exactly what we wanted to do. At the very least, we needed a good finish there; if everything had gone the right way, we could have clinched the title right there. As it was, we kept that black Chevrolet in sight and finished fifth. It put us in position to wrap up the title in Atlanta and also gave us the chance to race for a victory in the last race of the season.

I can't begin to tell you how hard this team worked during the season to make the Monte Carlos we raced as con-

sistent as they could be from race to race. And as the year went on, we learned from our mistakes and became more and more competitive.

When this team was formed, it wasn't done by recruiting a group of all-stars from different teams and assembling them to win the championship. Rather, the guys on the team were chosen because they wanted to work together and win races. Initially, none of them were stars in the garage area, but they have worked together and drawn from each other and become stars. No one paid much attention to them last year or even early this year. This season, it's been great to see the change as the crew members have begun to receive the praise and recognition they deserve and have worked hard to obtain.

I'll never forget the flak I took when I decided to join the Hendrick team three years ago. Drivers, other team members, some media and some other manufacturer's officials all said that I was going to a mediocre team and that the team would never win. The consensus was that Hendrick Motorsports had enough problems trying to run two teams and get them to win, let alone win with a third team. But I knew that the cars and engine program were good, and I also knew that Ray Evernham was coming

with me to be my crew chief. At the time, I just felt that the Hendrick opportunity was the right one for me. That has certainly turned out to be true.

So much of the success of the team this year is because of Ray. Everyone calls him crew chief, but he's a great coach and motivator as well. As the season wore on and we became the point leaders, Ray simply got more and more focused on what needed to be done on a race-to-race basis. Neither he nor any of our crew members sought out the public limelight. Instead, they concentrated on the task at hand, and Ray kept them thinking about how they could work together to make things stronger, rather than let the point race tear the team apart, like it has some teams in the past. He kept getting stronger and stronger throughout the season, and his example became something the entire team drew from.

Ray and I have been together since I started running stock cars, and it was strange that we met the way we did. I had been running in sprint cars and started looking around to try to figure out what I wanted to do next. Did I want to step out of the sprinters? I had seen some NASCAR Busch Series races on television and thought the racing was highly competitive.

I went to the Buck Baker School at Rockingham and, on the first lap in one of the school cars, I realized that this was where I wanted to be. It was the strangest thing. I had never been in a stock car before, but I knew right then and there that the high banks, the oval tracks, the power of the car and the intrigue of learning how to make this big, heavy thing do what I wanted it to was worth pursuing.

I was telling Buck that NASCAR Busch Series was something I wanted to do when he called another man over to join the conversation. His name was Hugh Connerty, and he was a former student of the school. He had liked his experience so much that he had gone out and bought a used Busch car and had it maintained at the school. When he could find time away from his restaurant businesses, he'd come to Rockingham and run some laps, just for fun.

Buck introduced us and asked Hugh if he'd mind if I took a few laps in his car. Hugh is a much bigger person than me, so after he said it was okay, we stuffed some pillows and pads down both sides of the seat and behind me, and I went out. On the third lap, I was more than a second faster than Hugh had ever driven the car, and when I got out, he said, "You and me need to go have lunch." We did, and he asked me if I'd like to drive his car in a couple of Busch races at the end of the year. I jumped on it, and that's how it started.

Leo Jackson was Hugh's son-in-law, so Hugh asked Leo if he'd give us a hand. Leo said yes and asked Phil and

Steve Barkdoll to help. Andy Petree, then Leo's crew chief for Harry Gant, said he knew this guy named Ray Evernham and asked him if he'd work as the crew chief for our little effort. Ray was quick to accept the offer. We worked on the body of the car, got an engine and went to Charlotte. We were fast enough to qualify, but the event got rained out. Next, we went to Rockingham, and we sat on the outside of the front row! People started asking, "Who is that kid?" and saying "Yeah, he's that kid who won on Saturday Night Thunder on ESPN in the sprint cars."

So Ray was there right from the beginning, and as time has gone by, he's become much more than a crew chief to me. We've become very good friends over the years, and that's just another reason why winning this championship is so special for all of us.

We all take a lot of pride in being the first team to win a NASCAR Winston Cup championship for Hendrick Motorsports. Winning The Winston Select for Rick and his wife Linda was pretty special, but being able to give him the opportunity to sit at the head table in the Waldorf-Astoria Hotel and climb onto the stage to accept the trophy as the champion car owner is something that every member of the crew is happy about. Rick is the one who has provided all the tools for us, and we're so delighted to be the ones to give him his first championship.

Another thing that makes it so special for me is that I have the opportunity to share it with my wife, Brooke. She's been such a great influence on me in the year since we've been married, and she's helped bring Christ into my life in a more meaningful way, as well as bring Him into our marriage and our home life. She's helped me understand how to have faith and be content with whatever the outcome is, and to realize that win or lose on Sunday, I'm a winner in the biggest race of all, no matter what happens on the track. She is such a source of strength for me, and with my life as hectic as it is, it's wonderful to have someone who is your best friend and who you love to share all of this with. We have some great memories of this season, and I'm fortunate to have someone like her to share them with.

I know that things are going to change even more now that we have won the championship. Life as we knew it will probably be changed forever. But we're going to try to make those changes good ones.

I'm looking forward to being the NASCAR Winston Cup champion; it's something I'm very excited about and very nervous about at the same time. I want to be a good champion and represent the sport and the championship

*A key component of any championship season is quick, consistent work on pit road, and the "Rainbow Warriors" distinguished themselves as being among the best at providing just that throughout their championship season. **(Inset)** In addition to their ability to communicate effectively, much of Jeff and Ray's success has been credited to Ray's ability to keep team members focused and motivated.*

well. I'm sure that I will get plenty of help from the people at Winston and NASCAR as well as at Hendrick Motorsports. They are all good people, and they will all offer good advice and help me make good judgments and choices during the coming season, I'm sure.

In closing, I'd like to salute the fans for their support of the sport. In the past, a lot of drivers have said that without the fans, there would be no sport for us to participate in. No one knows that better than me. Over the years, you have been the ones who have bought the tickets, supported the sponsors, tuned into the races on radio and television and helped the sport grow.

It wasn't long ago that I would go to a fan club meeting or an appearance and there would not be more than a dozen fans there. It enabled me to spend time with you on a more personal basis – something I really like to do. I know how important the fans are to Jeff Gordon, and I will continue to do my best to stay involved and make myself available to them.

I'd like to thank all of you – whether or not you are a Jeff Gordon fan – for your continuing support of the sport and the NASCAR Winston Cup Series. I am proud to be your Champion for the coming season, and I will do everything I can to make you proud that I had the opportunity to represent our sport in the champion's role.

Thanks again for your support of NASCAR Winston Cup racing.

Jeff Gordon
Jeff Gordon
1995 NASCAR Winston Cup Champion

DAYTONA 500

DAYTONA INTERNATIONAL SPEEDWAY
FEBRUARY 19, 1995
•••••

Throughout the winter months, Dale Earnhardt quietly had celebrated his seventh NASCAR Winston Cup title. He had savored the accomplishment of tying Richard Petty at the top of the championship heap. Dale knew that somewhere, his father, the late Ralph Earnhardt, was grinning with the knowledge that the Earnhardt name was now alongside the Petty name in the NASCAR record books.

After clinching the championship at Atlanta in November, Earnhardt and Richard Childress had discussed their goals for '95. For both driver and car owner, winning the 1995 championship was right at the top of the list. All efforts, once again, would be geared toward securing the most prestigious title in the world of stock car racing. Of course, they said, winning at Daytona would be a great way to start their championship quest. But they also pointed out that Daytona was a single race in a ten-month series of events that counted toward the ultimate goal, and every race paid the same number of points.

At Daytona, Dale Earnhardt is buckled into his "office" and prepared to begin his defense of his NASCAR Winston Cup title. He would not win the Daytona 500 for the 17th time, but he would have an awesome SpeedWeeks nonetheless. (Right) This time, it was Sterling Marlin who beat Earnhardt across the line. Marlin proudly displays the winner's trophy after notching his second-consecutive Daytona 500 victory.

But anyone who has ever spent a moment of time with either Earnhardt or Childress, or, for that matter, any member of the Goodwrench Chevrolet crew, knows that a victory in the "Super Bowl" of the sport — the Daytona 500 — ranks just as high as the championship on the team's list of goals.

And now, for the 17th time, Earnhardt watched as his car was unloaded from the transporter in Daytona's garage area. He had started this race 16 times in the past and, more than once, watched the race title slip from his grasp in the waning laps.

When asked if this was the year he would finally win the Daytona 500, his gaze turned from the black and white Chevrolet Monte Carlo and that wry, trademark grin deepened the smile crinkles around his gunfighter eyes. "Who knows?" he replied. "Ol' Darrell took himself 17 times to win this thing. Maybe 17 will work for me, too."

During the winter, Earnhardt had announced that he would no longer drive the Chevrolet owned by wife Teresa in NASCAR Busch Series, Grand National Division events. Instead, he had installed Jeff Green in the Goodwrench-sponsored machines, and for the first time in years, he would watch Daytona's Goody's 300 from pit road. His explanation for not driving in the NASCAR Busch Series any longer was that he wanted to focus his undivided attention on the chase for his eighth NASCAR Winston Cup.

(Right) Robert Pressley debuted Skoal's new paint scheme at Daytona; Pressley inherited the Leo Jackson-owned Chevrolet from the retired Harry Gant. Robert was a sensational fourth-fastest in the first round of qualifying. (Below) To the delight of the packed grandstand, two Dales lead the field to the green flag for the start of the Daytona 500. Dale Jarrett had won the pole and had Dale Earnhardt on his immediate right.

This year, Earnhardt had a new Monte Carlo to race, and the Goodwrench team planned to keep the Chevrolet at the leading edge of the field with its intensive testing and development program. Earnhardt was determined to win another championship for Childress, the team, Chevrolet and Goodwrench, and he'd need every advantage, given the increased competition from every team on the circuit.

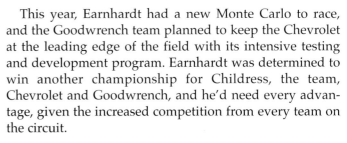

The field re-forms following a yellow-flag stop during the running of the Daytona 500.

The enormous turnover in personnel (see Preface) since last November meant that some of the teams would be much better than they had been last year. Earnhardt knew that the competition from Mark Martin, Rusty Wallace and the Robert Yates team — with Dale Jarrett behind the wheel of the wickedly-fast black Ford — would be intense in '95. He was also well aware of the Monte Carlo's potential — Childress' team had been a key participant in the car's two-year development before it became Chevrolet's flagship race car — and he knew that Sterling Marlin, Jeff Gordon, Ken Schrader, Terry Labonte and Bobby Labonte, now in the Interstate Batteries car, would all have the same Monte Carlo he and Childress had. Challenges for the championship could come from any of those drivers.

One question mark was the new Ford team headed by Bill Elliott. The Redhead

had reunited with his family at the team's shop in Dawsonville, Ga., and no one could foresee whether the Elliotts would emerge from the North Georgia pines with a killer effort (as they had in 1985), or if they would need some time to jell.

The Jarrett/Yates combination had been the fastest during the pre-season tests, and most expected Jarrett to win

Bill Elliott, in his new "Mac Attack" Ford, and Jeff Gordon, in the rainbow-hued DuPont Chevrolet, run side by side early in the race. Ironically, they would finish the race in this same order. Gordon's chance to win his first Daytona 500 was lost when his Chevrolet was damaged during a pit stop mishap. (Note the damage behind the left-front wheel.)

19

between the speeds that had captured the front row but were unsuccessful. The black Ford and the black Chevrolet were, for all intents and purposes (except on the stopwatch), equally fast.

Jarrett's speed was 193.494 miles per hour around the 2.5-mile track; Earnhardt's was 193.449 mph. The difference in speed between the two cars translated into a mere .011 seconds, an infinitesimal amount of time but just enough to award Jarrett the first pole position of his NASCAR Winston Cup career. That he had accomplished the milestone at Daytona, for the 500, in his first outing in the Yates Ford was all just icing on the cake.

Defending race champion Marlin slapped his Kodak Chevrolet in the third-fastest slot. Robert Pressley was surprisingly quick in his first outing as the retired Harry Gant's replacement in Leo Jackson's Skoal Chevrolet, claiming the fourth position on the grid. Their performances immediately proved that the new Monte Carlos were competitive on a superspeedway — the very type of track expected to be the new car's weakness.

Right behind Marlin and Pressley were the brothers Labonte; Terry was just a shade quicker than younger brother Bobby. Michael Waltrip was the fastest Pontiac driver, grabbing the seventh-fastest position with his Pennzoil-sponsored Grand Prix, and Lake Speed put Harry Melling's blue and yellow "Spam-mobile" in the eighth-fastest spot. Darrell Waltrip was ninth-fastest with his Western Auto Monte Carlo, and Phil Parsons surprised some by grabbing the final spot in the top 10 with the TriStar

(Above) As always, Rusty Wallace's pit crew served him well on pit road, but Rusty's luck went sour at Daytona anyway: Although he started the race seventh, he finished 34th. (Right) The technical inspection at Daytona was extremely thorough — NASCAR personnel made sure all cars fit the specs. The new Monte Carlos necessitated the use of new templates by the inspectors.

the pole for the Daytona 500. Sure enough, "The Other Dale" lived up to expectations and posted the fastest lap of the session to claim the first spot on the grid.

Right alongside, underscoring the seriousness with which he would compete for his first Daytona 500 victory, was "Dale Number One."

There wasn't much difference between the two black cars — a half-blink, a whisker, an eye lash. Media members tried to help their readers and listeners comprehend the difference

Motorsports Ford.

Aside from the front row, of course, the times were good only for starting positions in the Gatorade Twin 125s — always a pair of the most exciting races at SpeedWeeks. The results of the Gatorade Twins would, for the most part, determine the starting positions for the 500.

If Earnhardt had made a statement regarding his determination to have a superb SpeedWeeks by putting his Monte Carlo on the outside of the front row for the

(Above) Dale Jarrett's first NASCAR Winston Cup pole position coincided with his first ride in the Robert Yates-owned Ford. Jarrett and Rusty Wallace were heralded as Ford's two brightest hopes for victory, but it wasn't to be: Sterling Marlin stole the show. (Right) Freight-train lines of cars are the hallmark of NASCAR Winston Cup races at Daytona and Talladega.

start of the Daytona 500, then his performance in the 20-lap Busch Clash was an emphatic exclamation point.

For the sixth time in nine tries, he emerged as the winner of the Busch Clash, and once again, he did so in the style that has put the Kannapolis, N.C., native in a class by himself.

He drew the second starting position for the first of the two 10-lap segments and motored past pole-sitter Geoff Bodine in the first turn of the first lap. Only a slip in the second turn on the final lap of the segment kept him from crossing the finish line in the lead. Instead, he was forced to settle for second behind Jeff Gordon's DuPont Chevrolet. Both Monte Carlo drivers would go to the back of the field for the inverted start of the final 10-lap segment.

A quarter of the way through the second lap, Earnhardt was back at the front — he had passed eight cars in less than three miles of racing — and in the remaining eight-plus laps, no one could find anything for the black

Chevrolet. Marlin was a fighting second, and Elliott's "Mac Attack" Ford was an impressive third in its first outing. Gordon was fourth, followed by Todd Bodine, who had gained entry to the field by winning the wildcard draw from 1994's fastest second-round qualifiers.

Following the Busch Clash, everyone's attention turned to the Gatorade Twins. In the first race, Marlin set the stage for a Monte Carlo sweep of the 125s when he unlimbered the Kodak Chevrolet and ran away from the field. He led all but seven of the 50 laps en route to a four-car-length victory over Darrell Waltrip.

One down, one to go. Based on his Busch Clash prowess, Earnhardt was a favorite to win the second Twin 125, which would be his sixth consecutive 125 victory. Like Jarrett on pole day, Earnhardt didn't disappoint his followers: He blew everyone else away on his way to victory lane. Only Gordon appeared to have anything for the black Chevrolet, but after trailing Earnhardt for the final nine laps, Jeff was nearly three car-lengths behind.

For many teams, the Gatorade Twins had offered opportunities to overcome poor qualifying efforts and "win" their way into the Daytona 500 field. Drivers finishing in the top 15 in each Gatorade Twin gain entry to the 500 field. The remaining spots are then determined by the fastest qualifying laps of those who have not yet secured a starting position for the Sunday race.

Drivers who had bad luck in the Twins but were added to the field on the basis of their fast qualifying laps included Pressley, Parsons, Davy Jones, Jeff Purvis, Steve Grissom, Mike Wallace, Allen and John Andretti. NASCAR's new "provisional" starter rules for '95 allow four starters at the rear of the field, and those spots were taken by Brett and Geoff Bodine, Rick Mast and Steve Kinser.

For some teams, it was time to pack up and head for the interstate, and included in that group were some of the sport's stars. Jimmy Spencer, Kenny Wallace, Chad Little, Greg Sacks, Bobby Hillin and rookie contenders Mike Chase, Australian Terry Byers and Gary Bradberry couldn't get into the 500 field. Jim Sauter and Billy Standridge were others who found themselves watching CBS on Sunday afternoon. In all, 22 drivers were unable to qualify.

One who did make the field, however, was a delighted Dave Marcis. Carrying sponsorship from Olive Garden Restaurants on his Chevrolet, Marcis finished 10th in the first Gatorade Twin and earned his way into his 28th consecutive Daytona 500, breaking the record held by Richard Petty.

(Right) After watching the race's finish, Bill Elliott and the remainder of the Ford forces realized they had an enormous amount of work to do before they could catch the flying Chevrolets. (Below) The Daytona 500 boiled down to a battle for supremacy between two Monte Carlos; Sterling Marlin would manage to hold off a determined charge from Dale Earnhardt.

From the drop of the green flag, it appeared that the Monte Carlos were the strongest cars in the field. Among the fastest of the Chevrolets were Earnhardt, Marlin and Gordon. The trio had been the class of the field in the preliminary events, and the three drivers immediately began to prove that their earlier results were indicative of the strength of the new Chevrolets. The three cars led all but eight laps during the first half of the race.

Gordon's bid for victory was ended by an uncharacteristic mistake on pit road: The DuPont Chevrolet fell off the jack, damaging the side of the Monte Carlo. The resulting aerodynamic damage, coupled with a brush with the concrete wall, relegated the 23-year-old driver to a 22nd-place finish.

Gordon's difficulties left the race to Marlin and Earnhardt, and the two led all but three laps as they battled throughout the second half of the race.

With 10 caution flags interspersed throughout the event's 200 laps, half the field was able to remain on the lead lap until the end. That situation led to a crew chief's strategic nightmare when the final caution flew with 13 laps left (Bobby Labonte had spun between the first and second turns).

At the time, Marlin was the race leader and Earnhardt was third; Mark Martin's Valvoline Ford was the filling in the Monte Carlo sandwich.

The voices of crew chiefs filled the headphones of their car owners and drivers as they tried to decide whether or not to pit for tires with so few laps remaining. Fresh Goodyear Eagles meant quicker laps, but with so many cars on the lead lap, track position would be lost if the drivers pitted.

There was no discussion in the Earnhardt pit. No matter what the others did, Earnhardt was on his way to get new Goodyears. His team knew what he could do in 10 laps — they had seen him claw his way through the field in one-and-a-half laps in the Busch Clash.

Dale was the first of the leaders to pit; Sterling and Mark remained on the track. Seconds later, Earnhardt returned to the fray, and with just 11 laps remaining, the green flag flew. The pit stop had dropped the Goodwrench Chevrolet to 14th, so now it was up to the driver, his fresh

For the second-straight time and the third time in the last five years, Morgan-McClure Racing celebrated a Daytona 500 triumph in Daytona's victory lane.

Goodyears and a little luck to find a place to pass.

With the huge crowd on its feet, Earnhardt began his charge. During the next eight laps, he worked his way into second, but he simply couldn't catch Sterling's flying Monte Carlo. Earnhardt got some help from the lap-down Gordon, who became a drafting partner to help his fellow Chevrolet driver pass the Fords of Ted Musgrave and Mark Martin. But Jeff couldn't keep up with the black Chevrolet when it came to crunch time, and without help, Dale could only follow Marlin across the line.

For Sterling, it was a historic Kodak moment. Not only had he successfully defended his race title, but he had earned a unique distinction: The fact that the first two NASCAR Winston Cup triumphs of his career just also happened to be back-to-back Daytona 500 victories was a first in the stock car racing record books.

Predictably, Marlin and the Morgan-McClure Racing "Mighty-Mites" were jubilant in victory lane as they celebrated the team's third Daytona 500 win in the last five years. While Sterling planned his trip to nearby Disney World, reporters clustered around Earnhardt and third-place Martin. Although victory had escaped them, each was wearing a big grin. The source of Martin's smile was the fact that he had emerged from the Daytona race with a strong finish for the first time in his career. And Earnhardt and his team knew they had done all they could. More importantly, the charge from 14th to second had stamped the team as the logical choice for another title.

The Goodwrench Chevrolet's late-race dramatics and the nail-biting finish overshadowed some outstanding runs by other teams. Musgrave, with Howard Comstock back in his role as crew chief, posted a superb fourth place, and Jarrett encouraged the Texaco folks with a strong fifth place.

Michael Waltrip, who had fought his way to the front in his Pennzoil Pontiac, finished sixth, and Steve Grissom, with Buddy Parrott calling the shots from pit road, was seventh, ahead of Hendrick Motorsport teammates Terry Labonte and Ken Schrader. Morgan Shepherd claimed the final top-10 spot with his Wood Brothers Citgo Ford.

Earnhardt, with victories in the Busch Clash, the Gatorade Twin 125 and the first round of the Dodge IROC series (in a brilliant last-lap win over Al Unser Jr.) as well as a fighting second place in the Daytona 500, had proven to everyone that "complacency" was not in his vocabulary, even though he had won his seventh NASCAR Winston Cup the previous season.

And Earnhardt was not the only one to make an auspicious debut: The sleek sled otherwise known as Chevrolet's Monte Carlo had swept the Gatorade Twins, the Busch Clash and the Daytona 500.

Not too bad for right out of the box.

Daytona 500
Race #1 — Final Race Results

Fin. Pos.	Str. Pos.	Car #	Driver	Team
1	3	4	Sterling Marlin	Kodak Film Chevrolet
2	2	3	Dale Earnhardt	Goodwrench Service Chevrolet
3	6	6	Mark Martin	Valvoline Ford
4	12	16	Ted Musgrave	The Family Channel Ford
5	1	28	Dale Jarrett	Texaco Havoline Ford
6	15	30	Michael Waltrip	Pennzoil Pontiac
7	35	29	Steve Grissom	Meineke Chevrolet
8	11	5	Terry Labonte	Kellogg's Chevrolet
9	9	25	Ken Schrader	Budweiser Chevrolet
10	30	21	Morgan Shepherd	Citgo Ford
11	17	15	Dick Trickle	Ford Quality Care Ford
12	13	42	Kyle Petty	Coors Light Pontiac
13	18	10	Ricky Rudd	Tide Ford
14	16	9	Lake Speed	Spam Ford
15	21	31	Ward Burton	Hardee's Chevrolet
16	14	41	Ricky Craven	Kodiak Chevrolet
17	37	27	Loy Allen	Hooters Ford
18	25	43	Bobby Hamilton	STP Pontiac
19	27	80	Joe Ruttman	Hover Motorsports Ford
20	40	7	Geoff Bodine	Exide Batteries Ford
21	41	1	Rick Mast	Skoal Ford
22	4	24	Jeff Gordon	DuPont Auto Finishes Chevrolet
23	10	94	Bill Elliott	McDonald's Ford
24	28	8	Jeff Burton	Raybestos Brakes Ford
25	39	11	Brett Bodine	Lowe's Ford
26	31	33	Robert Pressley	Skoal Bandit Chevrolet
27	38	37	John Andretti	Kmart/Little Caesars Ford
28	26	66	Ben Hess	DuraGloss Ford
29	24	22	Randy LaJoie	MBNA America Pontiac
30	20	18	Bobby Labonte	Interstate Batteries Chevrolet
31	22	12	Derrike Cope	Straight Arrow Ford
32	5	17	Darrell Waltrip	Western Auto Chevrolet
33	33	77	Davy Jones	Jasper/USAir Ford
34	7	2	Rusty Wallace	Miller Genuine Draft Ford
35	29	98	Jeremy Mayfield	RCA Ford
36	19	71	Dave Marcis	Olive Garden Chevrolet
37	8	75	Todd Bodine	Factory Stores Ford
38	34	44	Jeff Purvis	Jackaroo Chevrolet
39	36	90	Mike Wallace	Heilig-Meyers Ford
40	42	26	Steve Kinser	Quaker State Ford
41	32	19	Phil Parsons	Ultra Custom Wheels Ford
42	23	87	Joe Nemechek	Burger King Chevrolet

GOODWRENCH 500

NORTH CAROLINA MOTOR SPEEDWAY
FEBRUARY 26, 1995
•••••

Just five days after Sterling Marlin's victory shuffle in Daytona's winner's circle, teams unloaded at North Carolina Motor Speedway for the second race of the 1995 NASCAR Winston Cup season.

All were delighted to hear that the weekend would mark their last visit to The Rock's old-fashioned garage area. General manager Chris Browning was eager to spread the news that the present garage would be dismantled and renovated by the time the teams returned for the October race. Media members were overjoyed to learn that a new, state-of-the-art media center also would be constructed near the garage area and that the outdated press box would be completely remodeled, as would some corporate suites. More seats would be built for fans, complete with concession stands and rest rooms.

The changes would all be made by October, but that was nine months away.

The task at hand was the Goodwrench 500. Everyone knew that Dale Earnhardt and the members of the Richard Childress team would leave no stone unturned as they tried to win the race sponsored by the company whose name was displayed on the hood and flanks of their Monte Carlo.

Congratulations, grins and high fives greeted Marlin, crew chief Tony Glover and the rest of the Kodak team — winners of the Daytona 500 — at one end of the garage. At the other end, however, members of Junior Johnson's Lowe's team went about their work on the "11" car with heavy hearts. Jackman Sidney Willingham had been killed in a one-car

*Thanks in part to his crew's outstanding work on pit road, rookie Steve Grissom posted a superb sixth place at Rockingham. (**Right**) Jeff Gordon had everyone's number at The Rock, and nothing Rusty Wallace (2), Dale Earnhardt (3) or Ricky Rudd (10) did was enough to derail the DuPont Express.*

highway accident after leaving work on Tuesday evening. He had worked with Johnson's team part-time for 18 months and had been hired full-time at the beginning of the 1995 season.

Despite the wide range of emotions, a race remained to be won, and Chevrolet's hopes for a second-straight victory were high. Pre-event testing had proven that the Bowtie Brigade's latest offering was among the fastest of the fast cars. All along, most had expected the Monte Carlo to be a superb intermediate and short-track car. Now that it had proven its prowess on the superspeedways with its dominant performance at Daytona, the Chevrolet teams could-

n't wait to unleash the new cars on Rockingham's 1.017-mile track.

From the start of the first practice session, it was evident that the pre-event tests were legitimate: The Monte Carlos were clustered at the top of the list of practice times. And by the time qualifying had begun for the 46 cars attempting to make the field, most eyes had locked on the rainbow-hued DuPont Chevrolet and driver Jeff Gordon.

Gordon's impressive showing at Daytona — where he had piloted one of the fastest cars in the field and contended for the victory until a mid-race pit-road incident ended his chances — seemed destined to be repeated at The Rock.

Without a doubt, Gordon was strapped into a rocketship at Rockingham, and despite the pressures associated with posting the fastest practice times, he captured the first pole for Monte Carlo. As for the driver, this pole was the third of his NASCAR Winston Cup career but the first for the 23-year-old at a track other than Charlotte Motor Speedway.

Jeff's run broke the record set by Ricky Rudd last October, but not by much: Gordon's time was less than a

(Left) Bill Elliott's group explodes into action to service the McDonald's Ford. (Below) Prior to the start of the Goodwrench 500, crew members toed the line for the national anthem.

tenth of a second faster than Rudd's previous time. Ricky just missed his old mark but still qualified fast enough to claim the other front row position.

Brett Bodine and his Lowe's teammates honored the memory of teammate Willingham by putting the Junior Johnson-owned Ford third on the grid for Sunday's race. Brother Geoff posted the fourth-fastest lap. The performance of the two Fords had vastly improved since Daytona — both had been forced to take provisionals to get into the 500 field.

Ken Schrader gave the Budweiser folks something to cheer about with his fifth-place starting spot, and Derrike Cope did the same for his Mane & Tail followers when he claimed the sixth spot with the Bobby Allison/Ron Zook Ford. Behind them, John Andretti grabbed his share of the headlines by claiming the inside of the fourth row with the Kranefuss/Haas Kmart Ford. Ricky Craven was the fastest rookie in the

(Right) Morgan Shepherd and John Andretti battle at the front of a pack that includes Mike Wallace (90), Geoff Bodine (7), Bobby Labonte (18), Dave Marcis (71), Dale Jarrett (28) and Mark Martin (6).
(Below) Crew chief Tony Furr and driver Joe Nemechek take a long, hard look at Nemechek's Burger King Chevrolet during practice at Rockingham.

field; with his Kodiak Chevrolet, he lined up alongside Andretti in eighth. The final top-10 spots were occupied by Rick Mast and Todd Bodine — the Skoal and Factory Stores Fords had increased the Blue Oval bunch's total of Thunderbirds in the first 10 positions to seven.

Not as lucky as those top-10 qualifiers was 1994 NASCAR Winston West Series champion Mike Chase, who had been signed to drive Dean Myers' Active Trucking Chevrolet. Within minutes of the conclusion of the first qualifying session, Chase found himself out of a ride. Chase had failed to qualify for the Daytona 500 (as did 21 others), and when he posted the slowest qualifying time during the first round at Rockingham, he was released from his contract. Myers said the team was "in a hurry and needed to have someone with more experience to drive the car." Jimmy Hensley was pressed into service and put the Chevrolet into the field during Saturday's second round of qualifying.

While Chase was packing his uniform bag, plenty of other drivers and teams in the garage area were scratching their heads in bewilderment. Among those failing to qualify during the first round were Daytona winner Marlin, defending series champion Earnhardt, Dale Jarrett, Bill

None of the drivers in this pack asked for or was given any quarter. At the conclusion of the Goodwrench 500, Dale Earnhardt (3) finished third, Jeff Gordon (24) posted his first win of the season, and Ricky Rudd (10) crossed the line fourth. Kyle Petty (42) notched his first top 10 of the new season while sporting his new Coors Light colors.

Elliott, Kyle Petty, Jimmy Spencer, Darrell Waltrip and Lake Speed!

Earnhardt seemed the least concerned of the group. Because his team is the defending champion, it always has first pit choice, and Earnhardt knew that the combination of his team's performance on pit road and the fact that they could pit on the frontstretch would enable him to get into the thick of things quickly.

For the others, however, qualifying was extremely important. Only the top 26 cars would pit on the frontstretch, and everyone knew how difficult it would be to win if they had to pit on the backstretch. Steve Grissom led the second round of qualifying, and Jarrett and Petty turned identical lap times as they competed for the final frontstretch spot. Jarrett claimed the spot because the Robert Yates team had finished above Kyle's Felix Sabates-owned team in the final 1994 NASCAR car owner's point standings.

Steve Kinser was forced to use his second provisional in as many races to make the field. Other provisionals were used by Loy Allen, Ward Burton and Dave Marcis. Ben Hess, Gary Bradberry, James Hylton and Billy Standridge failed to make the field.

Once qualifying had been completed, the focus naturally shifted to the race itself. By starting from the pole, Gordon had an opportunity to turn the Rockingham race into another major payday. The Unocal Challenge bonus had swelled to $91,200, but it was payable only if Jeff could post the victory after starting from the pole.

Gordon immediately showed the field that his qualifying time was a true indicator of his Monte Carlo's potential. Ricky Rudd led the first two laps, but then Jeff rocketed past and pulled away from the field. He led seemingly at will, only occasionally yielding the lead (due to pit stops), and when the event finally settled into its rhythm, it became clear that Jeff and the DuPont Chevrolet would dominate. He led more than 150 of the first 250 laps of the race, and then he really started putting the field away. From lap 279 on, he was displaced from the point only three times. Earnhardt led a lap, Morgan Shepherd led one and Bobby Labonte led 35. Gordon was at the point for 213 laps, including the final 83.

In the final 100 laps, Bobby Labonte was the only driver in a position to challenge Gordon, and the native Texan gave it everything he had. He spun in the second turn with less than 60 laps to go — which brought out the final caution flag — but he managed to get the Interstate Batteries Chevrolet pointed in the right direction and moving quickly enough to keep from losing a lap. On the restart, he was right behind Gordon again, and with less than 30 laps remaining, he took his best shot at passing the DuPont Chevrolet. Lapped traffic came into play, but Gordon maneuvered his way through it and held onto the lead.

Finally, Bobby was able to close to within a car-length, but then Gordon unleashed his knock-out punch and eased away from the black and green Chevrolet. He eventually pulled away to a 1.19-second victory.

Behind those two, Earnhardt had been working his way toward a rock-solid third place. As the day wound down, the track had tightened up, and Earnhardt's Chevrolet did the same. Despite his crew's best efforts to loosen the car and free it up in the corners, their changes had no effect. But third place was good enough to move Earnhardt into the point lead after two races. As for the remaining race finishers, Rudd trailed Earnhardt in fourth place. His efforts to win had been hampered by the fact that his Tide Ford had begun pushing in the corners during the late stages of the race.

Finishing a lap down in fifth was Jarrett, whose Texaco Ford had emerged victorious from a race-long battle with rookie Grissom's Chevrolet. Mark Martin finished seventh, two laps behind, and Cope, Ward Burton and Petty claimed the final top-10 positions, all three laps behind.

The DuPont driver's third career NASCAR Winston Cup win paid handsomely ($167,000, including the

After winning a late-race battle with Bobby Labonte, Jeff Gordon pulled away to a one-second victory in the Goodwrench 500 at Rockingham — his third career win. The icing on the cake was the Unocal Challenge bonus, awarded for winning from the pole.

Unocal Challenge bonus). The Rockingham trophy now would join those from the Coca-Cola 600 and the Brickyard 400, both won last season, on Jeff's mantle. More importantly, the win moved him from 22nd to seventh in the point standings and had bolstered his team's morale. (Emotionally, the DuPont team had fallen to an all-time low following the pit-road mistake at Daytona.)

While Gordon celebrated his victory at The Rock, Ford team members dispiritedly pushed their equipment back to the garage area. Chevrolet's new Monte Carlos had been 1-2 at Daytona and now had swept the first three positions at The Rock. Suddenly, Ford's 1994 record — 20 wins in 30 races — seemed like ancient history.

Goodwrench 500

Race #2 — Final Race Results

Fin. Pos.	Str. Pos.	Car #	Driver	Team
1	1	24	Jeff Gordon	DuPont Auto Finishes Chevrolet
2	15	18	Bobby Labonte	Interstate Batteries Chevrolet
3	23	3	Dale Earnhardt	Goodwrench Service Chevrolet
4	2	10	Ricky Rudd	Tide Ford
5	26	28	Dale Jarrett	Texaco Havoline Ford
6	21	29	Steve Grissom	Meineke Chevrolet
7	19	6	Mark Martin	Valvoline Ford
8	6	12	Derrike Cope	Straight Arrow Ford
9	41	31	Ward Burton	Hardee's Chevrolet
10	27	42	Kyle Petty	Coors Light Pontiac
11	24	94	Bill Elliott	McDonald's Ford
12	22	4	Sterling Marlin	Kodak Film Chevrolet
13	7	37	John Andretti	Kmart/Little Caesars Ford
14	3	11	Brett Bodine	Lowe's Ford
15	31	90	Mike Wallace	Heilig-Meyers Ford
16	8	41	Ricky Craven	Kodiak Chevrolet
17	11	30	Michael Waltrip	Pennzoil Pontiac
18	34	98	Jeremy Mayfield	RCA Ford
19	18	8	Jeff Burton	Raybestos Brakes Ford
20	29	81	Kenny Wallace	TIC Financial Ford
21	4	7	Geoff Bodine	Exide Batteries Ford
22	14	15	Dick Trickle	Ford Quality Care Ford
23	42	71	Dave Marcis	Terramite Chevrolet
24	16	2	Rusty Wallace	Miller Genuine Draft Ford
25	20	22	Randy LaJoie	MBNA America Pontiac
26	30	5	Terry Labonte	Kellogg's Chevrolet
27	39	26	Steve Kinser	Quaker State Ford
28	40	27	Loy Allen	Hooters Ford
29	13	87	Joe Nemechek	Burger King Chevrolet
30	28	23	Jimmy Spencer	Smokin' Joe's Ford
31	10	75	Todd Bodine	Factory Stores Ford
32	33	9	Lake Speed	Spam Ford
33	25	16	Ted Musgrave	The Family Channel Ford
34	12	21	Morgan Shepherd	Citgo Ford
35	9	1	Rick Mast	Skoal Ford
36	17	43	Bobby Hamilton	STP Pontiac
37	36	77	Davy Jones	Jasper/USAir Ford
38	37	17	Darrell Waltrip	Western Auto Chevrolet
39	5	25	Ken Schrader	Budweiser Chevrolet
40	32	32	Jimmy Hensley	Active Trucking Chevrolet
41	35	40	Greg Sacks	Kendall Pontiac
42	38	33	Robert Pressley	Skoal Bandit Chevrolet

PONTIAC EXCITEMENT 400

RICHMOND INTERNATIONAL RACEWAY

MARCH 5, 1995

•••••

L ess than a week after the Goodwrench 500, the teams unloaded their transporters in Richmond for the spring event on Paul Sawyer's mini-superspeedway. For at least one driver, the brief break between races had seemed unusually long; no driver was more eager to begin the upcoming weekend's event than Rusty Wallace.

Wallace desperately had hoped to get off to a good start in 1995 and be one of the drivers in contention for the NASCAR Winston Cup title right from the beginning. But his well-documented history of Daytona difficulty once again had raised its ugly head, and an accident at The Beach had relegated him to 34th place in the season-opener.

Nonetheless, he had traveled to Rockingham with high hopes for posting a good finish — after all, he had garnered much success there in the past — but an overheating engine ended his day 40 laps from the end of the race. He was classified 24th in the final rundown. After just two races, he was 32nd in the NASCAR Winston Cup standings and nearly 200 points behind leader Dale Earnhardt.

Despite the numbers, Wallace had reason to crack his familiar smile now and again. Richmond marked the first short-track race of the season, and Rusty knew he would have a great chance to run at the front of the field for the 400-lapper in the Capital of the Confederacy. His short-track record over the past four years was the best on the circuit, and he was taking his favorite car, "Midnight," to the three-quarter-mile oval.

*By the time his team rolled his Miller Ford out for the Richmond race, Rusty Wallace was desperate to make amends for his early-season disappointments. His determination was rewarded with a third-place finish. (**Right**) Flat-track specialist Terry Labonte put the whip to his Kellogg's Chevrolet to capture his first win of the season.*

He knew that a victory would not come easily — others such as Terry Labonte, Mark Martin, Earnhardt, Dale Jarrett and Sterling Marlin would be in the hunt for victory as well. He also knew he would have to contend with the blazingly-fast Jeff Gordon. But Wallace liked his chances, and if he could avoid the bad luck that had plagued him in the first two events, he could take a big step up the point ladder with a strong finish at Richmond.

A few miles away from the Penske South shop, the Kellogg's crew was putting the finishing touches on Labonte's Monte Carlo. The team's winning performances at North Wilkesboro and Phoenix at the end of the '94 season had branded Terry the master of the flat track, and Richmond, with its 14-degree banked corners, fell right into that category. Terry had won the September race under Richmond's arc-lights, and if all went well, the team felt Terry could move up from his 12th place in the standings.

Less than an hour east of Charlotte, Richard Childress and his team were loading the Goodwrench Monte Carlo onto the transporter. The painstaking preparation of the Goodwrench-sponsored car was finished, and the car was as ready as it could be for action on the track. Although Earnhardt hadn't posted a victory in the first two events of the season, his second and third places had vaulted him to a 29-point lead over Martin's Valvoline Ford team.

As anxious as he was to increase his point lead, Earnhardt (and all the other competitors) would have to wait. Friday's track activity consisted of card games, video watching and chitchat, interspersed with reviews of Weather Channel forecasts. Outside the transporters, a cold rain turned into sleet and then snow; it was obvious early in the day that there would be no track action on Friday. Saturday and Sunday's forecasts didn't look much better, but everyone hoped a weather window would allow the race to be run as scheduled and prevent the teams from having to stay extra days. Atlanta was scheduled for the coming weekend, and every minute lost in Richmond would mean added difficulty in preparing for the Purolator 500.

(Left) Friday's track activities were canceled when early-season rain, sleet and snow greeted the teams. (Below) Dale Earnhardt (3) and Rusty Wallace (2) waged a war during the Pontiac Excitement 400, although it was for second place behind Terry Labonte rather than the win. Earnhardt beat Wallace to the checkered flag after Wallace broke a right-rear shock absorber just laps from the finish.

The NASCAR Winston Cup tour's visit to Paul Sawyer's "mini-superspeedway" always provides the tens of thousands of fans in attendance with plenty of exciting action.

Saturday dawned cold and blustery, but the precipitation had stopped. The problem facing most teams now was the abbreviated practice session; either the cars would be right for qualifying or they would be loaded back onto the transporters. They would have only one chance — one qualifying session — to make the field.

There was absolutely no margin for error. A total of 47 cars were vying for the 38 spots available in the field. It was banzai qualifying at its best: One shot — make the field or go home.

Gordon had little to fear after he blazed a trail around the Sawyers' amphitheater — he had won his second-straight pole position. His front-row mate was a major surprise — Hamilton had slapped the Petty Enterprises STP Pontiac in second place with a lap just fractions of a second better than Wallace's. Ted Musgrave indicated that he hadn't forgotten how to get around Richmond by clocking the fourth-fastest lap, and Derrike Cope continued to impress with a lap good enough to grab the fifth starting spot. Ken Schrader

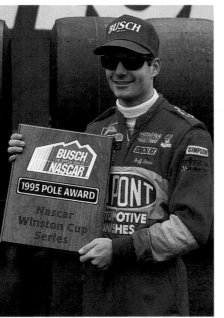

Jeff Gordon won his second-consecutive Busch Pole Award based on his qualifying performance at Richmond.

would start on Derrike's right, and Dick Trickle and Marlin filled the fourth row. Martin and Lake Speed completed the top-10 positions on the scoring sheets.

Again, Earnhardt had trouble qualifying (he managed only the 26th-fastest lap), but again, Dale knew that if he could stay out of trouble in the early stages of the race, he could work his way into contention by using his crew, his car and his pit choice to his advantage.

Michael Waltrip and Loy Allen brought up the rear of the field. Both had been forced to use provisionals, and Allen had done so for the second-straight race. The Quaker State camp's situation was even more distressing. Steve Kinser, for the third time, had been forced to use a provisional, so the team had just one left until Sears Point. Randy LaJoie was the fourth provisional starter.

Jimmy Hensley, driving the Active Trucking Chevrolet for the second time, missed the field, as did Kenny Wallace (in the TIC Financial Ford). Billy Standridge again left for home early, as did Jay Hedgecock, who had driven a Ford owned by country music's Diamond Rio. Steve Grissom, who was fifth in the point standings after superb runs at Daytona and

Mike Wallace (90) hoped to present his car owner, Richmond resident Junie Donlavey, with a great performance in the Pontiac Excitement 400, but in the end, no one could match the power of Terry Labonte's Chevrolet at the three-quarter-mile oval.

Rockingham, also headed out the back gate. His team, owned by Gary and Carolyn Bechtel, had not finished high enough in the '94 point standings to use a provisional.

Gary Bradberry had failed to get Jimmy Means' Ford into the field for the third-straight time, and Ben Hess' lap in the RaDiUs Ford wasn't fast enough either. Eric Smith and Davy Jones, who piloted the USAir/Jasper Engines Ford, also went home.

Those who survived qualifying still had to deal with Wallace. From the start, Rusty indicated that he was ready to break out of his slump. (The last time his Miller Ford had visited victory lane was last September at Martinsville.) On the second lap, Rusty bolted to the point and pulled away to lead the first quarter of the race.

But not everyone in the wall-to-wall crowd of more than 75,000 was watching the black and yellow Ford at the front of the field. Many were watching another black car work its way up from its 26th starting position — Earnhardt was taking no prisoners in his charge to the front. In just over 30 laps, he had cracked the top 10, and less than 30 laps later, he was up to fifth. When Martin cut a tire, Dale moved to third, and on lap 90, Earnhardt replaced Gordon in second place. Then Dale caught Rusty, and what ensued during the next 30 laps was the stuff of NASCAR Winston Cup racing legends.

Two drivers with great respect for each other's ability, driving equally matched race cars on a track that encourages side-by-side racing, waged one of the fiercest duels of the year. Wallace and Earnhardt were doorhandle to doorhandle, scraping and bumping occasionally, but clearly enjoying themselves. The sport's superstars grinned at each other as they put on a show that caused the immense throng to stand, cheer and high-five their neighbors. It didn't matter if you were a Wallace fan or an Earnhardt supporter. This stuff was fabulous!

Rusty finally eased away, but Dale had made his point. His Goodwrench Monte Carlo was capable of claiming its first victory, and he would be a factor for the remainder of the race.

Because of the two black cars battling at the point, Terry Labonte went largely unnoticed as he worked his way toward the front from his 24th starting position. The quiet Texan picked his spots, passed those in front of him and used excellent pit crew work to gain positions. By lap 150, Terry was in fifth place.

By then, everyone on pit road had noticed the Kellogg's Chevrolet, and Wallace and Earnhardt knew that they would have to contend with what Terry had under the hood of his Monte Carlo sometime during the final half of the Pontiac Excitement 400.

Todd Bodine's Factory Stores Ford kissed the third-turn wall on lap 151 after being tagged by Morgan Shepherd, and Labonte's crew used the opportunity presented by the caution to put Terry back on the track for the restart in third place. On lap 220, Labonte moved outside Wallace, and after a lap of side-by-side racing, Terry pulled away.

Less than 60 laps later, Robert Pressley cut a tire, spun and collected Jarrett in the process. During the ensuing caution, Labonte lost the pit road battle to Wallace and Earnhardt and consequently lined up third for the restart. But with just over 80 laps remaining, the fifth and final caution flag flew after Jimmy Spencer was sent spinning by Brett Bodine. The Gary DeHart-led Kellogg's crew, which had saved its best for last, leapt into action and made the most of the opportunity.

The red and yellow-clad Corn Flakes boys gave Labonte four new Goodyears and two cans of Unocal in just 16.97 seconds and sent the Monte Carlo to the front for the restart. Nothing Wallace or Earnhardt had would be enough to catch the fleet Chevrolet.

With a clear track ahead, Terry had his way with the rest of the field and pulled away to a 1.25-second victory. Behind him, Earnhardt and Wallace battled for the scraps. In the end, Dale eased home second ahead of the Miller Ford; Rusty struggled home third with a broken right-rear shock absorber. Schrader was a distant fourth, ahead of Marlin, Cope and Darrell Waltrip, all of whom finished on the lead lap. Martin, never able to make up the lap he lost from a flat tire, still managed to finish in eighth place, ahead of Hamilton and Andretti. Richmond marked the first top-10 finish of John's brief NASCAR Winston Cup career.

Other contenders suffered from a wide variety of problems, ranging from Brett Bodine battling the flu all weekend to Jeff Gordon's fuel pump problems. Jarrett was eliminated by the accident with Pressley. Kyle Petty's shifter broke off. Geoff Bodine cut a tire early in the race, lost a

The Morgan-McClure crew — still riding an emotional high from its Daytona 500 victory — provided championship-calibre service on the Kodak Chevrolet. Sterling Marlin finished fifth at Richmond, which bumped him up to second behind Earnhardt in the point standings.

lap and was never able to work his way back into contention.

As the teams readied for the trip home, Earnhardt and his Goodwrench crew were all smiles. They hadn't won the race, but Dale had demonstrated the fire needed to run at the front and the maturity to take the best he could for a day's work. His second place at Richmond had extended his point lead to 53 over the now-second-place Marlin.

Even more important to the Bowtie Brigade was the fact that the Monte Carlos had won again as well as posted another 1-2 sweep. The score was now Monte Carlo 3, Thunderbird 0. Nonetheless, the Ford forces were heartened by Wallace's Richmond performance. Wallace had proven that a Blue Oval could front the field. Maybe things weren't quite as bad as they had originally appeared to the Thunderbird camp.

Pontiac Excitement 400
Race #3 — Final Race Results

Fin. Pos.	Str. Pos.	Car #	Driver	Team
1	24	5	Terry Labonte	Kellogg's Chevrolet
2	26	3	Dale Earnhardt	Goodwrench Service Chevrolet
3	3	2	Rusty Wallace	Miller Genuine Draft Ford
4	6	25	Ken Schrader	Budweiser Chevrolet
5	8	4	Sterling Marlin	Kodak Film Chevrolet
6	5	12	Derrike Cope	Straight Arrow Ford
7	17	17	Darrell Waltrip	Western Auto Chevrolet
8	9	6	Mark Martin	Valvoline Ford
9	2	43	Bobby Hamilton	STP Pontiac
10	21	37	John Andretti	Kmart/Little Caesars Ford
11	20	7	Geoff Bodine	Exide Batteries Ford
12	7	15	Dick Trickle	Ford Quality Care Ford
13	4	16	Ted Musgrave	The Family Channel Ford
14	10	9	Lake Speed	Spam Ford
15	14	21	Morgan Shepherd	Citgo Ford
16	25	94	Bill Elliott	McDonald's Ford
17	28	98	Jeremy Mayfield	RCA Ford
18	15	11	Brett Bodine	Lowe's Ford
19	27	40	Greg Sacks	Kendall Pontiac
20	29	71	Dave Marcis	Olive Garden Chevrolet
21	30	10	Ricky Rudd	Tide Ford
22	33	31	Ward Burton	Hardee's Chevrolet
23	35	30	Michael Waltrip	Pennzoil Pontiac
24	23	23	Jimmy Spencer	Smokin' Joe's Ford
25	13	28	Dale Jarrett	Texaco Havoline Ford
26	16	90	Mike Wallace	Heilig-Meyers Ford
27	37	22	Randy LaJoie	MBNA America Pontiac
28	36	26	Steve Kinser	Quaker State Ford
29	38	27	Loy Allen	Hooters Ford
30	18	18	Bobby Labonte	Interstate Batteries Chevrolet
31	22	8	Jeff Burton	Raybestos Brakes Ford
32	34	87	Joe Nemechek	Burger King Chevrolet
33	19	42	Kyle Petty	Coors Light Pontiac
34	12	1	Rick Mast	Skoal Ford
35	11	33	Robert Pressley	Skoal Bandit Chevrolet
36	1	24	Jeff Gordon	DuPont Auto Finishes Chevrolet
37	32	75	Todd Bodine	Factory Stores Ford
38	31	41	Ricky Craven	Kodiak Chevrolet

PUROLATOR 500

ATLANTA MOTOR SPEEDWAY
MARCH 12, 1995
•••••

The Richmond results had shuffled the point standings considerably, and when the teams unloaded at track president Ed Clark's Atlanta Motor Speedway for the Purolator 500, Sterling Marlin's Kodak Chevrolet was parked next to defending series champion Dale Earnhardt's Goodwrench Monte Carlo.

Richmond winner Terry Labonte and Rusty Wallace also had moved up in the garage pecking order. Terry had climbed from 12th place to fourth following his victory, and Wallace had moved from 32nd to 17th, thanks to his third place! Amazing how a good finishing position can move a team in the early stages of the season!

Mark Martin was now third in the standings, and Dale Jarrett was fifth. Steve Grissom, after missing the show at Richmond, had taken a huge tumble, falling from fifth place all the way to 24th. And Jeff Gordon's fuel pump problem had dropped the DuPont Chevrolet from seventh to 13th on the point list.

The Purolator 500 was the first event affected by NASCAR's new ride- and spoiler-height rules. The sanctioning body's changes, which were designed to slow the cars slightly, would be put to the test on the bowl-shaped, high-speed 1.5-mile oval. The front air dams on the cars had been raised a quarter-inch, and the rear spoilers had been trimmed a quarter-inch. These minor

In honor of the '96 Centennial Olympic Games, Atlanta track president Ed Clark presented the top three finishers in the Purolator 500 with gold, silver and bronze medals. Jeff Gordon (center) won the gold, Bobby Labonte (left) took the silver and Terry Labonte (right) carted home the bronze. (Right) A full house was on hand to witness the running of the Atlanta 500-miler, and the fans were treated to an unbeatable combination: a great show and great weather. Hometown favorite Bill Elliott (94) flashes past the crowd as he approaches the first turn.

changes were expected to be followed by several other changes as NASCAR worked to lessen downforce and cornering speeds on the tracks.

While teams were working out the chassis adjustments made necessary by the new regulations, a wave of relief swept from crew to crew. Word had spread that Harry Gant had been released from a Charlotte hospital after being treated for broken ribs and a torn spleen following a highway accident. Gant and friends were en route to Daytona Beach for "Bike Week" — during which Harry was scheduled to make a personal appearance at a Harley dealership — when Gant was forced to swerve and "dump" his Harley to avoid running into a friend's Jeep. Immediately following the accident, Harry made light of his injuries, but he later had to be transported by ambulance to a hospital. Surgery to repair his spleen was contemplated but later deemed unnecessary.

Back at the track, most teams expected qualifying speeds to be higher than those of last year's March race because Atlanta had been repaved prior to the November season finale. Some crew chiefs, however, felt that the pole speed would be a little slower because the ride height and spoiler changes mandated by NASCAR would reduce speeds a little.

*(**Right**) Richard Petty kept a watchful eye on driver Bobby Hamilton from pit road during the Purolator 500. (**Below**) Bobby Labonte (18), Jeff Gordon (24) and pole-sitter Dale Earnhardt (3) rocket through the turns of the repaved oval. Add one Labonte (Terry), and you've got the top four finishers.*

Projections for faster qualifying speeds proved true during the first qualifying session. The pole speed was more than five miles per hour faster than last spring but off the mark posted by Greg Sacks last November when he had slapped his Hoosier-shod USAir Ford on the pole.

The big qualifying surprise was Earnhardt's performance; he had shaken his two-race "qualifying blues" and put his Monte Carlo on the pole. The Purolator 500 would be the first time the Goodwrench team had fronted the field since the DieHard 500 at Talladega the previous July.

Grabbing the pole was not an easy task — Dale had to squeeze everything he could out of the black Chevrolet to claim his 18th career pole. Beside him on the front row, just five one-thousandths of a second slower, was Bobby Labonte, who continued to impress behind the wheel of the Interstate Batteries Chevrolet.

Jeff Gordon, aboard yet another rocketship from the DuPont stable, grabbed the inside of the second row. Alongside Gordon was Darrell Waltrip, who had produced an outstanding qualifying run for fourth, beating Richmond winner Terry Labonte's fifth-fastest lap.

Ricky Rudd, breaking the Monte Carlo string at five, put his Tide Ford on the outside of the third row, ahead of Marlin. Derrike Cope, now seventh in the point standings, continued his impres-

sive season by parking the Bobby Allison/Ron Zook-owned Mane & Tail Ford in the eighth spot for the start of the Purolator 500. Bobby Hamilton extended his string of good qualifying runs with the ninth-fastest lap, just ahead of Dick Trickle's Quality Care Ford (from Bud Moore's stable).

Further back in the field, Steve Kinser had reason to celebrate after he captured the 22nd starting position. The

(Above) Bobby Allison has a tall tale or two for D.K. Ulrich in the Atlanta garage area. (Left) It didn't take Dale Jarrett long to move up through the field from his 18th-place starting position. He led a train of cars into contention and stayed there, finishing fifth.

Quaker State team was heartened by Kinser's qualifying performance, which marked the first time the 14-time World of Outlaws sprint car champion had gotten into the field without the help of a provisional. The Pontiac forces, on the other hand, had taken it on the chin in qualifying: Michael Waltrip, Kyle Petty and Randy LaJoie all were forced to use provisionals to make the field. Jimmy Spencer, in Travis Carter's Smokin' Joe's Ford, used the fourth provisional.

For the second-straight time, a driver in the top 10 in points failed to make the race. Steve Grissom had been the unlucky one at Richmond; at Atlanta, Ward Burton and his crew dejectedly loaded their Hardee's Chevrolet into the transporter. Other drivers leaving early were Gary Bradberry, who again failed to get Jimmy Means' Ford into the field, Loy Allen, Ken Bouchard, Johnnie Chapman, Ben Hess, Kenny Wallace and Pancho Carter.

Immediately after Honorary Starter Ernie Irvan dropped the green flag on Sunday, it appeared that Earnhardt was on his way to his first victory of the season. He blasted away to lead the first 62 laps, but then the handling on his Goodwrench Chevrolet began to fade. When it did, young Gordon and Bobby Labonte were right there to take advantage.

The two Chevrolet drivers left the black Monte Carlo in their dust and turned the 500-mile affair into

*(**Right**) Morgan Shepherd pulled away from this group on his way to a sixth-place finish. (**Middle**) Steve Kinser didn't fare as well: His Quaker State Ford came home on the hook after a collision. (**Below**) Kyle Petty did his best Steven Seagal impression but could only fight his way to 14th.*

their own show. Of the two, Gordon was the best, and he steadily pulled away to lay waste to the field.

The rainbow-hued car was so dominant that, at one point, Gordon had built his lead to 18 seconds and left the Labonte brothers and Earnhardt as the only other drivers on the lead lap. He might have finished with an even greater margin of victory were it not for Ken Schrader connecting with the Atlanta concrete 28 laps from the finish, produc-

ing the race's final caution period.

On the restart, Gordon again flew away from the field, leaving the battle for second place to the Labontes. Bobby finally got the best of older brother Terry and then set out after Gordon. Labonte nipped, nibbled and finally closed the gap to two car-lengths with just three laps remaining. But then, Bobby's green and black Chevrolet tightened up, and no one else had a prayer of catching the DuPont Chevrolet. The .19-second lead with which Gordon did finish was, by all counts, deceptive; prior to Schrader's mishap, Jeff had given up the lead only on green-flag pit stops.

Gordon's second trip to victory lane in '95 was made in the same car he had taken to the winner's circle at Rockingham, and, once again, he had led another Monte Carlo sweep. This time the Monte Carlos had claimed the top four positions, and Jeff celebrated Chevrolet's first victory at Atlanta since 1991 with a flourish. Car owner Rick Hendrick could be excused for his impromptu mini-jig in victory lane. Jeff's victory was the eighth Hendrick Motorsports triumph in the last 29 races, and even when Rick hadn't visited victory lane, he had been nearby; dur-

Joe Nemechek (87) and Rick Mast (1) battled throughout the day and to the finish: Mast crossed the line 11th, Nemechek 16th.

ing that same time period, his cars had produced 24 top fives and 44 top-10 finishes.

Bobby and Terry claimed second and third places, and Earnhardt man-handled his Chevrolet home fourth, the final car on the lead lap. Jarrett posted his third top-five finish in the Texaco Ford, ahead of Morgan Shepherd's Citgo Ford. Marlin finished seventh, ahead of Rudd, who had the final car a lap down. Martin, after running out of gas, and Wallace, without the juice needed to contend, claimed the final top-10 positions with their Fords.

As a result of the Chevrolet 1-2-3-4 lead-lap sweep, and with the score now Chevrolet 4, Ford 0, frustration was beginning to set in for the Blue Oval teams. After four straight races, the teams finally had a weekend off to prepare for tricky Darlington, but the Ford teams wondered if the additional time would be enough to figure out a way to stem the tide of the Chevrolet juggernaut.

Fans were beginning to wonder if this Jeff Gordon thing was for real. Everyone acknowledged that "The Kid" was extremely talented, he had good equipment and his crew had overcome the Daytona pit road mistake. But was the DuPont team really ready to challenge for the championship, or was this just an aberration?

A pair of poles, a brace of victories and good runs in the other two races (despite a fuel-pump problem at Richmond and the pit road mishap at Daytona) was surely a great start to the season for any team, but could he and the team maintain their momentum? Could he handle one of the most difficult tracks on the circuit — Darlington — or any of the short tracks? The next two races would certainly shed some light on those questions.

Jeff Gordon's team debuted its "Refuse to Lose" T-shirts in Atlanta's victory lane.

Purolator 500

Race # 4 — Final Race Results

Fin. Pos.	Str. Pos.	Car #	Driver	Team
1	3	24	Jeff Gordon	DuPont Auto Finishes Chevrolet
2	2	18	Bobby Labonte	Interstate Batteries Chevrolet
3	5	5	Terry Labonte	Kellogg's Chevrolet
4	1	3	Dale Earnhardt	Goodwrench Service Chevrolet
5	18	28	Dale Jarrett	Texaco Havoline Ford
6	17	21	Morgan Shepherd	Citgo Ford
7	7	4	Sterling Marlin	Kodak Film Chevrolet
8	6	10	Ricky Rudd	Tide Ford
9	13	6	Mark Martin	Valvoline Ford
10	12	2	Rusty Wallace	Miller Genuine Draft Ford
11	19	1	Rick Mast	Skoal Ford
12	32	41	Ricky Craven	Kodiak Chevrolet
13	8	12	Derrike Cope	Straight Arrow Ford
14	40	42	Kyle Petty	Coors Light Pontiac
15	21	9	Lake Speed	Spam Ford
16	20	87	Joe Nemechek	Burger King Chevrolet
17	9	43	Bobby Hamilton	STP Pontiac
18	16	29	Steve Grissom	Meineke Chevrolet
19	27	16	Ted Musgrave	The Family Channel Ford
20	15	37	John Andretti	Kmart/Little Caesars Ford
21	37	75	Todd Bodine	Factory Stores Ford
22	10	15	Dick Trickle	Ford Quality Care Ford
23	31	11	Brett Bodine	Lowe's Ford
24	25	77	Davy Jones	Jasper/USAir Ford
25	36	47	Billy Standridge	WCW Ford
26	35	94	Bill Elliott	McDonald's Ford
27	29	25	Ken Schrader	Budweiser Chevrolet
28	33	71	Dave Marcis	Olive Garden Chevrolet
29	24	40	Greg Sacks	Kendall Pontiac
30	34	7	Geoff Bodine	Exide Batteries Ford
31	30	33	Robert Pressley	Skoal Bandit Chevrolet
32	42	23	Jimmy Spencer	Smokin' Joe's Ford
33	28	8	Jeff Burton	Raybestos Brakes Ford
34	4	17	Darrell Waltrip	Western Auto Chevrolet
35	39	30	Michael Waltrip	Pennzoil Pontiac
36	14	98	Jeremy Mayfield	RCA Ford
37	22	44	Jeff Purvis	Jackaroo Chevrolet
38	11	32	Jimmy Hensley	Active Trucking Chevrolet
39	41	22	Randy LaJoie	MBNA America Pontiac
40	26	90	Mike Wallace	Heilig-Meyers Ford
41	23	26	Steve Kinser	Quaker State Ford
42	38	19	Phil Parsons	Tri-Star Motorsports Ford

TranSouth 400

Darlington Raceway
March 26, 1995
•••••

This time last year, when the NASCAR Winston Cup teams headed for Darlington and the annual spring TranSouth 400, Dale Earnhardt had yet to score a victory in '94. But Earnhardt was quick to remedy that problem with that very event. He did everything right to secure his first '94 victory: He started from a top-10 slot, led the most laps and showed the rest of the field the bumper of his Goodwrench Chevrolet in the process of writing his much-anticipated victory in the record books with a 7.4-second margin over second-place finisher Mark Martin.

This year, Dale and the Richard Childress team had come to the pioneer super-speedway with the same goal as last year: They intended to score their first victory of the season at the track where Dale has become something of a legend. In all, he has amassed nine victories at the storied facility — just a single win behind all-time Darlington master David Pearson.

But Earnhardt, as well as the other competitors, would have a few changes to contend with this time. Darlington president Jim Hunter had introduced a new wrinkle for the 1995 competitors — the entire surface of the facility had been repaved (the first time since Johnny Mantz won the first Southern 500 in history, back in 1950). The paving job had been described as "smooth as a billiard table" by Ricky Rudd and necessitated pre-event testing sessions by nearly every team. During one of those sessions, Ernie Irvan returned for a few practice laps, this time behind the wheel of his own NASCAR Busch Series car.

Sterling Marlin visited victory lane for the second time in 1995 following the TranSouth 400, and the champagne at Darlington tasted just as good at it had at Daytona. (Right) Jeff Gordon spent much of the race in this pose, leading from the pole position, but after fronting the field for more than 150 of the first 200 laps, he was taken out in an accident.

42

way between the first and second turns on the egg-shaped oval.

As teams prepared for the first qualifying session at Darlington, the media members in attendance passed the time digesting the grist produced by a plethora of between-race events. Gary Bradberry, unable to qualify Jimmy Means' Ford for any of the first four races of the season, resigned as the driver of the Advanced Communications RacePage Thunderbird. Brad Teague was nominated to drive the Ford for the weekend.

Another major development also came courtesy of NASCAR: NASCAR announced that a car representative of each make would be impounded at the conclusion of the TranSouth 400 and taken to the Lockheed wind tunnel in Marietta, Ga. (where Ford leases time for aerodynamic work) and then to the General Motors wind tunnel in Warren. Mich. The sanctioning body hoped to determine the "real" numbers regarding lift, drag and downforce. And the Ford, Chevrolet and Pontiac teams were more than willing to cooperate to put an end to the questions about whether one make of car had a major advantage over the other two.

(Left) Since 15 caution flags interrupted the event, pit-work was a key ingredient all day long. (Below) Ernie Irvan, sharing a quick word with Dale Earnhardt before the start of the race, is never far from a track. Before the Darlington event, he had run some laps while testing his NASCAR Busch Series car.

"Just wanted to see how I was doing," Ernie explained, grinning, as he climbed from behind the wheel of the Ford. His laps, despite the expected rustiness (he had not been behind the wheel of a race car since the previous August), were faster than the track record for the Busch machinery. All things considered, a pretty amazing feat!

At the conclusion of the pre-event test sessions, Robert Pressley led the list of unofficial times — he also had become the first driver in Darlington's history to crack the 170-mile-per-hour barrier. Earnhardt, meanwhile, loaded a battered Goodwrench Monte Carlo into his transporter for a trip to the team's shop in Welcome, N.C. Earnhardt had cut a tire during a practice lap, brushed the first-turn concrete wall and then backed the car into the wall mid-

Rockingham as well as at Atlanta the previous week, might soon be called "Predator" if it continued its string of awesome performances!

Gordon's lap, combined with Terry Labonte's second-fastest time and Ken Schrader's third-quickest lap, gave car owner Rick Hendrick reason to walk proudly through the garage area. His teams had swept the first three positions on one of the most difficult tracks on the NASCAR Winston Cup tour. They also had kept Rudd's Ford out of the top three. Ricky posted the fourth-fastest lap, good enough for the outside of the second row; he was the only

(Above) In this fish-eye view, the field heads through Darlington's first turn. (Right) Ken Schrader fronts a group that includes Bobby Hamilton (43), Jimmy Spencer (23) and Lake Speed (9).

At the conclusion of the first qualifying session on the track's new surface, the 170-mph barrier officially had been broken. And who claimed the pole for the TranSouth 400? None other than the hottest thing on the circuit so far in '95: Jeff Gordon. Gordon, driving a car nicknamed "Blacker," had notched his third pole of the young season. Crew chief Ray Evernham was quick to explain the car's name: "When we tested it last winter, we just painted it black and put a skull and crossbones on it instead of a number. We gave the car its name because we knew it would be chasing all those black cars." The aforementioned Monte Carlo, the same Chevrolet that had won at

Ford driver able to crack the top seven positions.

Daytona 500 winner Sterling Marlin was fifth in line for the start. Darrell Waltrip continued his string of strong performances with a lap good enough for the outside of the third row. Ward Burton, who had been unable to qualify at Atlanta the previous week, made sure he got into the field this time by posting the seventh-fastest lap, just a tick better than Rusty Wallace. Robert Pressley and Joe Nemechek filled the fifth row. Some of the biggest names in the sport had been relegated to the second half of the field.

Earnhardt would start 23rd, but he once again would use his Champion's choice of pit location and his team's pit road

(Left) Frenzied, makeshift repairs enabled Mark Martin to return to action following an accident — note the artistry of the car number! *(Above)* Jeff Gordon was not as lucky; his team could do nothing to repair the DuPont Chevrolet after he was involved in the same mishap.

excellence to move to the front. Dale Jarrett would start 26th and pit on the backstretch along with Michael Waltrip, Jimmy Spencer and Geoff and Todd Bodine. Chuck Bown returned to racing to pilot the Active Motorsports Chevrolet, replacing Jimmy Hensley. Rick Mast, Dave Marcis, Mike Wallace and, once again, Loy Allen were forced to use provisionals to make the field.

Kenny Wallace and Brad Teague were unable to qualify their Fords for the race.

Following the weekend's other events — Martin led all but three laps to cruise to the Dodge IROC Series victory on Saturday, and Larry Pearson scored his first victory of the season in the Mark III Vans 200 NASCAR Busch Series race — it was finally time to see if Gordon's DuPont Chevrolet could post its third victory of the season.

As expected, the repaving of Darlington resulted in faster speeds. The Goodyear tires adhered particularly well to the new asphalt, which allowed drivers to maintain higher speeds in the corners. Carrying more speed out of the corners resulted in additional straightaway speeds. In turn, faster straightaway speeds resulted in carrying yet more speed into the next corner. That cycle spelled trouble for those drivers who had forgotten how tricky old Darlington could be. The net result was a new record — 15 caution flags flew during the 400 miles. The old event record for cautions was five (set in 1967 and equaled in 1971 and 1994).

The 15 yellow flags also marked a new track record, erasing the old mark of 14 set during the Mountain Dew Southern 500 in 1982 and matched in 1985. By the end of the 1995 TranSouth 400, at least 30 cars carried scars from racing at the 1.366-mile track.

From the start, it looked as though Jeff Gordon would be the driver to beat for the victory. Jeff put "Blacker" at the point for more than 150 of the first 200 laps. But Jeff's hopes for a third victory were shattered when he was involved in an accident on a restart following the 11th caution period of the race. Bobby Labonte tapped Randy LaJoie, turning Randy around, and the two further col-

A real "Kodak Moment" at Darlington. Sterling Marlin and the entire Morgan-McClure team celebrate their second victory of the season, a triumph in the TranSouth Financial 400.

lected Dale Earnhardt, Morgan Shepherd, Dick Trickle and Gordon. Jeff's day was finished.

Sterling Marlin, who had brought his Kodak Chevrolet to the point for the first time on lap 160, managed to stay safely ahead of the accident. Once Gordon was eliminated from the race, the event became a duel between Earnhardt and Sterling. Dale moved to the front of the field after his Goodwrench crew turned him off pit road first during the final caution of the race, but Dale had been fighting a loose chassis throughout the day, and the Goodwrench Chevrolet simply wasn't handling well enough to deal a knock-out blow to the competition. Marlin fought, scrambled, diced and battled, and finally, with just 12 laps remaining in the race, the Kodak yellow Chevrolet passed the black Monte Carlo in the third turn. From that point on, Marlin unloaded his own haymaker.

By the time the checkered flag flew, Marlin was more than a full second ahead. The win was his third career victory and his second of the season.

Ted Musgrave, who had kept his Family Channel Ford in the lead pack throughout the final third of the race, posted a superb third behind Earnhardt — the best finish of his NASCAR Winston Cup career — ahead of an equally impressive run by Todd Bodine. Cope finished solidly in fifth place, ahead of Steve Grissom and Michael Waltrip. Morgan Shepherd and Bobby Hamilton were the remaining cars on the lead lap, and John Andretti claimed 10th place, the first car a lap in arrears.

Mark Martin and Rusty Wallace took big hits in the point race after suffering extensive damage to their respective Fords. Both were involved in an early-race accident (resulting in the third caution of the event) which began when Mark bumped the rear of Michael Waltrip's Pennzoil Pontiac during a restart. Crewmen turned Rusty's Miller Ford into a Modified-looking machine, and Mark's had aluminum sheet metal tacked onto the driver's door with a wobbly, hand-fashioned "6" on the bare aluminum. Rusty and Mark both were running at the finish but were classified 23rd and 37th.

In victory lane, Marlin's Kodak team celebrated its first Darlington win. Earnhardt, meanwhile, was grinning widely after he had changed his clothes in the Goodwrench transporter. He had posted his third second place of the season and his fifth top-five finish in as many races. Sterling had gained only five points during the afternoon, so Dale still had a commanding 67-point lead when the teams headed for Bristol's high banks.

In the garage area, NASCAR officials impounded Sterling's Chevrolet, Cope's Ford and Hamilton's STP Pontiac, loaded the vehicles and headed for the Lockheed wind tunnel in Georgia for the first comparative wind tunnel tests in the history of the sport.

TranSouth Financial 400

Race #5 — Final Race Results

Fin. Pos.	Str. Pos.	Car #	Driver	Team
1	5	4	Sterling Marlin	Kodak Film Chevrolet
2	23	3	Dale Earnhardt	Goodwrench Service Chevrolet
3	18	16	Ted Musgrave	The Family Channel Ford
4	31	75	Todd Bodine	Factory Stores Ford
5	13	12	Derrike Cope	Straight Arrow Ford
6	24	29	Steve Grissom	Meineke Chevrolet
7	28	30	Michael Waltrip	Pennzoil Pontiac
8	16	21	Morgan Shepherd	Citgo Ford
9	25	43	Bobby Hamilton	STP Pontiac
10	15	37	John Andretti	Kmart/Little Caesars Ford
11	3	25	Ken Schrader	Budweiser Chevrolet
12	21	11	Brett Bodine	Lowe's Ford
13	27	7	Geoff Bodine	Exide Batteries Ford
14	36	47	Billy Standridge	WCW Ford
15	41	90	Mike Wallace	Heilig-Meyers Ford
16	33	22	Randy LaJoie	MBNA America Pontiac
17	17	94	Bill Elliott	McDonald's Ford
18	42	27	Loy Allen	Hooters Ford
19	20	8	Jeff Burton	Raybestos Brakes Ford
20	34	77	Davy Jones	Jasper/USAir Ford
21	6	17	Darrell Waltrip	Western Auto Chevrolet
22	30	40	Greg Sacks	Kendall Pontiac
23	8	2	Rusty Wallace	Miller Genuine Draft Ford
24	40	71	Dave Marcis	Terramite Chevrolet
25	7	31	Ward Burton	Hardee's Chevrolet
26	39	1	Rick Mast	Skoal Ford
27	11	18	Bobby Labonte	Interstate Batteries Chevrolet
28	19	15	Dick Trickle	Ford Quality Care Ford
29	22	9	Lake Speed	Spam Ford
30	9	33	Robert Pressley	Skoal Bandit Chevrolet
31	35	98	Jeremy Mayfield	RCA Ford
32	1	24	Jeff Gordon	DuPont Auto Finishes Chevrolet
33	10	87	Joe Nemechek	Burger King Chevrolet
34	2	5	Terry Labonte	Kellogg's Chevrolet
35	38	42	Kyle Petty	Coors Light Pontiac
36	29	23	Jimmy Spencer	Smokin' Joe's Ford
37	12	6	Mark Martin	Valvoline Ford
38	26	28	Dale Jarrett	Texaco Havoline Ford
39	37	32	Chuck Bown	Active Trucking Chevrolet
40	32	26	Steve Kinser	Quaker State Ford
41	4	10	Ricky Rudd	Tide Ford
42	14	41	Ricky Craven	Kodiak Chevrolet

FOOD CITY 500

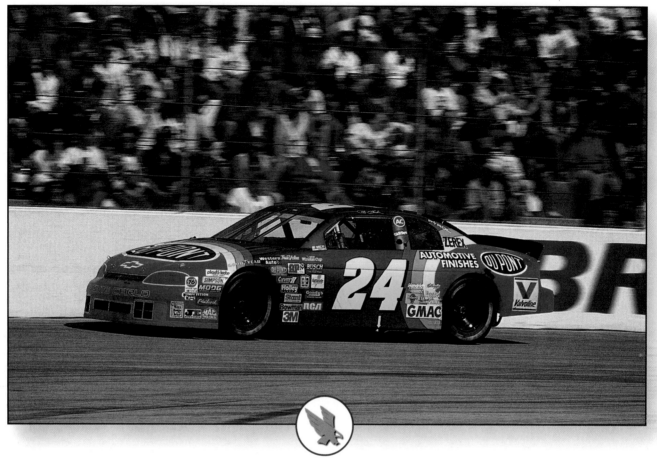

BRISTOL INTERNATIONAL RACEWAY

APRIL 2, 1995

•••••

Just five days after the TranSouth 400 at Darlington, the teams unloaded their short-track cars for the Food City 500 at Larry Carrier's steep-sided Bristol International Raceway.

Carrier continues to add seats at Bristol and his seats are sold almost before the last bolt is tightened. Until you see it, it's hard to believe that more than 75,000 fans could be seated around a half-mile oval. But Carrier continues to build, and by the time the expansion is completed, nearly 100,000 will be able to watch the non-stop action at Bristol.

Much had happened in the few days between Darlington and Bristol. NASCAR had taken the STP Pontiac, the Straight Arrow Ford and the Kodak Chevrolet for two days of intensive wind-tunnel testing at Lockheed and in Warren. Although questions regarding the test results were on everyone's mind, NASCAR officials were unable to supply any answers. The information gathered was very technical, and it would take weeks not only to decipher the results, but organize them in a meaningful format.

*Jeff Gordon, here on his way to his third victory of the season, jumped from 23rd to fourth in the early-season point standings based on his masterful performance at Bristol. (**Right**) During practice sessions, teams worked from an active pit road.*

Before practice opened on Thursday, Kenny Bernstein's Quaker State team announced that Hut Stricklin had been hired to work with the green Fords and driver Steve Kinser. Stricklin had been brought on board as a coach and consultant, and the team hoped he could speed Kinser along his learning curve as he made the transition from light sprint cars to heavier NASCAR Winston Cup machinery.

But before Hut could give a single lesson, he was pressed into service by the Hooters team. On Friday morning, Loy Allen (who had won three poles in 1994, including the Daytona 500) announced that he had resigned from his seat in the Junior Johnson-owned Ford the night before. Allen explained that he felt he needed more experience and believed he was holding back the whole team. So, Hut was retained as the driver for just this one race.

Allen's wasn't the only departure. Ben Hess was released from his ride in the Ray and Diane DeWitt-owned Ford. Hess had been unable to qualify for four of the season's first five races, so Butch Miller had been nominated to replace Hess, beginning with Bristol. But Miller made it clear that he would not drive for RaDiUs for the remainder of the season because he had a "great package" for the entire NASCAR SuperTruck Series by Craftsman that would preclude him from racing in NASCAR Winston

Cup "for the next couple of years."

The departures of Allen and Hess raised the number of driver changes in 1995 to five. At Rockingham, Mike Chase had been dropped from the Active Motorsports team and replaced by Jimmy Hensley. Hensley was replaced by Chuck Bown at Darlington. Gary Bradberry had left the Jimmy Means team at Atlanta and was replaced by Brad Teague.

Amidst the shuffling was a spot of good news: John Andretti was accepting congratulations from everyone on behalf of himself and wife Nancy after the birth of their daughter, Olivia Elizabeth. John was surprised and pleased by the outpouring of sentiment from fans, teams and drivers and commented that he felt like he was part of the NASCAR Winston Cup family. "I'm really proud to consider myself a [NASCAR] Winston Cup driver now and not an Indy car driver," John explained.

As the teams headed for the Goodyear garage for tires, they learned of an additional incentive for giving the race all they had: The name of this weekend's winning driver would automatically be written into the record books. The Food City 500 would mark Goodyear's 1,000th NASCAR Winston Cup triumph, a string that stretched back more than three decades. It would no doubt be very special to record the Eagles' long-sought-after 1,000th victory.

Of course, what the drivers wanted most from a victory was the points, and by the time the drivers took the track for the first practice session, everyone had committed the point table to memory. Although he had not yet won a race, Dale Earnhardt had put together five top-four finishes and carried a 67-point lead over Daytona 500 winner Sterling Marlin into Bristol. Mark Martin was third in the points but already 212 behind. Derrike Cope was fourth in the standings after taking the Straight Arrow Fords to three top-10 finishes in the first five races. Cope, the surprise of the early season, was merely two points behind Martin.

Terry Labonte was fifth in the standings, just three points behind Cope, and Ted Musgrave, another pleasant surprise, was just 19 points behind Labonte, in sixth place. Morgan Shepherd was seventh in the standings, just nine points behind Musgrave, and Jeff Gordon, on the strength of two victories in five races, was eighth in the standings. Dale Jarrett trailed Gordon by only seven points. Andretti held the final top-10 position but was barely ahead of Bobby Labonte and Ricky Rudd.

Some drivers expected to be leading the point standings by now were well down the list. Rusty Wallace had climbed to 16th but still trailed Earnhardt by more than 300 points. Brett, Todd and Geoff Bodine were all disappointed with their early-season performances, as were Bill Elliott, Kyle Petty, Dick Trickle, Jimmy Spencer and Darrell Waltrip.

Since the Chevrolet Monte Carlos had won

(Right) *John Andretti celebrated the arrival of his daughter with a special message on his Kmart Ford's spoiler.*
(Below) *Following an unwelcome meeting with the wall, Dale Earnhardt's Chevrolet spent 20 laps behind another wall — the pit wall — while his team made repairs.*

every pole since the Daytona 500, Martin and the Jack Roush team decided to let it all hang out in qualifying and post a pole of their own. Mark was the last driver to attempt to qualify during the first session, and he knew which driver he had to beat. Twenty-three-year-old Jeff Gordon had already made his case for the pole, piloting yet another rocketship from the Hendrick Motorsports shop. Martin, resorting to past experience, slung the Valvoline Ford around the oval in 15.399 seconds — just nipping Gordon's fast lap of 15.419 seconds. It was the first pole for Mark and the Roush Valvoline effort since last August's event at Watkins Glen.

Kyle Petty, determined to gain a pit slot on the frontstretch, turned in the third-fastest lap. Derrike Cope and David Green, who was qualifying for the injured Bobby Labonte, turned identical laps as they competed for the fourth position on the grid. Cope won the spot based on car owner points. Bobby would start the race but

would turn the car over to Green as soon as possible.

Musgrave qualified sixth-fastest, Ricky Craven seventh and Andretti eighth. Andretti's good showing in the Kranefuss/Haas Kmart "Blue Light Special" — whose rear spoiler exclaimed "It's A Girl" — was a fine way to celebrate the arrival of his daughter. Rusty Wallace and Jeff Burton claimed the final spots in the top 10, just nudging Geoff Bodine and Darrell Waltrip.

Terry Labonte, Rick Mast and Randy LaJoie were all absent from the first round of qualifying because their cars exceeded NASCAR's maximum rear-end wheel camber specifications. And Bill Ingle, the crew chief for Ricky Rudd's Tide Ford, was fined $1,000 after the car failed its pre-qualifying inspection; inspectors had found an A-frame and ball-joint assembly that was offset. After the necessary changes were made, Rudd qualified 13th fastest.

Terry Labonte, LaJoie and Mast all made it into the field during the second round of qualifying. Michael Waltrip, however, was forced to take a provisional to get into the field (it was the third provisional he had used this year). Steve Grissom, Ward Burton and Dave Marcis used the other provisionals to fill the 36-car field. Many others weren't as fortunate; Jeremy Mayfield, Joe Nemechek, Steve Kinser, Billy Standridge, Stricklin, Miller and Teague went home after being unable to get their cars into the field.

Front-row mates Martin and Gordon were good from the start of the race, but Petty was a man on a mission, and he pushed his blue and red Coors Light Pontiac into the lead early. Then Martin and Gordon asserted themselves, trading the lead for the next 200 laps.

While the drama at the front of the pack was unfolding, fans kept an eye on another classic Earnhardt "charge through the field." Dale had qualified poorly, starting 25th, but had advanced all the way to third — under green

— by the 100th lap. Then, as he tried to pass Jeff Burton on lap 117, the two touched, and Earnhardt was sent spinning into the concrete wall. Dale got the Goodwrench Monte Carlo moving, limped back to the pits and waited while his crew made repairs. After 20 laps, he was back at full speed but minus the hood, fenders and nose-piece of his black Chevrolet. It was obvious that the NASCAR Winston Cup standings again would be scrambled by the end of the race.

Martin and Gordon continued to dominate, and Rusty Wallace also joined the fray at the point. Wallace and Martin would jump away from the DuPont Chevrolet on the restarts after caution flags, but the longer the race ran, the better Gordon's car became. And since there were only seven caution flags during the race, Gordon's car just kept improving. With just over 100 laps to go, Gordon started cutting into Martin's lead, and on lap 402, Jeff went by the Ford and pulled away.

The youngster, knowing that Martin was his biggest threat, tried to put as much distance on the Ford as he could. While comfortably in the lead and with only 66 laps remaining, the DuPont Chevrolet began misfiring. His heart leapt into his throat because he thought he was running out of fuel. But crew chief Ray Evernham assured him he had plenty to make it to the end and told Gordon to switch ignition boxes. He did, and sure enough, the Chevrolet started purring again.

Gordon built his lead to more than five seconds. With nine laps to go, Jeff was told via radio that Martin had pitted for tires because his were worn out. "I wore the rubber off the tires — and then the cords off — trying to keep up," Mark said afterward. "Finally, the air just went out, and I had to come in."

That left only Wallace to contend with, but Gordon's worries weren't over yet. Four laps from the end, he started sliding in the corners and realized his own right-rear tire was worn out. He slowed considerably in the final laps, but there wasn't enough time for Wallace to catch the blue Chevrolet. Gordon finished the race with a 5.74-second lead over the black Miller Ford.

Behind Wallace came Darrell Waltrip, finishing solidly in third, followed by Bobby Hamilton, who posted his career-best finish in the Petty Enterprises Pontiac. It was the team's best performance on an oval track since 1988.

Rudd was fifth, and Jarrett was sixth in the Robert Yates Texaco Ford — the final car on the lead lap. Terry Labonte beat Martin for seventh place, and Sterling Marlin finished ninth. Marlin had been running fifth and was ready to take over the point lead when a tire lost its air with two laps to go. He had limped around the track for the final mile rather than come in for replacement tires and lose more positions. Robert Pressley was 10th in the Skoal Chevrolet.

Earnhardt, who lost only one additional lap after repairs had been made to his Chevrolet, finished 25th and managed to cling to the NASCAR Winston Cup point lead after all. But his lead was down to just 17 points over Marlin.

For Gordon and his "Rainbow Warriors," the third victory of the season was a most pleasant surprise. Since their best previous Bristol finish was an admitted "undistinguished" 17th, the team had arrived at Bristol "just hoping to take a complete car back home with us!"

Instead, for the third time in six races, Gordon made the trip to the winner's circle. He had been 21st in the point standings after Daytona, but he was now fourth, just a single point behind Martin.

It wasn't until after the team had returned to its shop and torn down the motor that Gordon and his mates found out how close they had come to not winning their third race of the season. A small screw from the carburetor base plate had loosened and fallen into the engine, where it rattled around from cylinder to cylinder. The pistons were battered and the valves were bent in every direction. It was amazing that the motor had even lasted through the final laps of the race!

Goodyear arrived at Bristol in great anticipation of a milestone: The Food City 500 would mark the Eagle's 1,000th victory in NASCAR Winston Cup competition.

Food City 500

Race #6 — Final Race Results

Fin. Pos.	Str. Pos.	Car #	Driver	Team
1	2	24	Jeff Gordon	DuPont Auto Finishes Chevrolet
2	9	2	Rusty Wallace	Miller Genuine Draft Ford
3	12	17	Darrell Waltrip	Western Auto Chevrolet
4	17	43	Bobby Hamilton	STP Pontiac
5	13	10	Ricky Rudd	Tide Ford
6	19	28	Dale Jarrett	Texaco Havoline Ford
7	21	5	Terry Labonte	Kellogg's Chevrolet
8	1	6	Mark Martin	Valvoline Ford
9	31	4	Sterling Marlin	Kodak Film Chevrolet
10	18	33	Robert Pressley	Skoal Bandit Chevrolet
11	34	29	Steve Grissom	Meineke Chevrolet
12	24	22	Randy LaJoie	MBNA America Pontiac
13	4	12	Derrike Cope	Straight Arrow Ford
14	20	94	Bill Elliott	McDonald's Ford
15	30	1	Rick Mast	Skoal Ford
16	23	23	Jimmy Spencer	Smokin' Joe's Ford
17	28	9	Lake Speed	Spam Ford
18	6	16	Ted Musgrave	The Family Channel Ford
19	8	37	John Andretti	Kmart/Little Caesars Ford
20	32	21	Morgan Shepherd	Citgo Ford
21	35	31	Ward Burton	Hardee's Chevrolet
22	33	30	Michael Waltrip	Pennzoil Pontiac
23	11	7	Geoff Bodine	Exide Batteries Ford
24	26	77	Davy Jones	Jasper/USAir Ford
25	25	3	Dale Earnhardt	Goodwrench Service Chevrolet
26	27	25	Ken Schrader	Budweiser Chevrolet
27	14	11	Brett Bodine	Lowe's Ford
28	10	8	Jeff Burton	Raybestos Brakes Ford
29	7	41	Ricky Craven	Kodiak Chevrolet
30	22	15	Dick Trickle	Ford Quality Care Ford
31	16	32	Chuck Bown	Active Trucking Chevrolet
32	5	18	Bobby Labonte	Interstate Batteries Chevrolet
33	29	75	Todd Bodine	Factory Stores Ford
34	36	71	Dave Marcis	Terramite Chevrolet
35	3	42	Kyle Petty	Coors Light Pontiac
36	15	40	Greg Sacks	Kendall Pontiac

FIRST UNION 400

NORTH WILKESBORO SPEEDWAY
APRIL 9, 1995
•••••

Enoch Staley's North Wilkesboro Speedway had taken on a new look by the time the race teams arrived at the track to contest the seventh event of the 1995 season.

The five-eighths-mile oval sported a new pit road that was one of the most unique on the NASCAR Winston Cup circuit. Pit road had been elongated and now featured a total of 42 pit stalls stretching from the third turn to the first turn. The new configuration meant that drivers who wish to pit must now begin decelerating as they exit the track's second turn. Most crew chiefs estimated that, under green-flag conditions, the act of entering pit road, making a stop and accelerating out of pit lane to rejoin the action would cost drivers approximately three laps on the track, a much slower turnaround time than that of the old layout. If green-flag stops played a major role in an event — as is often the case at North Wilkesboro — then things would get very interesting for teams trying to complete strategic maneuvers during the race.

Hut Stricklin, who had tried to work as both a consultant (to Kenny Bernstein's Quaker State Ford team) and a driver (in Junior Johnson's Hooters Ford after Loy Allen resigned from the ride) the previous weekend, was back to single duty at North Wilkesboro. He had maintained his consultant's role with Bernstein's team and was trying to accelerate Steve Kinser's pace along his learning curve.

Johnson and the Hooters team chose Jeff Purvis to be their "driver of the week." The pairing was a natural choice

Jeff Gordon surprised many — himself included — by winning the North Wilkesboro pole, his fourth of the young season. Brett Bodine took the other front-row spot at the site of his lone NASCAR Winston Cup victory. But when the First Union 400 concluded, neither Jeff nor Brett made the trip to victory lane: It was Dale Earnhardt (right) who emerged with the victory — his first of the year.

Despite the fine service Lake Speed received from his crew on pit road, he was unable to capitalize on his fine sixth starting position and finished a disappointing 25th.

when one considered that the restaurant chain's principals also owned Eastern Foods, the producer of Jackaroo Barbecue Sauce, Purvis' regular sponsor.

Randy MacDonald was on hand to pilot Jimmy Means' Ford at North Wilkesboro; he would try to qualify the team for the first time this year. Gary Bradberry had made five attempts to qualify the team, but he was unsuccessful, as was Brad Teague, Bradberry's successor.

Forty-five teams were vying for a maximum of 36 spots, and it soon was clear that the first round of qualifying would go a long way toward determining the field for the First Union 400: Saturday's weather was projected to be much warmer than Friday's, so it would be much more difficult to turn a fast lap in the second session.

On Friday, Derrike Cope, who continued to surprise the garage residents with his performances behind the wheel of Bobby Allison's Straight Arrow Fords, set the pace early. But Cope's ranking at the top of the leader board lasted only until Brett Bodine rolled off the line in Junior Johnson's Lowe's Ford. Bodine gave thousands of Johnson's "home"

fans reason to cheer when he posted a lap faster than Cope's and moved the No. 11 to the top of the list. But the upstate New York native's hopes for a pole (which would've been his first since the June '93 Michigan race) were crushed late in the session (just three cars remained in the qualifying line). Unfortunately for Brett, one of the three was the rainbow-hued DuPont Chevrolet.

Although Jeff Gordon had won three poles already this season, he didn't expect to claim his fourth at North Wilkesboro. The best he had qualified at the roller-coaster track in the past was a seventh in '93 — he was 12th for the start of both races in '94. His team was hoping for a "decent starting position," but Jeff was so sure of a mediocre showing that he had convinced wife Brooke not to come to North Wilkesboro for the first round of qualifying!

On his initial lap, the car pushed

Brett Bodine arrived at North Wilkesboro hoping to give his team a much-needed boost in front of its hometown fans. Brett started second and led briefly, but the handling on Junior Johnson's Ford was off a bit. In the end, Brett finished ninth, one lap off the pace.

toward the wall entering the first turn, and the 23-year-old "threw that lap out the window." During the second lap, "we rolled through and I didn't lose my momentum. I didn't think it was a great lap," Gordon said after his qualifying run, "but surprisingly, it was good enough for the pole — we were all very surprised."

Gordon's prowess pushed Bodine to the outside of the front row and Cope back to the inside of the second row. Cope shared the limelight with another surprisingly fast qualifier: Bobby Hamilton. Hamilton had cranked up the STP Pontiac and posted a lap just faster than the defending NASCAR Winston Cup champion, Dale Earnhardt.

Lake Speed claimed sixth place for the start with a strong qualifying run, just ahead of Mark Martin and Joe Nemechek. Nemechek had had a rather rough ride en route to his eighth-place start. On his first qualifying lap, Joe spun on the backstretch and tagged the new concrete pit wall in the third turn. Because he had not completed a lap, Joe was allowed to return to the track as the final driver in the first session. Obviously, he made the best of his

second chance. Ted Musgrave and Morgan Shepherd claimed the last of the top-10 positions, beating out Rusty Wallace and Ricky Rudd by fractions of seconds.

Following the first session, there was some serious head scratching and teeth gnashing in the garage area. Some high-profile drivers and teams — including Dale Jarrett, John Andretti, Bobby Labonte, Jeremy Mayfield, Kenny Wallace, Jeff Purvis, Davy Jones and Steve Kinser — were in danger of missing the race, particularly if Saturday's warmer temperatures arrived as predicted.

Sure enough, Saturday's weather arrived just as anticipated. Of the dri-

vers who didn't make the race on Friday, the first 14 stood on their times; they knew they could not go any faster in the warmer weather. But 11 others had absolutely no choice: They had to run again and hope they could find a way into the tight field.

Jarrett and Andretti decided to use provisionals to get into the field. Of those who ran for it, Dave Marcis led the times. He posted the fastest time of the session, but it still wasn't good enough to earn his way into the field. He also was forced to use a provisional. It was Marcis' final provisional for the first third of the season, which meant he was "naked" for the upcoming races at Martinsville and Talladega. When he went to Sears Point, however, he would receive another provisional for the second third of the season. The final driver to make the field via a provisional was Bobby Labonte. Mayfield, Kenny Wallace, Chuck Bown, Jay Hedgecock, Jones and Billy Standridge all loaded their cars for the journey home to watch the race on ESPN. Also, Purvis was unable to get the Hooters car into the field, so car owner Johnson was left with just a single race entry, driven by Brett Bodine. Steve Kinser also failed to make the field: A glum group of green-clad crew members could only load the Quaker State Ford back into the transporter. Although Jarrett was in the field, the Havoline Ford camp wasn't exactly marked by back-slapping delight. Jarrett's provisional was the first one taken by the Robert Yates-owned team since 1992.

(Left) Joe Nemechek and crew chief Tony Furr inspect the tires from Joe's Burger King Chevrolet. Excessive tire wear, caused by North Wilkesboro's abrasive surface, was a concern for all the teams.
(Below) Both Dale Jarrett (28) and Bobby Labonte were forced to use provisionals to make the starting lineup, but once in the race, they gave it all they had. Dale eventually finished 11th, four spots ahead of Labonte.

Greg Sacks (40) was already slightly under the weather when he started the race, and the strain of hustling the car around the tight North Wilkesboro oval — as he's doing here alongside rookie contender Robert Pressley — eventually took its toll. Sacks fell victim to fatigue and was forced to retire on lap 325.

One of the most disappointed drivers was MacDonald; he had been unable to wring a fast enough lap from Means' Thunderbird. Following Saturday afternoon qualifying, Means and car owner Bud Moore were seen huddled in the front of the Quality Care transporter, and the next day, Means announced he would not field his car for the next few races. He said he had reached his "frustration level" as car owner and instead would try a position as team manager for Moore's Thunderbirds, driven by Dick Trickle.

One of the few happy faces in the garage belonged to Mike Wallace. Wallace had given car owner Junie Donlavey a super 71st birthday gift by putting the Heilig-Meyers Ford solidly in the field.

When the field rolled out for the First Union 400, temperatures were in the mid-80s, and a gusting wind threatened to turn the umbrellas on pit road inside-out. The weather wouldn't be the only challenge: It was clear from practice that North Wilkesboro's gritty surface would take a toll on tires. Those who were best able to manage the wear on their Goodyear Eagles would benefit during long runs under green-flag conditions.

And few drivers are more savvy about tire wear than seven-time champion Earnhardt.

After the drop of the green flag, Gordon flashed to the front, while Brett Bodine faded slightly. Earnhardt, mean-while, bided his time and moved to the point for the first time on the 42nd lap. For the remainder of the race, Earnhardt remained a factor in the battle for the victory. One had only to review his career record at North Wilkesboro to rank him a favorite to win the race. Prior to Sunday's race, Dale had made 32 career starts at the track; in those starts, he had posted 28 top-10 finishes, 19 top fives and four victories. Earnhardt didn't disappoint.

In the first six races of the season, Earnhardt had posted three seconds, a third and a fourth — everyone knew it was just a matter of time before the black Chevrolet made its first victory lane visit of the season.

The clock ran out at North Wilkesboro.

Dale capitalized on the problems of some of his challengers and, with just three caution flags marring the afternoon, managed his tires better than his competitors. He finally took command of the race on lap 317 and steadily pulled away from the remainder of the field. Dale breezed to his 64th career victory by a margin of more than 13 seconds, two-thirds of a lap ahead of his nearest challenger. A delighted Gordon, whose best previous finish at North Wilkesboro had been an 11th, crossed the line second. Jeff had led for nearly a quarter of the race but fell away from the chase in the final quarter of the event when his tires were rendered useless after just 30 laps. In the end, Gordon had to contend more with Martin's Valvoline

Ford than Earnhardt's Goodwrench Chevrolet. Fortunately for Gordon, although Mark had drawn to within a car-length several times, he had been unable to find the mustard to draw alongside Gordon, let alone pass the DuPont driver. Martin was forced to settle for third place.

Rusty Wallace's challenge for the victory had fallen victim to a jammed air wrench — a lug nut had gotten stuck sideways in the socket during one of his stops. He finished fourth, ahead of Steve Grissom, who posted the best finish of his brief NASCAR Winston Cup career with his lead-lap fifth place.

Ted Musgrave, Sterling Marlin, Rick Mast and Brett Bodine all finished a lap in arrears. Darrell Waltrip soldiered his way to a 10th-place finish just ahead of Jarrett.

The heat and humidity also played a part in the final outcome of the event. Kyle Petty, already ill on race morning with flu-like symptoms, called for a relief driver. Although Mike Wallace, out via an accident after 225 laps, responded to the Coors Light pits, Kyle remained in the car. When he finally emerged, he was given fluids and oxygen and taken to the infield care center, from which he later was released. Jeff Burton and Greg Sacks were only two of several drivers who also were given medical attention following the event.

Of the 36-car field, 33 cars were running at the completion of the event, and due to the lack of attrition, tires had become scarce. NASCAR officials quickly had stepped in, controlling the distribution and mounting of new sets of tires to ensure that the teams contending for the victory all received the tires they needed. The officials' watchful eyes prevented some teams from "hoarding" tires on pit road and establishing what NASCAR considered a potentially unfair advantage over some of the other teams.

When all was said and done, it had taken seven races — much longer than most had expected — for Richard Childress' team to score its first victory of the season. Nonetheless, the Goodwrench team had displayed its championship mettle during the first half-dozen races of the season; it had been reliable and consistent enough to post five top-four finishes in that six-race string. Now the team had broken the '95 ice, and most expected this would be just the first victory in a skein of wins that would propel Earnhardt to another title.

Earnhardt was one of the few who disagreed.

"We've got to race these events one at a time," the defending champion noted. "We've gotten the consistency we need to be a contender, but there's a lot of the season left to race yet, and we all know that anything can happen. This is a sweet victory. But it's a long way from here to Atlanta in November."

First Union 400

Race #7 — Final Race Results

Fin. Pos.	Str. Pos.	Car #	Driver	Team
1	5	3	Dale Earnhardt	Goodwrench Service Chevrolet
2	1	24	Jeff Gordon	DuPont Auto Finishes Chevrolet
3	7	6	Mark Martin	Valvoline Ford
4	11	2	Rusty Wallace	Miller Genuine Draft Ford
5	15	29	Steve Grissom	Meineke Chevrolet
6	9	16	Ted Musgrave	The Family Channel Ford
7	20	4	Sterling Marlin	Kodak Film Chevrolet
8	13	1	Rick Mast	Skoal Ford
9	2	11	Brett Bodine	Lowe's Ford
10	22	17	Darrell Waltrip	Western Auto Chevrolet
11	33	28	Dale Jarrett	Texaco Havoline Ford
12	17	25	Ken Schrader	Budweiser Chevrolet
13	4	43	Bobby Hamilton	STP Pontiac
14	27	7	Geoff Bodine	Exide Batteries Ford
15	35	18	Bobby Labonte	Interstate Batteries Chevrolet
16	30	5	Terry Labonte	Kellogg's Chevrolet
17	34	37	John Andretti	Kmart/Little Caesars Ford
18	28	33	Robert Pressley	Skoal Bandit Chevrolet
19	10	21	Morgan Shepherd	Citgo Ford
20	8	87	Joe Nemechek	Burger King Chevrolet
21	25	75	Todd Bodine	Factory Stores Ford
22	23	30	Michael Waltrip	Pennzoil Pontiac
23	31	22	Randy LaJoie	MBNA America Pontiac
24	18	31	Ward Burton	Hardee's Chevrolet
25	6	9	Lake Speed	Spam/Melling Ford
26	14	8	Jeff Burton	Raybestos Brakes Ford
27	29	23	Jimmy Spencer	Smokin' Joe's Ford
28	16	94	Bill Elliott	McDonald's Ford
29	12	10	Ricky Rudd	Tide Ford
30	3	12	Derrike Cope	Straight Arrow Ford
31	24	42	Kyle Petty	Coors Light Pontiac
32	19	15	Dick Trickle	Ford Quality Care Ford
33	21	41	Ricky Craven	Kodiak Chevrolet
34	36	71	Dave Marcis	Olive Garden Chevrolet
35	32	40	Greg Sacks	Kendall Pontiac
36	26	90	Mike Wallace	Heilig-Meyers Ford

HANES 500

MARTINSVILLE SPEEDWAY
APRIL 23, 1995
•••••

The teams had enjoyed a brief respite from weekly competition with the Easter holiday, but the break in action didn't translate into a lack of topics of conversation. When the transporters were unloaded at Martinsville Speedway for the Hanes 500, crew members had plenty to talk about as they went about the business of preparing their mounts for the final short-track event of the first half of the season.

The most sobering — but encouraging — news was that Richard Petty successfully had undergone surgery on April 18. Petty would be released from the hospital the day following the Hanes 500.

Two days after the North Wilkesboro race, car owner Kenny Bernstein and driver Steve Kinser had parted company. Steve would return to the World of Outlaws series with Quaker State as his new team's sponsor. Kinser, unquestionably one of the finest driving talents in the motorsports world, had found the transition to the 3,400-pound NASCAR Winston Cup stock cars a difficult row to hoe. He had qualified for only two of the season's first seven events. Kinser had been forced to take provisionals to get into the field for three races and had failed to qualify fast enough to even rate a provisional at the other two events. It was an extremely difficult decision for both car owner and driver to make, but once the matter had been laid to rest, Bernstein announced that Hut Stricklin would be the "interim" driver for the Quaker State Thunderbird for the Hanes 500.

*Rusty Wallace and longtime friend and Penske Racing South co-owner Don Miller are happy to pose with their wares following a successful — albeit long — day at Martinsville. It was Wallace's first win of the season but his fourth in his last five starts at the Virginia half-mile. (**Right**) A throng of enthusiastic spectators outlasted Mother Nature and were treated to a fine show at Martinsville.*

founder. "We have the original furniture and many of his mementos that were in the office, so we're going to put it all back in his office, the way it was, and put a glass door on the doorway so fans can see it as a tribute to him," Geoff explained. "He built this place and it's a part of him and we don't ever plan to forget that."

The Morgan-McClure team and driver Sterling Marlin were breathing a collective sigh of relief. Engine builder Runt Pittman was continuing to improve following a close call. In a boating accident near Wilmington, N.C., Pittman had lost his balance, hit his head and fallen into the water. Runt had been knocked unconscious and nearly drowned. Only the quick assistance of others on the fishing boat kept the accident from becoming a tragedy. After five days in the hospital, he was released and was continuing his recovery at home.

But not all of the news from the holiday break

(Above) Steve Hmiel and Mark Martin keep a close eye — and watch — on the competition during practice for the Hanes 500. (Right) Bobby Labonte (18) captured the first-ever pole for the Interstate Batteries team (the second of Bobby's career), but his front-row vantage point was short-lived. On the first lap of the race, Bobby found himself chasing the entire field after he was tagged in the rear and sent spinning. He eventually finished 10th.

Elton Sawyer had been named to pilot Junior Johnson's Hooters Ford. Sawyer, the team's third driver in three races, could only say that he hoped the arrangement led to several drives on the NASCAR Winston Cup tour. He maintained, however, that his NASCAR Busch Series, Grand National Division ride, in a competitive Ford fielded by Atkin-Sutton Motorsports, was his first priority.

Immediately following the North Wilkesboro event, ground-breaking festivities had been held for Bruton Smith's new Texas Motor Speedway in Ft. Worth. Three notable drivers taking part in the ceremony were Bobby and Terry Labonte and Jeff Gordon. Also, Ernie Irvan had driven one of Robert Yates' Fords during a test at Road Atlanta as the team made preparations for the upcoming Sears Point race. The test drive was another phase in his step-by-step recovery from his '94 Michigan accident.

Geoff Bodine had celebrated his 46th birthday and announced that he was in the process of restoring Alan Kulwicki's office in his race shop as a tribute to the team's

was good. Ronnie Hopkins, a longtime chassis builder for several NASCAR Winston Cup teams, had died after a long illness, and Tom Ingram, the brother of five-time NASCAR Busch Series, Grand National Division champion Jack Ingram, had died on April 17. A former racer, Tom had built winning engines for Jack, Harry Gant, Tommy Houston, L.D. Ottinger and the late Butch Lindley, among others, in a career that had spanned more than two decades.

Soon however, discussion of the past gave way to talk of the present and future. Since Chevrolet had won the first seven races of the season, Ford and Pontiac teams were scrambling to find a way to beat the new Monte Carlos, and they hoped that Clay Earles' flat, half-mile Virginia track would prove to be an equalizer of sorts.

NASCAR officials had sorted through the seemingly endless reams of computerized findings from the wind tunnel tests of the Ford, Chevrolet and Pontiac cars and announced that the wind tunnel tests had shown the Monte Carlo body to provide superior downforce in the corners. NASCAR officials indicated that they were having conversations with crew chiefs from teams of all makes in hopes of making the three brands more equal on the track. Teams expected some changes to the nose ride heights and rear spoilers to be announced any day.

After the first seven races of the season, point leader Dale Earnhardt enjoyed a 26-point lead over Sterling Marlin. Jeff Gordon had moved all the way up to third in the standings; his second place at North Wilkesboro had allowed him to inch ahead of Mark Martin by just four points. Terry Labonte was fifth in the standings and Rusty Wallace was sixth, ahead of Ted Musgrave and Dale Jarrett. Steve Grissom continued to impress and held down ninth place in the standings despite missing the Richmond race. Derrike Cope, however, had fallen to 10th in the points following his 30th-place finish at North Wilkesboro.

Rusty came to Martinsville hoping to continue his outstanding performances on the short tracks. He had been the only driver to post top-three finishes in every previous short-track event (Richmond, Bristol and North Wilkesboro). The 1989 champion was hoping for a strong finish on the half-mile and a boost in the points.

Just prior to the first qualifying session, overcast skies gave way to warming sunshine, and those who ran early, before the asphalt and concrete had heated up, seemed to have the advantage. So after the 43 cars in search of a spot on the 36-car starting grid had turned laps, the top 10 could best be described as unusual. Missing from that group were the likes of Jeff Gordon, Wallace, Earnhardt and others expected to start at the front of the field.

Instead, Bobby Labonte had cranked off a lap fast enough for his second career NASCAR Winston Cup pole position and the first in the history of Joe Gibbs' Interstate Batteries team!

Outside Labonte was rookie contender Robert Pressley, who'd posted a brilliant lap in another green and black car, this one owned by Leo Jackson and sponsored by Skoal. Greg Sacks had planted his right foot on the floor of his Kendall Pontiac and surprised everyone — including himself — by putting the Grand Prix on the inside of the second row. Darrell Waltrip had displayed the firepower of his Western Auto Monte Carlo and grabbed the fourth position, alongside Sacks, for the start of the 500-lapper.

Mark Martin had the fastest Ford, and Bobby Hamilton continued to impress with the STP Pontiac; he had captured the sixth spot, barely beating out Kyle Petty's Coors Light Pontiac. It was the first time this season that three Pontiacs had qualified in the top 10. Ricky Rudd had turned the eighth-fastest lap, and Sawyer justified his selection as the driver of the Hooters Ford by snagging the inside of the fifth row. Jarrett and the Havoline Ford rounded out the top 10.

On just the fifth lap of the Hanes 500, Terry Labonte and Morgan Shepherd ran out of real estate. Labonte was unable to continue and finished last (36th). Dale Earnhardt, who was sandwiched between Labonte and Martinsville's concrete wall, limped back to the garage for repairs (inset) and returned to the track 19 laps later. He was credited with a 29th-place finish.

Again, the second round of qualifying turned into a game of strategy. Nine drivers, including Michael Waltrip and Randy LaJoie, stood on their Friday times. Fourteen others decided to run for one of the last 16 positions in the field. Dick Trickle turned the fastest lap to claim the 21st starting position, but many others were not as fortunate. Both Michael and Randy were bumped from the field; Waltrip used a provisional to make the field, but LaJoie had none available and had no choice but to go home. Cope, John Andretti and Geoff Bodine also were forced to use provisional starts to make the field.

Certainly, if nothing else, those drivers were grateful that their car owners were high enough on the list to make using a provisional a possibility. If they needed to be reminded of their good fortune, they needed only to watch the others, whose crews dispiritedly loaded their transporters. Todd Bodine, Jimmy Spencer, Chuck Bown, Jay Hedgecock, Jeff Burton and Davy Jones all were unable to turn a lap fast enough to get into the field for Sunday's Hanes 500.

When the crews arrived at the spit-and-polish bullring on Sunday morning, there was doubt as to whether or not the race would be held. The teams might very well have been forced to while away the day in their transporters, waiting through the rain and waiting for a postponement of the event until Monday. Storms were raging throughout the Southeast, and the chances of running enough laps to get the Hanes 500 into the record book appeared marginal at best. Clay Campbell, the usually affable track president, had a harried look on his face. He and wife Kim had welcomed their first son, William Clay, into the family just a few days before race weekend, and Clay was teased unmercifully by members of the NASCAR family who wanted to know if the tired look on his face was from trying to keep the Hanes 500 on schedule or from being up night after night with the newborn. Clay simply smiled, accepted the congratulations offered by everyone and said he hoped the weather would clear enough to get the race on the books.

More than two-and-a-half hours past its scheduled starting time, the Hanes 500 finally began, but within five laps, the race had taken on a totally unexpected look.

Terry Labonte tried to force his way past Morgan Shepherd, and the two collided, only to separate and then hit again. Earnhardt was simply too close for comfort and had nowhere to go when the drama unfolded. All three cars suffered extensive damage.

Earnhardt eventually was forced to pull his Goodwrench Chevrolet behind pit wall, where his black-clad crew members swarmed all over the Monte Carlo like ants on sugar. At first, it looked as though Earnhardt was out for the day, but yeoman-like work by his crew enabled him to return to action just 19 laps later despite a battered front end. He made the best of the situation and fought his way to a 25th-place finish. Shepherd did the best he could with what remained of the Wood Brothers Thunderbird and, after extensive repairs, came home 31st. Labonte wasn't quite as fortunate. His day had ended for good after he'd completed just four laps, and as a result, he would tumble all the way to ninth in the point standings.

Robert Pressley was the early race leader, but it didn't take long for Wallace to pull his Miller Ford into contention for the victory (if he succeeded, the win would be his fourth in the last five Martinsville races). Eventually, the race evolved into a battle between the black and yellow Ford and a surprise contender, Darrell Waltrip, whose Chevrolet was running on rails.

But on lap 184, rain began falling again, and NASCAR officials dropped the red flag while Wallace was leading and Waltrip was in second place. Officials hoped the showers would pass in time to dry the track and complete the race. In the next two hours, the track somehow did dry enough to allow a restart, and as the cars circled around under the caution, completing the drying process, team radios crackled with terse conversations about strategy for the rest of the race.

Sterling Marlin's Morgan-McClure Chevrolet suffered front-end damage when Sterling ran into the back of Rick Mast during the lap-five incident. Although the "Mighty-Mites" quickly returned Sterling to the fray, the episode cost Sterling a lap which he was never able to regain.

The cars had not returned to the track until 6 p.m., and since the low clouds reduced the available light, it was obvious to everyone that the full 500 laps would not be completed.

Waltrip gambled that NASCAR would only allow the event to run barely past the 250 laps needed for a race to be "official": He stayed on the track while the remainder of the leaders pitted for new tires and fuel on lap 206. Once the race went green on lap 219, Darrell hoped he could hold off the drivers behind him and "steal" a victory.

For the next 20 laps, he held the point, but finally, Wallace passed him just 12 laps before halfway in a determined move that said, "If this thing ends at 251, I'm gonna be the guy at the front!"

Darrell's gamble had failed, and on used tires, he could only float backwards through the field. He finally made a stop on lap 292, but because he did so under green-flag conditions, he was a lap down when a caution flew just four laps later. However, he made up the lap in ensuing cautions and worked his way back to fourth place, but that was as high as he could get.

Wallace was determined to capitalize on the fact that he was fronting the field, and when NASCAR officials informed the drivers on lap 346 that the race would end in 10 laps due to darkness, Wallace prepared to personally end Chevrolet's string at seven.

He wouldn't do it without a bit of a scare, however. Three laps later, Ward Burton and Kenny Wallace spun in the fourth turn. The ensuing yellow allowed the field to close the gap Rusty had created, and when the green flag appeared on lap 354, the Miller Ford driver looked in his mirror only to see a strong-running Musgrave locked on his bumper. But Wallace hammered the throttle, pulled away to a small margin and then worked his way around the track to post an eight-car-length victory over the Family Channel Ford.

Behind Musgrave came Gordon, who barely beat back Waltrip's determined charge. Martin was fifth, giving Jack Roush two cars in the top five, and Ken Schrader slipped past Jarrett to claim sixth. Bobby Hamilton and Kyle Petty finished eighth and ninth, the final cars on the lead lap, and Bobby Labonte claimed 10th, the first of eight cars a lap in arrears. Hamilton's eighth was his fourth top-10 finish in the last six races, and Petty's ninth was his best since he had finished 10th at Rockingham in the second race of the season.

Wallace's victory was more than just the first Thunderbird win of the season. He had led the most laps, and when his prowess was combined with Earnhardt's problems, he had chopped 109 points off Dale's lead. Rusty couldn't be blamed for wishing that the rest of the season would be contested on short tracks!

Hanes 500

Race #8 — Final Race Results

Fin. Pos.	Str. Pos.	Car #	Driver	Team
1	15	2	Rusty Wallace	Miller Genuine Draft Ford
2	32	16	Ted Musgrave	The Family Channel Ford
3	12	24	Jeff Gordon	DuPont Auto Finishes Chevrolet
4	4	17	Darrell Waltrip	Western Auto Chevrolet
5	5	6	Mark Martin	Valvoline Ford
6	13	25	Ken Schrader	Budweiser Chevrolet
7	10	28	Dale Jarrett	Texaco Havoline Ford
8	6	43	Bobby Hamilton	STP Pontiac
9	7	42	Kyle Petty	Coors Light Pontiac
10	1	18	Bobby Labonte	Interstate Batteries Chevrolet
11	11	11	Brett Bodine	Lowe's Ford
12	14	94	Bill Elliott	McDonald's Ford
13	17	4	Sterling Marlin	Kodak Film Chevrolet
14	30	87	Joe Nemechek	Burger King Chevrolet
15	35	30	Michael Waltrip	Pennzoil Pontiac
16	19	98	Jeremy Mayfield	RCA Ford
17	2	33	Robert Pressley	Skoal Bandit Chevrolet
18	25	41	Ricky Craven	Kodiak Chevrolet
19	26	29	Steve Grissom	Meineke Chevrolet
20	9	27	Elton Sawyer	Hooters Ford
21	28	81	Kenny Wallace	TIC Financial Ford
22	3	40	Greg Sacks	Kendall Pontiac
23	23	71	Dave Marcis	Olive Garden Chevrolet
24	21	15	Dick Trickle	Ford Quality Care Ford
25	29	31	Ward Burton	Hardee's Chevrolet
26	24	9	Lake Speed	Spam/Melling Ford
27	31	90	Mike Wallace	Heilig-Meyers Ford
28	33	12	Derrike Cope	Straight Arrow Ford
29	20	3	Dale Earnhardt	Goodwrench Service Chevrolet
30	8	10	Ricky Rudd	Tide Ford
31	18	21	Morgan Shepherd	Citgo Ford
32	34	37	John Andretti	Kmart/Little Caesars Ford
33	27	26	Hut Stricklin	Quaker State Ford
34	22	1	Rick Mast	Skoal Ford
35	36	7	Geoff Bodine	Exide Batteries Ford
36	16	5	Terry Labonte	Kellogg's Chevrolet

WINSTON SELECT 500

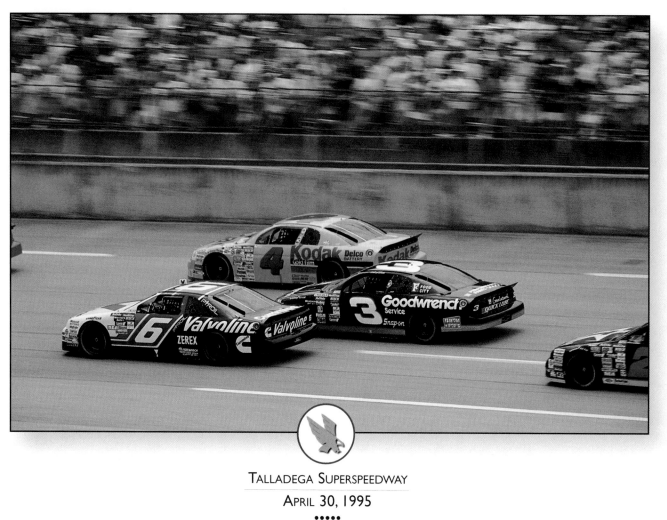

TALLADEGA SUPERSPEEDWAY
APRIL 30, 1995
•••••

While Dale Earnhardt was manhandling his Goodwrench Chevrolet to a 29th-place at Martinsville, Sterling Marlin was struggling with his own mount. The driver of the Kodak Chevrolet finished 13th (a lap down to winner Rusty Wallace), a finish just high enough to keep the Tennessean in second place in the NASCAR Winston Cup standings as the teams headed for the mammoth Talladega Superspeedway and the Winston Select 500.

Marlin, the winner of the Daytona 500 and the TranSouth 400 at Darlington, was primed for a third win when crew chief Tony Glover and the rest of the Morgan-McClure "Mighty-Mites" rolled their yellow Monte Carlo off the tailgate at track president Grant Lynch's 2.66-mile oval.

Sterling trailed Earnhardt by just eight points in the battle for the top rung of the point standings, and as if that weren't enough pressure, Marlin also was staring a cool $100,000 bonus in the face. His Daytona victory had qualified him for the Winston Select Million program, in which R.J. Reynolds posts a $1 million bonus payable to the driver able to win three of four selected events on the tour in a single season. And that wasn't all: The first driver able

At the start of the Winston Select 500, Dale Earnhardt, Sterling Marlin, Jeff Gordon and Mark Martin sat atop the point standings, and it didn't take the foursome long to demonstrate why. Early in the race, Martin (6), Earnhardt (3) and Marlin make it three-wide as they set sail.

(Right) Darrell Waltrip plots his strategy prior to the Winston Select 500. Whatever his plan, it worked! Although Darrell started a less-than-stunning 21st, he had worked his way up to fourth by the conclusion of the race.

to win two of the four "crown jewel" events would receive a $100,000 bonus (a "consolation" prize if no driver was able to clinch three of the four selected events). If Marlin won at Talladega, he automatically would win the $100,000; plus,

he effectively would have eliminated all other drivers from contention for the bonus million. Clearly, a win in the Winston Select 500 would put him in the catbird's seat for the Million — he would then only have to win either Charlotte's Coca-Cola 600 or the Mountain Dew Southern 500 at Darlington in September to secure the biggest payoff of his career.

Marlin knew the task was a difficult one. Last year, he had been faced with the same situation: He had won the Daytona 500 but then come up empty in the three remaining races. But this year, Sterling felt that the new Monte Carlo body, combined with engine builder Runt Pittman's exotic-sounding engine (which had taken him to victory lane at Daytona), greatly improved his chances over last year's, at least to win the $100,000 bonus. Pittman, who had spent several days in the hospital recovering from a

(Above) Shortly after Ricky Rudd arrived at Talladega, NASCAR inspectors found an unapproved device on the Tide Ford and slapped Rudd with a record fine.
(Right) Jeff Purvis (44), Jeremy Mayfield (98) and Brett Bodine (11) ride seemingly in formation in front of the record crowd. Of the three, Mayfield finished highest — 14th. Purvis and Bodine finished 29th and 30th, respectively.

boating accident, was back on the scene at Talladega. But the team was missing its manager and co-owner. Larry McClure had suffered fractures of his lower left arm in a highway accident on April 26 and was unable to come to Talladega.

While Marlin was dreaming of the $100,000 bonus, Earnhardt also had visions of 100 Big Ones dancing in his head. The driver leading the points at the conclusion of the Winston Select 500 would pocket a

$100,000 bonus from RJR as part of the revised point fund payoff. Needless to say, Earnhardt was determined to protect his eight-point lead.

On the strength of three wins and five top-five finishes in the first eight races of the season, Jeff Gordon had moved near the top of the point heap. He was now third — 70 points behind Earnhardt and 19 ahead of Mark Martin. Martin, incidentally, was the highest-placed Ford driver in the standings. Rusty Wallace's victory in the weather-shortened Martinsville race had moved him to fifth in the standings, where he trailed Earnhardt by 129. Ted Musgrave had continued to perform well; he held sixth in the standings, just 22 markers behind Rusty. Dale Jarrett was seventh, 30 points behind Musgrave, and Bobby Hamilton, Terry Labonte and Steve Grissom held down the final positions in the top 10.

Within an hour of unloading the Tide Ford from its transporter, crew chief Bill Ingle and owner/driver Ricky Rudd were deep in conference with NASCAR officials in the garage area. A NASCAR inspector had found an illegal hydraulic system built into the Ford; the system allowed the rear of the car to be lowered, which reduced the aerodynamic drag and increased the car's speed. Rudd and Ingle were fined a total of $50,000 — the largest fine in the history of the sport. Ricky was hit for $20,000 as the driver and $25,000 as the car owner, and Ingle's total came to $5,000. It was the second time in less than a week that fines had been levied on Ingle. He had been fined $250 the previous week for striking Ted Musgrave following the conclusion of the Hanes 500. In addition, Ingle had been fined $1,000 at Bristol when an offset A-frame suspension part was found on Rudd's Ford during inspection.

Morgan Shepherd (21) and Kyle Petty (42) split Lake Speed (9) and Davey Jones (77) as they blast through Talladega's trioval. Shepherd, who finished third, would eventually play a significant role in the outcome of the race — and the points.

To be sure, NASCAR's inspectors were busy at Talladega. During pre-practice inspections, they found "spreader" devices in several fuel cells; the devices are designed to act as a baffle and distribute fuel evenly in the cell. The sanctioning body confiscated the implements from the cars of Darrell Waltrip, Ken Schrader, Davy Jones, Ricky Craven, Mike Wallace, Jimmy Spencer, Bill Elliott and Elton Sawyer.

Speaking of Sawyer (but in a more positive context), his performance at Martinsville had earned him another ride in the Hooters Ford. Elton and crew chief Mike Hill, assuming things would go well at Talladega, already were trying to figure out how many events Elton could drive for Junior Johnson during the remainder of the season (i.e. the NASCAR events that did not conflict with the NASCAR Busch Series, Grand National Division events). As expected, NASCAR officials advised teams of new nose and rear-spoiler heights introduced to make Pontiacs, Fords and Chevrolets more equal on the track. Prior to the upcoming Sears Point race, all the cars' air dams would be trimmed one-fourth of an inch on the front, and rear spoilers would be dropped from 6.25 inches to 5.75 inches in height. Following the Sears Point race, Fords and Pontiacs would return to the 3.75-inch clearance under the air dam and would increase the spoiler height to six inches. The Chevrolets would maintain four inches of clearance at the nose and 5.75 inches of spoiler at the rear.

For some drivers, turning a qualifying lap is merely the activity preceding motel check-in. That's what qualifying had become for Terry Labonte over the past four years. He'd strap in, give it a shot, get out of the car in the garage, change into street clothes and head for the highway. It's been a long time — since the 1991 Budweiser at The Glen, in fact — since Terry needed to worry about staying for a pole-winner's interview.

At Talladega, Terry did his usual thing. One lap then another, with the second a little quicker, and coast to the garage area. But when he discovered that he'd clocked a lap at more than 196 mph, he was persuaded to hang around the Kellogg's transporter for a while, at least until someone ran faster, he reasoned. He waited and waited and waited, but it became clear that unless someone completed a Herculean task, Terry would find himself in the eye of the media hurricane.

Labonte did indeed grab his first pole in nearly four years. In fact, his lap of 196.532 mph was merely the fastest qualifying speed turned at Talladega since Bill Elliott rattled off a 199.388 for the 1990 Winston 500.

So with a grin on his face and his self-deprecating humor wrapped around him like a shroud, Terry meandered over to the infield press facility to answer questions about his Busch Pole run.

Although Labonte had guaranteed himself a portion of the headlines, another driver also was surrounded by a phalanx of media representatives. Loy Allen, who had resigned his seat in the Hooters Ford, made a triumphant return to the sport with his arrival at Talladega in the

Gordon's second-place finish in the Winston Select 500, combined with Earnhardt's last-lap spin and subsequent 21st place, locked the two drivers in a dead heat in the NASCAR Winston Cup points. Gordon, by virtue of the tie-breaker (most victories) pocketed the $100,000 bonus from R.J. Reynolds.

him a good luck charm: a rabbit's foot that had been carried by General Norman Schwartzkoff in the Gulf War. Rusty hoped it would be just the ticket to change his notoriously poor Talladega and Daytona luck.

Although there were the usual battles at the front involving several drivers, it was clear from the beginning of the Winston Select 500 that the best cars on the track belonged to Martin, Marlin, Gordon and Earnhardt. Only a very strange set of circumstances would enable any of the others in the field to notch the victory, but then again, Talladega has a long and storied history of exactly those types of circumstances, as well as of rewarding drivers who were not ranked as odds-on favorites.

TriStar Motorsports Ford, complete with Healthsource sponsorship. To top it all off, Allen rocketed the Ford to the outside of the front row; he missed the pole by less than a half-mile per hour.

Martin, who had vented his frustrations at North Wilkesboro, saying he couldn't wait to get to the bigger tracks where his team "could strut our stuff," underscored the competitiveness of the Jack Roush-owned Valvoline Ford by claiming the third-fastest spot on the grid. Bobby Labonte, fresh from his pole-winning run at Martinsville, indicated that Joe Gibbs' Chevrolets could run on the superspeedways as well; Labonte grabbed the outside of the second row with a lap just a tick faster than Dale Jarrett's. Gordon, the season's leading pole winner with four, turned the sixth-fastest lap, and Marlin whipped his Chevrolet around the track to the seventh starting position. Dick Trickle surprised everyone with the eighth-fastest lap in Bud Moore's Thunderbird, and Robert Pressley took the inside of the fifth row. Michael Waltrip's Pennzoil Pontiac would start on Pressley's right.

Following the second day of qualifying, Steve Grissom and Ward Burton, along with Brett and Geoff Bodine, were forced to take provisional spots to get into the Winston Select 500 field. Ritchie Petty, Billy Standridge, Joe Nemechek, Steve Seligman and Delma Cowart weren't as fortunate. They were forced to head home after they failed to qualify.

But qualifying was the least of Rusty Wallace's concerns. Rusty's difficulties at the sport's biggest tracks are well-documented. Everyone knows of the engine failures and poor finishes that have contributed to his inability to repeat his 1989 NASCAR Winston Cup title. Wallace's problems are so widely known that one of his fans sent

Another Talladega twist is that the favorites usually reap more than their fair share of the problems. Marlin's hopes for victory were crushed on lap 82 when he pulled the Kodak Chevrolet behind the wall with a broken rocker arm. Repairs were made and he was able to return to action, but he was classified 39th at the end of the race.

Since the race was interrupted by only two caution flags — the second of which ended with 63 laps of green-flag racing still remaining — the event boiled down to strategy. Teams tried to stretch the mileage of the fuel remaining in their cars but were left to calculate if they could go the distance on what was left in their tanks, or if they should pit for a few critical seconds-worth of fuel. Martin, Earnhardt, Morgan Shepherd and Gordon had formed a four-car train at the front of the field and held more than a 10-second lead when the final series of green-flag stops began.

Gordon peeled off and hit pit road on lap 170. Four laps later, the remaining three cars in the train headed for splashes of Unocal. Rusty found himself alone at the point, and although the Miller Ford driver knew it would be a tight squeeze, he stroked the rabbit's foot and sent a few words aloft anyway, hoping for divine intervention. It didn't work.

With a 15-second lead and only four laps remaining, Rusty's Ford sputtered. Rusty had no choice but to head for pit road. For a split-second it seemed as though Rusty actually had a chance: As Rusty coasted to the pits, Terry Labonte spun in the fourth turn. Unfortunately for Rusty, the spin would not be his saving grace; Terry recovered from the spin and no caution interrupted the final laps. Wallace eventually fell to 20th place.

Earnhardt, accompanied by Martin, was comfortably in

the lead when Sterling Marlin came off pit road like a shot. Those repairs had apparently done the trick, and although he was out of contention for the victory, he was prepared to use this new-found power to his "teams'" advantage. Marlin charged in front of Gordon and Shepherd and quite literally pulled them to the front of the field. As soon as Sterling had placed them in a position to battle for the lead, he dropped them off. The struggle for the victory then became a torrid, four-car affair. Headed for the white flag, Martin pulled to the inside of Earnhardt, and Gordon followed the red, white and blue Ford. Mark and Jeff eased past the black Chevrolet exiting the second turn, but then Morgan tagged Earnhardt, and the Goodwrench Chevrolet was suddenly spinning backwards. Dale recovered, righted the car and continued to the checkered flag, but in the process, he had fallen from third to 21st place, the final car on the lead lap.

Martin maintained his advantage to the finish line, beating Gordon by couple of car lengths to post the first victory in a restrictor-plate race in Roush Racing's history. Gordon finished second, Shepherd third, and for the second-straight race, Darrell Waltrip came home fourth. Bobby Labonte was fifth, just beating a rousing run by Bill Elliott, and Geoff Bodine came all the way from his provisional starting spot to claim seventh. Younger brother Todd was eighth, and Jimmy Spencer claimed ninth place. Rounding out the top 10 in a scintillating return to the sport was Allen and the TriStar Ford.

Earnhardt, who had won the Talladega round of the Dodge IROC series with a fabulous drive on Saturday, was extremely frustrated by his Winston Select 500 finish. He was even more frustrated once the NASCAR Winston Cup points were calculated following the event.

Mark Martin and Jack Roush were delighted to be in victory lane. After years of near-misses that had resulted only in heartbreak, they had finally conquered one of NASCAR's giant superspeedways.

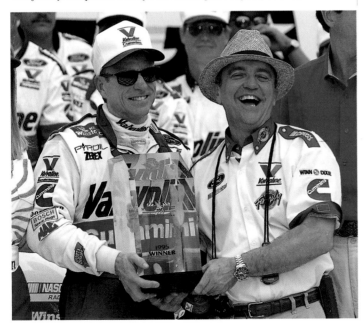

Earnhardt's poor finish, via the last-lap spin and Gordon's second place, had moved the two drivers into a tie for the top spot in the point standings following the first nine races of the season. And, to add insult to injury, the $100,000 point bonus from RJR went to Gordon, not Earnhardt, because Jeff had won more races in this leg of the season than Dale. (Gordon's three victories to Earnhardt's one had broken the tie. The scenario was the same as if two drivers had completed the year tied for the championship; the number of victories during the season would be the first tie-breaker.)

It would be a long ride back to North Carolina for the seven-time champion.

Winston Select 500

Race #9 — Final Race Results

Fin. Pos.	Str. Pos.	Car #	Driver	Team
1	3	6	Mark Martin	Valvoline Ford
2	6	24	Jeff Gordon	DuPont Auto Finishes Chevrolet
3	14	21	Morgan Shepherd	Citgo Ford
4	21	17	Darrell Waltrip	Western Auto Chevrolet
5	4	18	Bobby Labonte	Interstate Batteries Chevrolet
6	24	94	Bill Elliott	McDonald's Ford
7	41	7	Geoff Bodine	Exide Batteries Ford
8	12	75	Todd Bodine	Factory Stores Ford
9	19	23	Jimmy Spencer	Smokin' Joe's Ford
10	2	19	Loy Allen	Healthsource Ford
11	11	16	Ted Musgrave	The Family Channel Ford
12	10	30	Michael Waltrip	Pennzoil Pontiac
13	18	22	Randy LaJoie	MBNA America Pontiac
14	33	98	Jeremy Mayfield	RCA Ford
15	30	43	Bobby Hamilton	STP Pontiac
16	15	9	Lake Speed	Spam/Melling Ford
17	38	41	Ricky Craven	Kodiak Chevrolet
18	9	33	Robert Pressley	Skoal Bandit Chevrolet
19	5	28	Dale Jarrett	Texaco Havoline Ford
20	35	2	Rusty Wallace	Miller Genuine Draft Ford
21	16	3	Dale Earnhardt	Goodwrench Service Chevrolet
22	26	10	Ricky Rudd	Tide Ford
23	27	90	Mike Wallace	Heilig-Meyers Ford
24	17	26	Hut Stricklin	Quaker State Ford
25	37	8	Jeff Burton	Raybestos Brakes Ford
26	1	5	Terry Labonte	Kellogg's Chevrolet
27	31	27	Elton Sawyer	Hooters Ford
28	13	1	Rick Mast	Skoal Ford
29	28	44	Jeff Purvis	Jackaroo Chevrolet
30	40	11	Brett Bodine	Lowe's Ford
31	29	42	Kyle Petty	Coors Light Pontiac
32	42	31	Ward Burton	Hardee's Chevrolet
33	22	77	Davy Jones	Jasper/USAir Ford
34	36	71	Dave Marcis	STG Chevrolet
35	32	40	Greg Sacks	Kendall Pontiac
36	23	81	Kenny Wallace	TIC Financial Ford
37	39	29	Steve Grissom	Meineke Chevrolet
38	8	15	Dick Trickle	Ford Quality Care Ford
39	7	4	Sterling Marlin	Kodak Film Chevrolet
40	20	25	Ken Schrader	Budweiser Chevrolet
41	34	37	John Andretti	Kmart/Little Caesars Ford
42	25	12	Derrike Cope	Straight Arrow Ford

SAVE MART SUPERMARKETS 300

SEARS POINT RACEWAY
MAY 7, 1995
•••••

The only way things could have been more exciting for the NASCAR Winston Cup fans in northern California was if Ernie Irvan had been slated to make his return to competition as the defending champion in the Save Mart Supermarkets 300.

Over the last six years, the NASCAR Winston Cup tour has played to larger and larger crowds at the winding, 2.52-mile Sears Point Raceway road course, nestled in the northern California wine country. The Napa and Sonoma Valleys offer a wonderful respite for the weary traveler, and if the idea of rolling vineyards, wonderful wineries and countryside almost as lovely as that surrounding Watkins Glen doesn't get your motor running, then merely slide down the road a half-hour to bask in the wonders of the Bay Area.

There, you have the artistic beauty of Sausalito, towering redwoods, the Golden Gate Bridge and the spectacle of San Francisco, one of the world's most beautiful cities in either the daytime or evening. Surely, among Nob Hill, Fisherman's Wharf, Chinatown and cable car rides, you'll find something that appeals to your senses.

On race day, arrive at the track early, choose your seat on the hillsides overlooking the course and watch the world's best stock car racers have fun on the asphalt. Sears Point is unique in that spectators are able to see significant portions

Dale Earnhardt spent most of his day at Sears Point chasing Mark Martin, but when the race was on the line, the seven-time champion was right where he needed to be. Dale's flawless performance earned him his first-ever road course victory. (Right) Mike Wallace slings Junie Donlavey's Ford around turn five and heads for the Carousel with Ken Schrader in hot pursuit. Wallace started a fine 10th, but a rear-end problem in the Heilig-Meyers Thunderbird slowed him to a disappointing 34th-place finish, nine laps behind the leaders.

Mart Supermarkets 300 one of the best events on the tour.

In the few days since the completion of the Winston Select 500 at Talladega, everyone had come to realize that the point battle had become just that: a battle. Gordon and Earnhardt were locked in combat for the top rung of the ladder, but they weren't the only ones grappling for positions and points. One look at the standings showed that Martin's victory merely had capped a drive over the past several races that had pulled him to within eight points of the leaders. Sterling Marlin was just 53 points behind Mark and only 62 out of the lead. Rusty Wallace was now 126 behind thanks to the costly stop for fuel in the waning laps at Talladega. Wallace shared the fifth-place spot with a pilot who had been surprisingly strong of late: Ted Musgrave. Dale Jarrett, in seventh place, was 175 behind Earnhardt.

Attention soon turned from the point chase to the race itself. For the third-straight race, Elton Sawyer was on hand to drive the Hooters Ford for Junior Johnson; it was beginning to look as though the NASCAR Busch Series regular had found a semi-permanent home in the Thunderbird. A welcome addition to the field was Wally Dallenbach, who would make his first NASCAR Winston Cup start since last August, when he left Richard Petty's team

(Above) No surprises at the front of this field! Ricky Rudd and Terry Labonte are two of the smoothest drivers on the tour, and Mark Martin (starting third) has proven his road-course skills many times over. Starting fourth is Dale Earnhardt, hungry for his first road-course win. (Right) In the background, a sea of passenger cars blankets the California hillside as Ted Musgrave leads a pack of stock cars into the Carousel. Ted had a fine run in his Jack Roush-prepared Ford and finished a sparkling sixth.

of the entire track from any one vantage point, unlike nearly every other road course in the country. The hillside areas, in some cases, allow fans to see as much as 80 percent of the track.

When you combine the aesthetic qualities of the scene with the fact that young Jeff Gordon, born and raised for some years just down the road from Sears Point, was tied for the NASCAR Winston Cup point lead with seven-time champion Dale Earnhardt, you had the recipe for a huge crowd.

Stir in some Ricky Rudd and Rusty Wallace, two of the best road racers on the tour, and add a dash of Mark Martin, Bill Elliott, Terry Labonte, Darrell Waltrip and Geoff Bodine — all of whom have proven time and again that they can run with the best on a road course — and suddenly you have all the ingredients to make the Save

following the Watkins Glen event. He would pilot a Chevrolet owned by Bill Strauser, and both Dallenbach and Strauser hoped this initial effort would lead to regular appearances on the circuit during the 1996 season.

In the event's first six years, Ricky Rudd had proven himself to be a master of the road course, and during the first round of qualifying for this year's Sears Point event, Rudd only reaffirmed his knack for finding the correct (and fast!) line around the serpentine track. He slung the Tide Ford around the corners, up and down hills, and through "the Carousel" to a new track record in excess of

92 miles per hour. But he had needed every single fraction of a second to keep Terry Labonte from notching his second-straight pole. Terry was just two-tenths of a second slower around the 2.5-mile course.

Martin proved that car owner Jack Roush can prepare a road-racing car just as well as a superspeedway machine by grabbing the third-quickest lap, barely beating Earnhardt. Gordon's performance was one of the surprises of the session; he notched the fifth-fastest lap

at a track where he was not expected to excel. Wallace plunked the Miller Ford on the outside of the third row, serving notice that he would be a contender once again (he won at Sears Point in 1990).

Ken Schrader and Kyle Petty claimed the fourth row, and Dale Jarrett proved that the Robert Yates-owned team's test session at Road Atlanta two weeks prior was time well spent; he turned the ninth-fastest time. Mike Wallace slapped Junie Donlavey's Heilig-Meyers Furniture Ford on the outside of the fifth row, surprising both Geoff Bodine and Ted Musgrave, who were 11th and 12th, respectively.

It wouldn't be Sears Point without one of these shots! This year, it was Michael Waltrip captured in mid-air. Michael wrestled with an ill-handling car all day long but managed to bring home a top-10 finish.

The top 25 positions were locked in during the first session. John Andretti grabbed the final spot available in the first session; that left 12 positions to be won outright in the second session, as well as six provisionals. (Four provisional spots were for the regular NASCAR Winston Cup teams, but two provisional spots had been added for the West Coasters, since the race was a combined event for NASCAR Winston Cup and NASCAR Winston West.)

Following the second session, Bobby Labonte, Rick Mast, Dick Trickle and Ricky Craven used the "regular" Cup provisionals, and Doug George and Dan Obrist were added to the field via the "West" provisionals.

Despite the provisionals, several drivers were left out in the cold. Greg Sacks, Jeremy Mayfield and Elton Sawyer were the "regular" runners who could only watch as their crews loaded the cars into the transporters for the transcontinental drive back to the shop. Others who did

Road-racing star Davy Jones, driver of the Jasper Racing Thunderbird, was looking forward to showcasing his skills on the California road circuit, but Lady Luck wasn't on his side. Here, his crew pushes him back to the pits after the car stalled on pit road; later, he fell victim to an accident. Davy finally was credited with 36th place.

not make the race were Scott Gaylord, Garrett Evans, St. James Davis and Derrike Cope's cousin, Ernie.

Regardless of how they fared in qualifying, competitors were delighted to see Irvan strolling through the garage area on Sunday prior to the start of the race. Ernie had undergone successful endovascular surgery at the University of California San Francisco Medical Center on Friday; the two procedures performed were expected to assist Ernie in recovering from his Michigan injuries. Unfortunately, the procedures also delayed what Ernie had hoped would be his return to racing by three months, but all indications were that the surgery, performed by a team of expert interventional neuroradiologists, was completely successful.

The Brothers Labonte had very different Sears Point experiences. Terry (on left) qualified on the front row, ran with the lead group and finished a very strong fifth. Bobby, forced to use a provisional to start 38th, spent the day working his way through the field and finally wound up 13th.

From the start of the event on Sunday, Rudd acted as though he was about to engineer a flag-to-flag victory. But in the last corner of the fifth lap, the Virginian missed a shift and allowed Mark Martin to squeeze by. From then on, Mark looked as though he was the one wired for victory. The Valvoline Ford driver seemingly led at will. He had no one in front of him to cause problems, and no one close enough behind him to challenge. He gave up the lead only when he made a green-flag stop for tires and fuel. After his final stop on lap 51, he emerged ahead of Earnhardt and Gordon, the only drivers close enough to have a chance at the flying Ford driver.

But a full-course yellow flag allowed the pack to catch him on lap 61, and less than a lap later, the yellow reappeared for a collision involving Rusty Wallace, Jarrett and Davy Jones. Wallace limped back to the pits to have sheet metal pulled away from a tire. Jarrett, meanwhile, could only "hang around" for corner workers to arrive. The Ford had landed on its side, and Jarrett could only hang sideways in his safety harness until someone pushed his Havoline Ford back on four wheels. Once the car was righted, Jarrett merely drove it back onto the track!

With just eight laps remaining, the green flew for the final time, and Mark was still at the point. But Earnhardt was right behind him and looking for an opening. For what seemed an eternity, Martin closed the door in the corners lap after lap, thwarting Earnhardt's every thrust.

But then, with just two-and-a-half laps remaining, Dale found the hole he needed. Headed into the Carousel, Mark slipped in a patch of rear-end grease, momentarily lost traction and slid to the outside of the turn. Earnhardt pounced.

The seven-time champ pulled inside Mark, streaked ahead exiting the downhill left-hander and then concentrated on not making a mistake himself. He knew Mark was good enough to beat him if he could find an opening, but Earnhardt was simply silky throughout the final five miles; he held his line and did not give Martin a single opportunity.

In the end, Dale won by three car-lengths. He immediately lowered his window net and began waving to the immense crowd lining the track.

One could excuse his exuberance.

His career had encompassed every honor — 65 wins, seven championships, Driver of the Year titles, IROC championships and on and on and on.

But he had never won a race on a road course. For 17 years, he had gone to the post at Riverside, Sears Point and Watkins Glen but been unable to visit a road course victory lane. So understandably, he simply bubbled in the winner's circle. Even the fans who pull for other drivers realized that something very special had happened on the northern California hillsides.

Dale's only regret was that car owner Richard Childress was not present to help celebrate the team's first road course victory. Childress was in Africa on a long-ago planned hunting safari.

Earnhardt was quick to note that if the only way the team could win at a road course was if Childress was absent, then the first thing he was going to do after his victory lane celebration was make a telephone call.

Dale was planning to call Childress' travel agency and book his car owner on another African safari — but this one would coincide with the February running of the Daytona 500! "If that's what it takes to win that race, then Richard will be in Africa instead of [at] the Daytona 500,"

Earnhardt, Wallace, Petty and Gordon played "follow the leader" with Mark Martin for 66 of the race's 74 laps. Mark bobbled only once, but that's all it took for Earnhardt to get around him and steal the victory.

Earnhardt said with a grin. Somehow, though, you knew there was some truth to Earnhardt's jesting.

Martin came home second, and Gordon, who had fallen away from what became the Earnhardt/Martin saga, was third. Rudd, who had lost eight positions when his car bobbled in the early going, fought his way back to a solid fourth. Terry Labonte was fifth, and Ted Musgrave came home sixth, further strengthening his claim to a top-five position in the point standings. Marlin and Todd Bodine were seventh and eighth, ahead of Ken Schrader and Michael Waltrip.

In addition to Earnhardt capturing his first road course victory, another "first" was written into the NASCAR record book: A total of 29 cars were on the lead lap at the conclusion of the race.

After all the excitement, a good night's sleep was on the agenda of those who would begin their ride with Kyle Petty the next morning. A core group of motorcycle riders would begin their cross-country ride from San Francisco to Charlotte for, among other charities, the NASCAR Winston Cup Racing Wives Auxiliary.

Not many milestones remain for Dale Earnhardt, but winning on a road course was one of them. Dale and Teresa were elated to be in victory lane in northern California.

Save Mart Supermarkets 300
Race #10 — Final Race Results

Fin. Pos.	Str. Pos.	Car #	Driver	Team
1	4	3	Dale Earnhardt	Goodwrench Service Chevrolet
2	3	6	Mark Martin	Valvoline Ford
3	5	24	Jeff Gordon	DuPont Auto Finishes Chevrolet
4	1	10	Ricky Rudd	Tide Ford
5	2	5	Terry Labonte	Kellogg's Chevrolet
6	12	16	Ted Musgrave	The Family Channel Ford
7	20	4	Sterling Marlin	Kodak Film Chevrolet
8	26	75	Todd Bodine	Factory Stores Ford
9	7	25	Ken Schrader	Budweiser Chevrolet
10	13	30	Michael Waltrip	Pennzoil Pontiac
11	25	37	John Andretti	Kmart/Little Caesars Ford
12	15	12	Derrike Cope	Straight Arrow Ford
13	38	18	Bobby Labonte	Interstate Batteries Chevrolet
14	21	43	Bobby Hamilton	STP Pontiac
15	27	21	Morgan Shepherd	Citgo Ford
16	39	1	Rick Mast	Skoal Ford
17	34	23	Jimmy Spencer	Smokin' Joe's Ford
18	23	8	Jeff Burton	Raybestos Brakes Ford
19	19	94	Bill Elliott	McDonald's Ford
20	6	2	Rusty Wallace	Miller Genuine Draft Ford
21	14	31	Ward Burton	Hardee's Chevrolet
22	11	7	Geoff Bodine	Exide Batteries Ford
23	9	28	Dale Jarrett	Texaco Havoline Ford
24	40	15	Dick Trickle	Ford Quality Care Ford
25	41	41	Ricky Craven	Kodiak Chevrolet
26	28	29	Steve Grissom	Meineke Chevrolet
27	37	71	Dave Marcis	Olive Garden Chevrolet
28	8	42	Kyle Petty	Coors Light Pontiac
29	31	11	Brett Bodine	Lowe's Ford
30	29	33	Robert Pressley	Skoal Bandit Chevrolet
31	42	07	Doug George	Olson Technology Ford
32	30	22	Randy LaJoie	MBNA America Pontiac
33	16	26	Hut Stricklin	Quaker State Ford
34	10	90	Mike Wallace	Heilig-Meyers Ford
35	17	17	Darrell Waltrip	Western Auto Chevrolet
36	24	77	Davy Jones	Jasper/USAir Ford
37	18	87	Joe Nemechek	Burger King Chevrolet
38	36	09	Terry Fisher	Pontiac
39	32	45	Wally Dallenbach	Star Race Computers Chevrolet
40	22	9	Lake Speed	Spam/Melling Ford
41	35	91	Ken Pedersen	Coors Ford
42	33	38	Butch Gilliland	Ultra Wheels Ford
43	43	72	Dan Obrist	Chevrolet

THE WINSTON SELECT

&

Winston Select Open

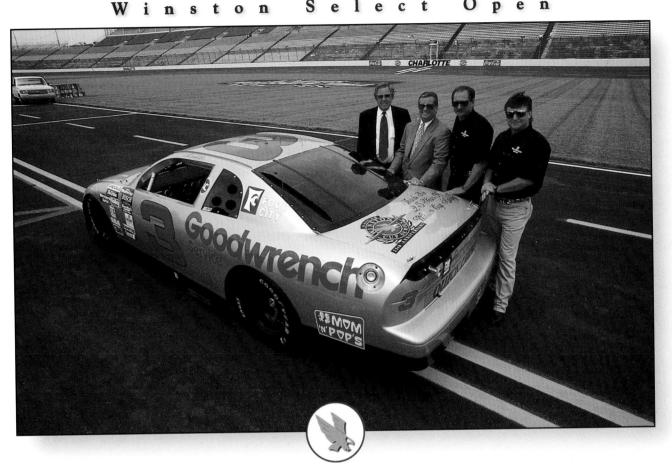

CHARLOTTE MOTOR SPEEDWAY
MAY 20, 1995
• • • • •

It took some time, but in the end, a herd of more than 200 motorcycles pulled into the Sandwich Construction Company's parking lot, just a mile or so northeast of the city of Charlotte. The road-weary riders climbed from their Harleys, stretched, hugged and grinned. They had completed the ride from San Francisco and raised well over $300,000 for a variety of charities, including the NASCAR Winston Cup Racing Wives Auxiliary.

It was a fitting kick-off to the "Fortnight at Charlotte": In the next two weeks, teams would battle in The Winston Select Open, The Winston Select and the Coca-Cola 600 at Bruton Smith's speed palace.

While the likes of Kyle Petty, Geoff Bodine, Michael Waltrip, Harry Gant, Steve Grissom and others had been traveling across the country in stages (stops included Los Angeles, Las Vegas, Phoenix, Dallas/Ft. Worth, Memphis and Nashville), the teams had been busy remodeling their cars to fit the newly instituted NASCAR rules regarding air-dam and rear-spoiler levels. During the test sessions prior to the opening of official practice at Charlotte, the changes had seemed to result in slower speeds, but the real story would be told when the engines were fired in anger during race week.

Prior to The Winston Select, Richard Childress and Dale Earnhardt unveiled this limited-edition Monte Carlo to commemorate the 25th anniversary of R.J. Reynolds' sponsorship of the NASCAR Winston Cup Series. Also on hand were NASCAR President Bill France (left) and T. Wayne Robertson, President of RJR's Sports Marketing Enterprises. (Right) An elated Jeff Gordon had added yet another accomplishment to his brief but impressive NASCAR Winston Cup resume: a win in The Winston Select.

Ricky Rudd had appealed the $50,000 fine levied on him at Talladega for the illegal hydraulic machinery in his Tide Ford, but the appeals board had upheld the fine. Buddy Parrott, after completing the cross-country ride with Petty, headed for the hospital to have arthroscopic surgery on his left knee; the procedure would correct a cyst that had troubled him for years.

Davy Jones was trying to become the second driver in two years to compete in both the Indianapolis 500 and the Coca-Cola 600 on the same day. His highest priority, however, was making the Indy 500 field, so when weather curtailed the sessions at Indianapolis, Bobby Hillin had been pressed into service to drive the USAir/Jasper Ford for

On pole night, Bobby Labonte was super-fast on the track — the first of his three qualifying laps was the quickest of the evening — but he absolutely "lit up" pit road when he came in for his required pit stop. Between his on- and off-track speeds, he wound up capturing the pole for The Winston Select.

Davy in The Winston Select Open.

Two new paint schemes were unveiled when the first practice session began at Charlotte. John Andretti's Ford had changed from white and red to purple and red. But the most eye-catching transformation was the work of Dale Earnhardt's crew: Dale would drive a silver Goodwrench Chevrolet at Charlotte.

Earnhardt and car owner Richard Childress had presented the car during a press conference and explained that the reason they were racing in silver — for the first and only time — was to recognize the many things R.J. Reynolds had done for the sport during the last 25 years.

"In honor of your 25th anniversary, I think it's only appropriate that we give you something silver," Earnhardt said after he had driven the car through a banner. "The people at RJR have done so much for me and my career during the 17 years that I've been racing in NASCAR Winston Cup events that we thought this would be something special for you to enjoy."

Earnhardt also said that his silver helmet, designed specifically for use in The Winston Select, would be presented to RJR's president, Jim Johnston, after the race.

In qualifying for The Winston Select Open (the race for those who haven't already qualified for The Winston Select with a victory), Michael Waltrip whipped his Pennzoil Pontiac around the 1.5-mile track at an average speed in excess of 180 miles per hour, knocking Lake Speed's Spam Ford off the coveted inside front-row spot. Michael was the only driver to crack the 30-second mark. Afterward, Michael said that one of the team's goals was

Bobby Labonte and Mark Martin battle down Charlotte's frontstretch with Dale Earnhardt applying pressure from behind.

Members of the Smokin' Joe's team pay special attention to preparing their motor in hopes that driver Jimmy Spencer can squeeze enough "Camel power" from it to win the rich, all-star race.

to make sure they were also in good shape for the following weekend's Coca-Cola 600 qualifying session. Joe Nemechek and Jeff Burton claimed the second row, and Hut Stricklin and Robert Pressley put their green machines on the third row. Rick Mast and Dick Trickle made up the fourth row, and Todd Bodine and Chuck Bown claimed the last positions in the top 10.

Then, those who had already qualified for the "Main Event," the rich, non-points running of The Winston Select, had their own qualifying session to determine who would start where. Again, qualifying consisted of three laps on the track under the clock, accompanied by a pit stop for right-side tires. The qualifying system, adopted several years ago, is unique to the sport. The reason the folks at R.J. Reynolds instituted such a system was to ensure that the entire team played a role in determining who sat on the pole for the all-star event.

The key to a fast average speed in qualifying is the pit stop, and since speed limits on pit road were temporarily suspended, the driver able to minimize the time lost while slowing down for and speeding up after the two-tire stop usually wins the pole — and the $50,000 that comes with it.

This year was no different. When qualifying had been completed for the 15 competitors with guaranteed spots in

the field, youth and daring had been rewarded over age and guile.

Bobby Labonte literally blasted on and off pit road. His daring, combined with his Interstate Batteries Chevrolet's speed on the track and a flawless stop by crew chief Jimmy Makar and the remainder of the green-and-white-clad crew, enabled Labonte to shock the enormous qualifying night crowd by putting the No. 18 at the top of the leader board. His crew's stop wasn't the fastest — the teams of Rusty Wallace and Dale Jarrett beat Makar and Co.'s stop by two seconds — but Labonte more than made up the difference with his fearless attack of the pit road asphalt.

Dale Earnhardt and Darrell Waltrip withheld nothing in the final segment, and this was the result.

Wallace won the outside of the front row, and Jarrett and Earnhardt claimed the second-row starting positions. Sterling Marlin and Ricky Rudd lined up fifth and sixth, ahead of Jeff Gordon and Mark Martin. Geoff Bodine and Darrell Waltrip made up the fifth row, ahead of Brett Bodine and Terry Labonte, and Bill Elliott and Elton Sawyer claimed the 13th and 14th positions. Following his pit stop, Jimmy Spencer dropped the clutch in his haste to return to the track and broke the rear end in his Smokin' Joe's Ford. He would start 15th.

Prior to The Winston Select Open, a delightful gathering of racing's "legends" thrilled the crowd with their skills — and antics — in the Legends of the Sport race. After holding off late-race challenges from Dick Brooks, Lennie Pond and Richard Brickhouse, Ramo Stott basked in the limelight in the winner's circle.

Then the tension began to mount: It was time to vie for one of the spots in The Winston Select. When The Winston Select Open field rolled off the line for the 75-mile race, every driver in the 36-car field was well aware that if he wanted to be in "The Show," he had to finish in one of the top five positions at the conclusion of the 50 laps. If he finished sixth, he was through for the night. Only the first five finishers would transfer into the high-dollar event and have a chance to battle with those already in the field for The Winston Select.

Many of the "big names" in the field were expected to easily qualify for the main event. Drivers such as Morgan Shepherd, Kyle Petty, Ted Musgrave, Derrike Cope, Darrell Waltrip, Lake Speed, Rick Mast and Hut Stricklin all were rated to have an excellent shot at moving up to The Winston Select.

But Ken Schrader and Todd Bodine had other ideas. Schrader, who had wrecked his Budweiser Chevrolet when it got away from him during qualifying, would have a lot of ground to make up; he would start from the back of the field. The popular driver was competing for the first time since losing part of his thumb the previous weekend in a freak accident. Bodine had less of a deficit to overcome; he'd qualified ninth. Regardless, it didn't take long for either driver to rocket past the back-sliding Waltrip, whose pole-sitting Pennzoil Pontiac lost its handling almost as soon as the green flag had dropped.

By half-distance, Bodine was at the point. He decided to pit for tires during a caution and returned to the track in eighth position with just 15 laps remaining. When Todd hit pit road, he had turned the lead over to Schrader. When the green flag dropped for the final time, Ken bolted away from the field. But Todd's decision turned out to be the right one in the long run — he clambered his way through the pack, took the whip to his Factory Stores Ford and shot past Schrader with three laps to go. Todd continued to draw away and insured his first visit to a NASCAR Winston Cup victory lane. Behind Todd came Schrader, Robert Pressley, Mike Wallace and Speed, all of whom claimed transfer spots to gain entry into The Winston Select.

After what seemed to be just a few minutes, driver introductions began for The Winston Select. As the field formed behind the pace car, no one knew quite what to expect. In the past, the event had been filled with fireworks more times than not, and since the winner's share ranged from $200,000 to $300,000 (depending on how drivers finish in the first and second segments of the three-part race), there was a huge incentive to toss gentlemanly conduct out the proverbial race car window.

During the first 30-lap segment, Gordon immediately established himself as having one of the fastest cars in the field. He whipped his DuPont Chevrolet past Earnhardt to take the lead on the sixth lap, and by the end of the 45 miles, he had pulled away to a margin of more than two seconds.

To no one's surprise, fans voted to invert the field for the start of the second 30 laps. Gordon, alongside a smoking Valvoline Ford driven by Martin, would start from the back of the field.

Two laps after the start, Jimmy Spencer and Schrader collided while battling for the lead. Both Earnhardt and Terry Labonte were also slightly involved. Earnhardt pitted to make sure his car was okay, so when the race resumed on the 37th lap, Dale was at the back of the field, although determined to make his way back to the front. On lap 40, he tapped the rear bumper of Jarrett's Ford and sent Jarrett spinning. Jarrett, in turn, collected Martin, Todd Bodine, Spencer, Marlin and Terry Labonte — again. Bodine, Jarrett and Martin were forced to the sidelines with damaged cars.

Once again, the race was restarted, and

Todd Bodine (75) had gained entry into "The Show" by winning The Winston Select Open and had a strong run going in the main event until he, along with Mark Martin (6) and others, were collected in the aftermath of Dale Jarrett's spin.

once again, Earnhardt found himself at the back of the field (this time, he had been hit with a pit road speeding penalty). But while all eyes focused on Dale, awaiting his expected charge, Gordon ripped away to the front. He passed Pressley on lap 47 and pulled away to win the second segment. Gordon had claimed the $50,000 bonus for each of the race's early segments, but more importantly, he was in the catbird's seat for the start of the final, 10-lap shootout.

Quickly, the field lined up for the start of the final 10 laps. Gordon knew he had a good car, but all he had to do was look to his right and then in his mirror to know that he was going to have his hands full.

Cagey Darrell Waltrip, who'd finished second in the second segment of the event, was on his right. Behind the DuPont Monte Carlo was the silver Chevrolet; Earnhardt's charge had resulted in a third-place finish.

Darrell tried to jump the start, so the field was brought back around for a restart. This time, Gordon controlled the start. As the field headed for the first turn, Gordon sensed that something was about to happen. Earnhardt drilled the Goodwrench Monte Carlo into the low groove and pulled alongside Gordon in the first turn. The three cars continued in that manner, side by side, down the backstretch. But entering the third turn, Jeff could see that Dale's entry into the corner was all wrong. Earnhardt was too deep, and it was obvious that he was going to drift up the track in the corner. On the other side, Waltrip was full-tilt boogie. Gordon made some instantaneous decisions and cracked the throttle. Sure enough, Earnhardt drifted up the track and clobbered Waltrip, who had run out of room and was up against the concrete wall. The two scraped and spun while Gordon, along with the remainder of the field, dropped low to avoid the mess. Lake Speed and Bobby Labonte weren't as fortunate as some of the others; both were caught up in the accident.

Finally, after two tries, the final segment was restarted. Although Marlin tried his best, he had no answer for Gordon. Jeff pulled away and went on to become the youngest winner of The Winston Select since its inception in 1985. The 10-lap segment payoff was another $200,000 — Gordon's winnings for the night's work had suddenly shot up to $300,000.

Amidst the fireworks, Gordon climbed from his DuPont Chevrolet in victory lane. He had celebrated his first career NASCAR Winston Cup victory in that exact spot the previous May after he'd claimed the Coca-Cola 600.

Behind Marlin was Rudd. Rusty Wallace was fourth and Geoff Bodine fifth. Bill Elliott finished sixth, and Pressley and Mike Wallace made a good account for themselves after advancing from The Winston Select Open by finishing seventh and eighth. Spencer was ninth and Brett Bodine 10th.

The Winston Select

Final Race Results

Fin. Pos.	Str. Pos.	Car #	Driver	Team
1	7	24	Jeff Gordon	DuPont Auto Finishes Chevrolet
2	5	4	Sterling Marlin	Kodak Film Chevrolet
3	6	10	Ricky Rudd	Tide Ford
4	2	2	Rusty Wallace	Miller Genuine Draft Ford
5	9	7	Geoff Bodine	Exide Batteries Ford
6	13	94	Bill Elliott	McDonald's Ford
7	18	33	Robert Pressley	Skoal Bandit Chevrolet
8	19	90	Mike Wallace	Heilig-Meyers Ford
9	15	23	Jimmy Spencer	Smokin' Joe's Ford
10	11	11	Brett Bodine	Lowe's Ford
11	12	5	Terry Labonte	Kellogg's Chevrolet
12	14	27	Elton Sawyer	Hooters Ford
13	10	17	Darrell Waltrip	Western Auto Chevrolet
14	4	3	Dale Earnhardt	Goodwrench Service Chevrolet
15	1	18	Bobby Labonte	Interstate Batteries Chevrolet
16	20	9	Lake Speed	Spam/Melling Ford
17	16	75	Todd Bodine	Factory Stores Ford
18	8	6	Mark Martin	Valvoline Ford
19	3	28	Dale Jarrett	Texaco Havoline Ford
20	17	25	Ken Schrader	Budweiser Chevrolet

WINSTON SELECT SEGMENT RESULTS – 1995

Segment One

1.	Jeff Gordon	11.	Darrell Waltrip
2.	Ricky Rudd	12.	Bill Elliott
3.	Mark Martin	13.	Mike Wallace
4.	Bobby Labonte	14.	Geoff Bodine
5.	Rusty Wallace	15	Lake Speed
6.	Todd Bodine	16.	Elton Sawyer
7.	Dale Earnhardt	17.	Jimmy Spencer
8.	Sterling Marlin	18.	Brett Bodine
9.	Terry Labonte	19.	Ken Schrader
10.	Dale Jarrett	20.	Robert Pressley

Segment Two

1.	Jeff Gordon	11.	Rusty Wallace
2.	Darrell Waltrip	12.	Robert Pressley
3.	Dale Earnhardt	13.	Bill Elliott
4.	Sterling Marlin	14.	Jimmy Spencer
5.	Mike Wallace	15.	Elton Sawyer
6.	Geoff Bodine	16.	Brett Bodine
7.	Ricky Rudd	17.	Todd Bodine
8.	Terry Labonte	18.	Mark Martin
9.	Bobby Labonte	19.	Dale Jarrett
10.	Lake Speed	20.	Ken Schrader

COCA-COLA 600

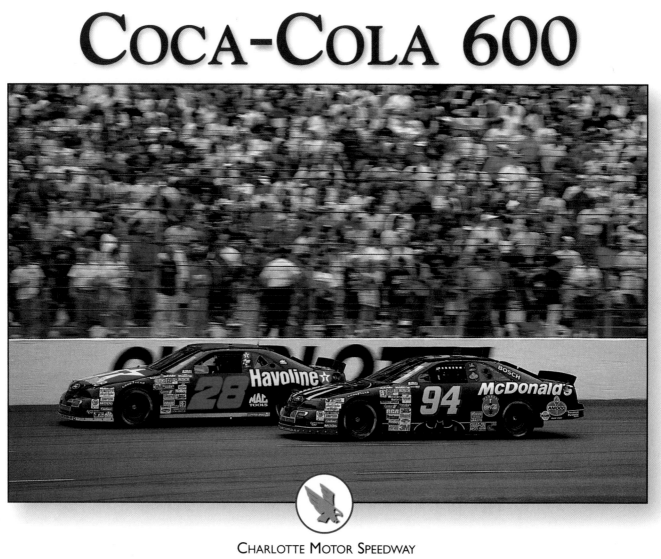

CHARLOTTE MOTOR SPEEDWAY

MAY 28, 1995

•••••

W hen we last saw Jeff Gordon, he was exultantly celebrating his victory in NASCAR's all-star race with lovely Brooke by his side. He'd clearly had the dominant car in the field for The Winston Select that Saturday night. So, crew chief Ray Evernham made a pretty logical decision: With a car that dominant, why switch horses when another big-money event was just a few days away?

So Evernham and the rest of the DuPont crew hauled the Monte Carlo up the road a mile or so, cleaned it, went over it with a fine-toothed comb and then brought it back to Charlotte. Now, Jeff would try to defend the Coca-Cola 600 title he won last May. The team already had deposited $300,000 of Charlotte's money, and if Jeff could win the pole and repeat his Coca-Cola 600 victory, another huge pile of dinero awaited the team.

The Monte Carlos' dominance in the previous weekend's events — not a single Grand Prix made it into The Winston Select — prompted NASCAR to give the Pontiac teams a little help. When practice opened, the Pontiac teams

To the delight of the capacity crowd at Charlotte Motor Speedway, Bill Elliott (94) draws his "ThunderBat" alongside Dale Jarrett. (Right) Prior to The Winston Select, Bobby Labonte had said that he didn't feel as though he "belonged" in the all-star race because he had yet to win a NASCAR Winston Cup event. One week later, he proved to everyone — himself included — that he indeed belonged by claiming his first big-time victory: a win in the prestigious Coca-Cola 600.

were busily adjusting their cars to conform with the newest specs: a 3.5-inch clearance on the front air dam and 6.25 inches of rear spoiler. NASCAR also reiterated that the 9:1 compression engines used this year in NASCAR Busch Series rac-

ing — whose use was originally scheduled to begin on the
NASCAR Winston Cup level
next season — would not be
mandatory for '96 after all.

Dale Earnhardt was back in
black, and no one seemed more
determined to win than the
seven-time champion. After the
problems he suffered the previous weekend, Earnhardt was

*(**Right**) Michael Waltrip dips under
Jimmy Hensley (driving in relief for
the other Waltrip — Darrell) on his
way to a strong, third-place finish. It
was the best finish of the year to date
for Michael, as well as for Pontiac.
(**Below**) Bill Elliott's day ended on
lap 135 when he cut a tire and
smacked the wall in turn one.*

clearly ready for a trip to victory lane, and the Coca-Cola
600 would be a fine place to make that journey.

Earnhardt had returned his Goodwrench Monte Carlo
to its familiar colors, but the Charlotte garage was home to
yet another upstart: This time, Bill Elliott had changed his
paint scheme for the 600. Elliott's usual red Thunderbird
had been painted black and had "thunderBat" written
across the nose where the Thunderbird lettering was usually displayed. The new colors and name were part of a
McDonald's promotion for the new Batman movie, which
would continue through the Pocono and Michigan races.
Elliott's appearance in a black driver's suit was one of the
strangest sights in the garage area!

It was strangely appropriate that Elliott and Earnhardt
were carrying black into battle because it matched the
somber mood of many NASCAR officials, as well as team
members and drivers. Enoch Staley, one of the sport's pio-

neers and longtime president of North Wilkesboro
Speedway, had passed away Saturday night after compli-
cations from a stroke. He had been a friend to all in the
garage area.

The Coca-Cola 600 was the third race of the four events
counting towards the Winston Million program, and if
either Mark Martin or Sterling Marlin wanted to cash the
$1 million bonus check from R.J. Reynolds, one of them
would have to win both the Coca-Cola 600 and the
upcoming Mountain Dew Southern 500 at Darlington. It
was showtime for the two drivers, and both Morgan-
McClure and Roush Racing came to Charlotte with the
best cars in their stables. If either won, he automatically
would win the $100,000 "consolation" prize, so both teams
left nothing to chance in their preparation for the longest
race on the schedule.

After making the field for the Indy 500, Davy Jones
returned to Charlotte in hopes of qualifying for the 600. If
he could get into the 600 field, he could match John
Andretti's feat (last year, Andretti became the first driver
in history to compete in both races in a single day).
Unfortunately, Davy lost control of the USAir/Jasper Ford
in the final practice session at Charlotte just minutes
before qualifying, and the team had no time to prepare the
back-up car. So Jones dejectedly flew back to Indy, unable
to complete his quest. He would eventually finish 23rd in
the 33-car Indy 500 field.

As the remainder of the teams began preparations for
the first round of qualifying for the 600, Darrell Waltrip
slumped, unmoving, in his transporter. The Winston
Select accident had banged him up more than he had originally thought. He was taped up for what was believed to
be a muscle tear, but after he qualified, X-rays showed that
he also had three broken right ribs.

And just those few qualifying laps had convinced Darrell that he would need some help for the 600 — he immediately retained Jimmy Hensley as his relief driver. Waltrip's plan was to start the 600 but get out of the Western Auto Monte Carlo as soon as possible. He felt the car — and his relief driver — were clearly capable of winning the race. Of course, Darrell declared a yellow flag to help with the driver change would be most helpful — obviously, he'd not lost his sense of humor, despite the pain from his injury.

The source of Darrell's pain was his ribs, but everyone else's pain could be traced to a certain rainbow-hued Chevrolet.

Everyone expected Gordon to be fast, but after he'd completed his qualifying lap, one could almost see the faces fall up and down pit road. Those yet to qualify knew they had been, in Michael Waltrip's words, "drilled." Gordon simply blew away the field, winning the pole with a lap more than a mile per hour faster than his closest competitor. Waltrip may have best summed up the general consensus:

"We had good power, the car worked real good, and I was real happy with the way it drove around the turns. But man, to do everything you can and have things work-

(Right) Jeff Gordon returns to the pits trailing a shower of sparks after losing a wheel on the backstretch. The Rainbow Warriors would make repairs and send Jeff back onto the track, but he would not repeat his Coca-Cola 600 victory of a year ago.
(Below) Kyle Petty, Ted Musgrave (16) and Mike Wallace (90) go three-wide in front of Jimmy Spencer, creating a colorful quartet down the frontstretch at CMS.

ing good, and then to get beat by three-tenths of a second — you just kind of flip out over that!" The Pennzoil Pontiac driver turned the fifth-fastest lap.

Alongside Gordon was Bobby Labonte, who continued to impress with his Interstate Batteries Chevrolet, owned by Joe Gibbs. Ricky Craven's performance was the surprise of the session; he celebrated his 29th birthday by stealing the inside of the second row from a hot-running Brett Bodine. Bodine and car owner Junior Johnson had taken on more of the responsibility for the car's preparation after crew chief Mike Beam had left the team to form his own business and build and maintain cars for Bill Elliott. The effects of Johnson's increased "hands-on" involvement and Bodine's chassis work had been evident immediately.

Ken Schrader was back in yet another Budweiser Chevrolet from the Hendrick Motorsport stable after tearing up two Monte Carlos during the previous weekend.

This one was obviously just as good: Ken slapped a lap on the board good enough for the sixth starting position.

Marlin was seventh-fastest, and Elton Sawyer, in the Hooters Ford once again, gave Johnson another reason to smile with his eighth-place starting position. Joe Nemechek had his Burger King Chevrolet tuned up, and he proved it by claiming the inside of the fifth row. Morgan Shepherd would start on Nemechek's right with the Citgo Ford from the Wood brothers' shop.

Some of the pre-race favorites — Rusty Wallace, Dale Jarrett, Martin and Earnhardt — found themselves in the second half of the field. Earnhardt, who'd suffered from a variety of problems during qualifying, would start 34th.

Steve Grissom, Kyle Petty,

(Above) Among the teams debuting new paint schemes during the weekends at Charlotte was Kranefuss-Haas Racing. They presented John Andretti's new Kmart/Little Caesars Ford — is it now the "Purple Light Special"? (Left) Outstanding rookie contender Ricky Craven receives some encouragement from veteran team manager Waddell Wilson. Must have been some speech! ... Ricky celebrated his 29th birthday by claiming the third spot in qualifying and an impressive top-10 finish in the Coca-Cola 600.

Randy LaJoie and Jeremy Mayfield were all forced to take provisionals, which meant that Greg Sacks, Bobby Hillin, Jimmy Hensley, Davy Jones, Jeff Purvis and Johnny Chapman would be unable to make the field.

Following his performance of the previous weekend, Gordon was the prohibitive favorite for Sunday's unique race, which would begin in late-afternoon sunshine and end under the lights. The number "24" was the most sought-after figure in every pool!

On Sunday, the battle began as soon as the green flag dropped. Bobby Labonte beat Gordon back to the line to lead the first lap, but in just seven more laps, Jeff had slashed to the point. Jeff occupied the point until the 45th lap, when he gave up the lead to "teammate" Schrader.

Gordon continued to run with the leaders until the 67th lap, when he lost two laps on pit road while his team worked on his front brakes. His chances of a second-straight 600 victory were slim to none.

And Gordon's luck only went from bad to worse. Less than 10 laps later, Gordon returned to pit road during a caution (the result of an accident involving leader Todd Bodine and Ward Burton), and while crew members were working on the DuPont Chevrolet, a brief fire broke out under the right-front wheel. His crew quickly extinguished the blaze, however, and Gordon headed back into action ... but not for long. Two laps later, the right wheel came off his Chevrolet. In a shower of sparks, he returned for more work and lost more than 30 laps while his crew replaced the entire spindle assembly.

With Gordon clearly out of contention, the race turned into one of the most furiously contested events of the season. By the time it was completed, a dozen drivers had exchanged the lead 32 times.

Throughout all the lead changes and the torrid dueling

Members of Robert Yates Racing held an impromptu team meeting in the CMS garage to discuss how they could turn what had thus far been a frustrating season around. But their bad luck only continued in the 600: The engine failed in the Texaco Havoline Ford, relegating Jarrett to a 32nd-place finish.

at the front of the field, it appeared that Earnhardt, Schrader and Bobby Labonte had the best cars. And Schrader, trying to win his first race in nearly four years, seemed the best of the three, leading seemingly at will. He took the Bud Chevrolet to the point time after time, but with just over 60 miles remaining, he slowed heading down the backstretch. His hopes for that elusive win disappeared with a rattle and a bang from the Hendrick power plant; after leading 169 laps, Ken was left to coast to the garage.

With Schrader out, Bobby Labonte became the leader. He had pulled out a six-second lead over Earnhardt before Schrader's engine had failed and was now home free. Once his older brother, Terry, pulled past Earnhardt for second place, the stage was set for a Labonte 1-2 and a great celebration the following day when the family gathered together for the Memorial Day holiday.

Earnhardt was stuck, and all he could do was hope for a caution. He didn't have enough fuel to make it to the finish, and if he was forced to stop under green, he would fall off the lead lap. But the hoped-for caution never fell, and Dale was forced to make a dash down pit road with just eight laps remaining. In the end, he fell from third to sixth but managed to boost his point lead nonetheless. The problems that plagued Gordon relegated him to a 33rd-place finish. Mark Martin didn't fare much better, finishing 28th, 10 laps behind.

Meanwhile, back at the front, Michael Waltrip, who had taken advantage of every break that had come his way throughout the race and run with the leaders the entire distance, came home with a hard-fought third place, his best (and Pontiac's best) finish so far this season. Marlin was fourth, a lap down; he had failed in his effort to take another step toward the Winston Select Million bonus. Rudd was fifth, just ahead of Earnhardt, and Hut Stricklin and Lake Speed posted their first top-10 finishes of the season, claiming seventh and eighth. Bobby Hamilton was ninth, and Craven grabbed the first top-10 finish of his career by beating Shepherd to the line.

After finishing second to Gordon twice this season and finishing second to him in the MAXX Rookie of the Year battle two years ago, Bobby Labonte finally was able to enjoy his moment in the moonlight. With fireworks exploding in the background, the quiet Texan emerged from his Chevrolet in the winner's circle. One of the first to hug him was his brother, who had exited his own Kellogg's Chevrolet and immediately headed — at a dead run — for victory lane.

Gordon had come to prominence by winning last year's Coca-Cola 600.

Was it Bobby Labonte's turn?

Coca-Cola 600

Race #11 — Final Race Results

Fin. Pos.	Str. Pos.	Car #	Driver	Team
1	2	18	Bobby Labonte	Interstate Batteries Chevrolet
2	13	5	Terry Labonte	Kellogg's Chevrolet
3	5	30	Michael Waltrip	Pennzoil Pontiac
4	7	4	Sterling Marlin	Kodak Film Chevrolet
5	18	10	Ricky Rudd	Tide Ford
6	34	3	Dale Earnhardt	Goodwrench Service Chevrolet
7	12	26	Hut Stricklin	Quaker State Ford
8	16	9	Lake Speed	Spam/Melling Ford
9	23	43	Bobby Hamilton	STP Pontiac
10	3	41	Ricky Craven	Kodiak Chevrolet
11	10	21	Morgan Shepherd	Citgo Ford
12	29	90	Mike Wallace	Heilig-Meyers Ford
13	39	29	Steve Grissom	Meineke Chevrolet
14	15	1	Rick Mast	Skoal Ford
15	27	16	Ted Musgrave	The Family Channel Ford
16	11	15	Dick Trickle	Ford Quality Care Ford
17	36	37	John Andretti	Kmart/Little Caesars Ford
18	21	17	Darrell Waltrip	Western Auto Chevrolet
19	26	12	Derrike Cope	Straight Arrow Ford
20	9	87	Joe Nemechek	Burger King Chevrolet
21	33	32	Chuck Bown	Fina/Lance Chevrolet
22	42	98	Jeremy Mayfield	RCA Ford
23	41	22	Randy LaJoie	MBNA America Pontiac
24	25	33	Robert Pressley	Skoal Bandit Chevrolet
25	8	27	Elton Sawyer	Hooters Ford
26	28	7	Geoff Bodine	Exide Batteries Ford
27	38	23	Jimmy Spencer	Smokin' Joe's Ford
28	32	6	Mark Martin	Valvoline Ford
29	40	42	Kyle Petty	Coors Light Pontiac
30	6	25	Ken Schrader	Budweiser Chevrolet
31	37	81	Kenny Wallace	TIC Financial Ford
32	22	28	Dale Jarrett	Texaco Havoline Ford
33	1	24	Jeff Gordon	DuPont Auto Finishes Chevrolet
34	24	2	Rusty Wallace	Miller Genuine Draft Ford
35	4	11	Brett Bodine	Lowe's Ford
36	31	19	Loy Allen	Healthsource Ford
37	35	71	Dave Marcis	Olive Garden Chevrolet
38	14	75	Todd Bodine	Factory Stores Ford
39	19	94	Bill Elliott	McDonald's Ford
40	20	8	Jeff Burton	Raybestos Brakes Ford
41	30	31	Ward Burton	Hardee's Chevrolet
42	17	97	Chad Little	Harris-Teeter Ford

MILLER GENUINE DRAFT 500

DOVER DOWNS INTERNATIONAL SPEEDWAY
JUNE 4, 1995
• • • • •

No matter the venue of a NASCAR Winston Cup race, thousands of behind-the-scenes workers, ranging from concession and parking personnel to ticket takers and sellers, are needed to make the event a reality.

Usually, their presence is largely unnoticed by the tens of thousands of race fans in attendance, but from time to time, a particular group of workers emerge during the event to become the "heroes" of the weekend.

That's what happened during the running of the Miller Genuine Draft 500 at Dover.

Track president Denis McGlynn and the management of Dover had undertaken a huge project since last September's race at the "Monster Mile": They had reconfigured the entrances and exits of the four corners and put a new racing surface of milky-white concrete down over the entire mile-long oval.

Front-row mates Jeff Gordon and Ward Burton parade the field around the new-and-improved Dover Downs. The pristine concrete surface — a sharp contrast to the old, black asphalt of the Monster Mile — inspired track officials to dub the speedway "White Lightning." (Right) Kyle Petty focuses his thoughts before heading into battle.

An entirely new, welded wire "wheel fence" had been installed around the track, and a walk-over bridge had been constructed in the second turn. Now, for the first time, competitors, media and the track's staff could move from inside the track to outside without having to wait for a caution flag and bolt across the start/finish line. More than 7,000 new seats had been added in the third- and fourth-turn grandstand, and work had been completed on the hospitality suites in the fourth turn.

(Above) Media crews snatch last-minute interviews as team members perform final preparations prior to the start of the race. (Right) After a less-than-stellar qualifying run, Kyle Petty and the entire Coors Light team had their work cut out for them. But on the strengths of a strong motor, excellent chassis setup and superior pit work, Kyle was able to slice through the field from his 37th starting position to take the win at Dover.

Following the first test session, track management had gone to work smoothing out the ridges in the new concrete surface by dragging a two-ton concrete "doughnut" around the track. Goodyear's engineers also had gone back to work in order to provide a different compound for the second test session. So, by the time teams unloaded for the NASCAR Busch Series and NASCAR Winston Cup doubleheader, everyone expected the concrete surface to produce a highly competitive pair of races.

But by Saturday morning, however, it had become apparent that the Eagles brought for the event weren't quite right. By noon, Goodyear's racing boss, Leo Mehl, had made the decision that turned the weekend around.

Goodyear had brought a total of 3,800 tires for the NASCAR Busch Series and NASCAR Winston Cup competitors, but before the Busch race had even begun, Mehl had made calls to the company's warehouses near Charlotte and Cleveland. A total of 400 different tires would be trucked overnight from Charlotte and some 700

from near Cleveland. It was hoped that these tire compounds would better handle the heat that built up as a result of the new Dover surface. Tires used in April at Darlington would be the "new" right-side tires, and tires used at Charlotte in '94 would be the "new" left fronts. The left rears would be tires used at Dover in '94.

The service crews, employed by Competition Tire East and West (the companies contracted by Goodyear to service the racing tires), have been known by team members through the years as "tire busters." They had come to Dover expecting the unexpected. The normal crew consists of 28-30 workers, more than half of whom are "weekend warriors," and a dozen tire-mounting and dismounting machines to service a race. Since this was the first time for the new Dover surface, the crew had been boosted to

40, and a total of 15 mounting machines were on hand.

Management's foresight turned out to be the saving grace of the weekend.

The phone lines around Dover crackled on Saturday afternoon as workers were called in to both the North Carolina and Ohio warehouses to load tires onto trucks for the 12-hour drive to Dover. While all that was going on, the service crews fell to in the Dover Goodyear area. A total of 1,800 tires already had been mounted for the NASCAR Winston Cup teams' use, and for each team, six sets of tires (24 tires x 42 teams) needed to be dismounted and the rims (1,008) readied for the substitute tires.

The service crews finished dismounting the tires at 10:30 p.m. and headed for the hotel for room service, a shower and some much-needed sleep. But by 4:30 Sunday morning, they were back at the track — the three tractor-trailers bearing the substitute tires were outside the track's gates. By the time the race crews began filing through the garage gate at 6 a.m., the first set of tires was mounted and waiting for each car. Each team would receive at least six sets of tires for the race, but it was up to the teams to manage those six sets of tires. By 12:10 p.m. — two laps into the Miller Genuine Draft 500 — the final tires had been mounted, balanced, stacked and distributed.

The service crews breathed a sigh of relief. Their task had been of near-Herculean proportions, but it was finally completed. There were no celebratory fireworks, no incentive bonuses split among the workers. It was simply a supremely competent job by workers who performed harmoniously under unexpected pressure. The workers were rewarded by the fact that the fans didn't even notice and the race went on as scheduled — not a single minute late. But everyone in the garage area recognized the huge effort that had gone into the overnight switch, and drivers, crew chiefs and car owners, not to mention NASCAR officials, stopped by the tire stations to say thanks for the job well done.

The fans had been too busy to notice the tire dilemma; they were still intently discussing the $60,000 fine levied on the DuPont Chevrolet team and crew chief Ray Evernham for the use of a non-approved hub on Jeff Gordon's Monte

The "Monster Mile" has always had an appetite for race cars, and those of Chuck Bown (inside) and Dave Marcis are graphic examples of how and why the Delaware speedway got its nickname.

Carlo at Charlotte. The part was discovered following Gordon's problems during the Coca-Cola 600, and Evernham took full responsibility for the use of the part on the car. It was the biggest fine in NASCAR Winston Cup history, surpassing the $50,000 fine levied on Ricky Rudd and his Tide Ford team earlier in the season.

NASCAR officials, hoping to give the Fords more downforce in the corners and make the Thunderbirds more equal with the Chevrolets, had increased the rear-spoiler height for the Ford Thunderbird teams by a quarter-inch between the Charlotte and Dover races.

And that wasn't the only newsworthy announcement made between the two races. Immediately following the Charlotte race, Kenny Bernstein had announced that his team was for sale but reiterated that he would fulfill his contractual obligations with Quaker State for the remainder of the season. Bernstein explained that after spending the last several years living out of a suitcase and more than 300 days a year on the road with his NASCAR Winston Cup and NHRA drag racing teams, he wanted "to cut back the workload, the travel schedule and relax a little." Ironically, he had announced his decision after his team's best finish of the season: Hut Stricklin's seventh place in the Coca-Cola 600.

At Dover, a different face appeared behind the window net of the USAir/Jasper Engines Ford when the car was rolled out for the first practice session. Saying "We have sponsors and people affiliated with our team [who] just can't continue at the pace we have been going," owner D.K. Ulrich had named Bobby Hillin to replace Davy Jones in

the Thunderbird. Ulrich noted, however, that Jones would compete in either NASCAR Busch Series or SuperTruck events (or a combination of both) later this season.

If anything, the huge fine levied on the DuPont team merely made the crew more determined to post a good showing at Dover, particularly since the Delaware track is the venue closest to sponsor DuPont's corporate headquarters, located less than an hour north of the track. Sure enough, Gordon, Evernham et al were vindicated during the first round of qualifying: They notched the team's sixth pole of the season with a record lap. While Gordon and his team were celebrating, Ward Burton and his Hardee's group also found cause to be pumped for Sunday. Burton's extensive testing sessions at Dover had paid off; his reward was the outside pole, his best qualifying position of the season. Bobby Labonte, sky-high following his Coca-Cola 600 win, grabbed the inside of the second row for Joe Gibbs' Interstate Batteries team, and John Andretti completed the "twentysomething" look of the front two rows by posting the fourth-fastest lap. Vets Sterling Marlin and Geoff Bodine made up the third row, and outstanding runs by Ricky Craven and Joe Nemechek resulted in the seventh and eighth starting positions. Hut Stricklin and Brett Bodine rounded out the top 10. Darrell Waltrip, Ken Schrader, Derrike Cope (in a back-up car because his race mount was damaged in a practice accident) and Greg Sacks were forced to use provisionals to make the 42-car field. Doug French was the only driver unable to make the field.

While Goodyear's service crews had been trying to catch a little shut-eye on Saturday night in preparation for their early-morning marathon, NASCAR Winston Cup crew chiefs had pulled out their black books, spread notes from previous Dover outings all over the beds in their hotel rooms and done their best to re-create chassis combinations from the past that they hoped would help them with the new Eagles on tap for Sunday. In an effort to help teams prepare for the grueling 500-lapper, NASCAR officials had given the teams an unprecedented Sunday-morning, 30-minute practice session which would begin at 8 a.m., prior to pre-race preparation.

For some, the extra practice session was still not enough. On just the second lap, Andretti, on the outside of the second row, got a little sideways exiting the fourth turn. Craven, who had nowhere to go, tapped Andretti, and chaos ensued behind them on the narrow track. When the dust and tire smoke had cleared, nearly half the field — 20 cars — had been damaged in one way or another. Among those involved in the chain-reaction accident were Wallace, Mark Martin, Dale Jarrett and Ricky Rudd. The melee was particularly devastating to Rusty Wallace, who had been expected to be a major factor in the Dover race. After all, he had been in pursuit of his fourth-consecutive victory on the "Monster Mile." Now, a Dover victory was nowhere to be seen in Wallace's future.

As one can imagine, the accident changed the complexion of the race. When it restarted, Gordon and the DuPont Chevrolet commanded the attention at the front of the field, while Jimmy Spencer was doing his best to move the Smokin' Joe's Ford to the front. Hardly noticed was a red, blue and silver Pontiac gradually moving through the field. By the 100-mile mark, however, the crowd had no choice but to take note of the Pontiac. Kyle Petty had taken the Coors Light Grand Prix to fifth place and obviously had one of the fastest cars in the field.

Car by car, Petty crept towards the leaders, and on lap 136, during a round of green-flag stops, Kyle became the race's third leader. As the race ground on, it became obvious that, for the first time this season, a Pontiac was a serious contender for a NASCAR Winston Cup event win. Petty did not waver from the front of the field, and as the race entered its final 100 laps, the third-generation driver clearly was comfortable with his vantage point.

Kyle made his final stop for tires and fuel with 70 laps remaining, and once the remaining cars in the field had cycled through their final green-flag stops, he regained the lead — 42 laps remained. Ted Musgrave and Bobby Labonte, however, weren't about to let the Pontiac cruise to victory lane without a fight, and both drivers battled their way to Petty's rear bumper in the final laps. Kyle had just enough for the green and black Chevrolet and the red, white and blue Ford. He hugged the inside of the track and left them to fight for

Petty was barely able to hold off the charges of Bobby Labonte and Ted Musgrave; he flashed across the finish line a mere two-tenths of a second ahead of the pair. Labonte barely nipped Musgrave for the runner-up spot.

In victory lane, an exhausted Kyle Petty climbed from the car and took a few minutes for some much-needed — and well-deserved — rest and water before participating in the victory celebration.

the scraps. His Pontiac came home the winner by two car-lengths, and Labonte just edged out Musgrave for the runner-up position.

Stricklin posted another strong finish with Bernstein's Quaker State Ford, claiming fourth ahead of Dale Earnhardt, the final driver on the lead lap. Earnhardt's crew had whistled him off pit road following his final stop of the race to help him regain the lead lap. Gordon and Marlin were the first drivers a lap down, in sixth and seventh place, and Michael Waltrip posted his third-straight top-10 finish by finishing eighth. Wallace soldiered home to ninth place — not exactly what he'd had in mind when he entered the track on Friday morning. Joe Nemechek captured the last spot in the top 10.

The victory was the first for a Pontiac since Rusty Wallace had won the November '93 Atlanta event and was the first for Petty since he'd won at Pocono in June '93, 59 races ago. The victory, a great belated birthday gift (Kyle had turned 35 just two days earlier!), ironically had come in the same Pontiac he had driven to a 30th-place, 20-laps-behind finish at Charlotte the previous week! The win was also an emotional one for everyone on the Felix Sabates-owned team, particularly crew chief Barry Dodson, who turned 42 on race day. Dover was Dodson's 19th career victory (his last win came with Wallace and Raymond Beadle's team in 1990). Dodson dedicated the victory to his children, Trey and Tia, who were killed in an automobile accident in Darlington, S.C., last November.

"Racing amazes me," Kyle said after his eighth career victory. "Here we were, totally out of it at Charlotte, and here we are, winning at Dover. Pretty amazing."

Then Kyle took a minute to say a few words — in his own, inimitable way — about the turn of events regarding the tires.

"My hat's off to Goodyear for having the kahunas enough to say, 'Look, these tires don't work. We're going to change things and get some different ones that will.' They did it all in one night. They came back with a tire they knew would work.

"It's times of crisis that show the class of people and the quality of a company. Leo Mehl and Goodyear showed a lot of class with what they did here in just over 24 hours, and how they handled it."

And then, for just a minute, Kyle sounded just like his daddy.

"Them cats over there," he said, jerking his thumb toward the Goodyear compound, "are the heroes of the weekend. I sit here, talking with you, and everyone's real excited about this win. But without those guys — those cats we call 'tire busters' and take for granted week after week — we wouldn't have been racing here today.

"Those guys are the real heroes."

Miller Genuine Draft 500

Race #12 — Final Race Results

Fin. Pos.	Str. Pos.	Car #	Driver	Team
1	37	42	Kyle Petty	Coors Light Pontiac
2	3	18	Bobby Labonte	Interstate Batteries Chevrolet
3	32	16	Ted Musgrave	The Family Channel Ford
4	9	26	Hut Stricklin	Quaker State Ford
5	23	3	Dale Earnhardt	Goodwrench Service Chevrolet
6	1	24	Jeff Gordon	DuPont Auto Finishes Chevrolet
7	5	4	Sterling Marlin	Kodak Film Chevrolet
8	12	30	Michael Waltrip	Pennzoil Pontiac
9	16	2	Rusty Wallace	Miller Genuine Draft Ford
10	8	87	Joe Nemechek	Burger King Chevrolet
11	40	25	Ken Schrader	Budweiser Chevrolet
12	41	12	Derrike Cope	Straight Arrow Ford
13	17	1	Rick Mast	Skoal Ford
14	31	90	Mike Wallace	Heilig-Meyers Ford
15	20	94	Bill Elliott	McDonald's Ford
16	36	29	Steve Grissom	Meineke Chevrolet
17	38	98	Jeremy Mayfield	RCA Ford
18	35	81	Kenny Wallace	TIC Financial Ford
19	33	33	Robert Pressley	Skoal Bandit Chevrolet
20	39	17	Darrell Waltrip	Western Auto Chevrolet
21	10	11	Brett Bodine	Lowe's Ford
22	7	41	Ricky Craven	Kodiak Chevrolet
23	22	22	Randy LaJoie	MBNA America Pontiac
24	14	43	Bobby Hamilton	STP Pontiac
25	21	8	Jeff Burton	Raybestos Brakes Ford
26	15	21	Morgan Shepherd	Citgo Ford
27	6	7	Geoff Bodine	Exide Batteries Ford
28	42	40	Greg Sacks	Kendall Pontiac
29	11	23	Jimmy Spencer	Smokin' Joe's Ford
30	26	75	Todd Bodine	Factory Stores Ford
31	29	10	Ricky Rudd	Tide Ford
32	24	15	Dick Trickle	Ford Quality Care Ford
33	30	32	Chuck Bown	Active Trucking Chevrolet
34	34	9	Lake Speed	Spam/Melling Ford
35	13	6	Mark Martin	Valvoline Ford
36	25	71	Dave Marcis	Olive Garden Chevrolet
37	19	5	Terry Labonte	Kellogg's Chevrolet
38	2	31	Ward Burton	Hardee's Chevrolet
39	4	37	John Andretti	Kmart/Little Caesars Ford
40	18	28	Dale Jarrett	Texaco Havoline Ford
41	27	27	Elton Sawyer	Hooters Ford
42	28	77	Bobby Hillin	Jasper/USAir Ford

'95

UAW-GM Teamwork 500

POCONO RACEWAY

JUNE 11, 1995

•••••

K yle Petty may have snapped his long, winless string at Dover the previous week, but one of the biggest winners in the garage area was Dale Earnhardt. On the surface, it didn't look as though he'd had the best of races: He had been involved in a multi-car accident in the early laps, been forced to pit several times so his crew could complete repair work during the cautions and fallen a lap off the pace later in the race.

But Earnhardt's determined driving, combined with a brilliant call by crew chief Andy Petree and car owner Richard Childress to take just two tires late in the race, propelled Dale back onto the lead lap. At the race's conclusion, he was fifth in the rundown and had gained points on every one of his nearest competitors — with the exception of second-place finisher Ted Musgrave.

It was the kind of performance Earnhardt had turned in time and time again en route to seven NASCAR Winston Cup championships — he simply took advantage of every opportunity and worked hard for the best possible finish, even if he was unable to win the race.

This time, Earnhardt's trademark performance had boosted him to a 100-point margin over Sterling Marlin in the points. As the teams headed for the scenic Pocono Mountains and their first date with the triangular superspeedway, unique in the world of motorsports, Jeff Gordon trailed Marlin by just six points. Mark Martin was fourth but just a single point ahead of Musgrave. The two Roush Racing drivers trailed Earnhardt by

Terry Labonte ended up in Pocono's victory lane after working his way up from the 27th starting spot to second behind a dominant Jeff Gordon. When a bobble by Jeff opened the door, Terry bolted through and slammed it shut to take his second win of the year. (Right) Ken Schrader had taken the pole at Pocono and was intent on ending a frustrating winless streak that dated back to 1991, but he could manage only third place.

182 and 183 points, respectively.

As the crews began unloading their mounts, the "buzz" which stretched from one end of the spacious garage area to the other grew steadily louder. Everyone was talking about Buddy Parrott's resignation; he had forfeited his position as crew chief for young Steve Grissom and the Diamond Ridge team.

The announcement had come as a surprise, especially since Parrott had immediately made an impact on Grissom's team after he'd left Penske South at the conclusion of the 1994 season. Parrott had been credited with helping the young Alabama driver post four top-10 finishes in the first 11 races of the season.

Young John Andretti, oblivious of the "buzz," was methodically working his way toward his Kmart Ford, but

in Myrtle Beach this weekend for the NASCAR Busch Series event.

Further down the line, Bill Elliott was decked out in black for the second time in three weeks, and his McDonald's Ford bore the black paint it had debuted at Charlotte. Pocono marked the second of three special appearances by the No. 94 team to promote the alliance of the new "Batman Forever" movie and McDonald's. Elliott hoped the second appearance of the "ThunderBat" would be even better than the first.

The tires Goodyear had brought to Pocono had slightly stiffer sidewalls than those used in the past, and teams scrambled during Friday's practice sessions to find the chassis settings that would enable the tires to perform at their optimum level. Some teams found the key right

In front of a packed grandstand at Pocono, Ricky Rudd (10) gives Mark Martin a little help as they try to overtake Geoff Bodine.

it was taking a while. John was stopping at the garage stall of every car involved in the Dover accident and apologizing for triggering the mishap. He was surprised to find that driver after driver, crew chief after crew chief and car owner after car owner told him, "That's racin'." At one point, John had wondered if he should wear his helmet when he made his apologies, so he was extremely pleased by the reaction he received, which was quite the opposite of what he had expected.

While all this was going on, teams were beginning to take note of a new face in the Hooters Ford garage. Jimmy Horton had been named to drive the second Junior Johnson-owned Thunderbird since Elton Sawyer, who had become the regular driver in the last few weeks, was

away, while others planned to use Saturday's practice sessions to dial in the chassis characteristics which best suited the tires.

During the first round of qualifying on the 2.5-mile track, Ken Schrader surprised many by notching what would be the fastest lap. Earlier, it had appeared that the Valvoline Ford driver would start the race from the inside of the front row: Halfway through the first session, Martin had bested Morgan Shepherd's quick lap to post the latest, fastest time. But then Schrader, the next-to-last driver in line, posted a lap in excess of 163.3 miles per hour. Schrader had ended a poleless string that had reached back to the 1993 Mountain Dew Southern 500 at Darlington, and Martin was forced to settle for the outside

of the front row.

Bobby Hamilton's performance also surprised many; he grabbed the inside of the second row. Ricky Rudd qualified fourth fastest, but he was disappointed with his lap. Jeff Gordon — the season's leading pole-winner with six — was fifth-fastest, just ahead of Geoff Bodine, who had spent 90 minutes of the practice session waiting while repairs were made to his Exide Ford following a meeting with the concrete wall.

Darrell Waltrip, whose broken ribs (courtesy of his Charlotte accident) were still healing, had bolted a new, supportive seat into his Western Auto Chevrolet. Darrell responded with the seventh-fastest lap and was confident of a solid run at Pocono. Rusty Wallace, brim-full of confidence as well, lined up on Darrell's right. Shepherd and Bobby Labonte made up the fifth row. Derrike Cope just missed the top 10.

After the first round, Kyle was 18th, Earnhardt was 24th, Elliott was 25th and Terry Labonte was 27th. Horton had clocked in 30th. Of course, everyone expected to improve their times on Saturday, after they'd had more time to work with the Goodyears.

But fog and misting rain throughout Saturday ended any hopes for improvement and presented crew chiefs with another problem to solve before the 200-lapper on Sunday. Out came the black books, and crew members discussed the events they had run in the past with a similar tire, comparing notes on the chassis settings that had been used for those events.

For some, it would be a guessing game. Terry Labonte arrived at the track on Sunday morning to find his Kellogg's Chevrolet looking like a discarded doughnut at

*As Ken Schrader prepares to take his Budweiser Monte Carlo into turn
one for the first time, the forty-two-car field fans out behind him five- and six-wide along Pocono's roomy frontstretch.*

a picnic. Crew members, carrying shocks and springs back and forth from the transporter to the garage area, were swarming around the red and yellow car. An entirely new chassis setup was going underneath the Chevrolet, and Terry and others like him wouldn't know if their crew chiefs were right or not until the green flag fell later in the day.

Before the first 100 miles of the UAW-GM Teamwork 500 had been completed, it was evident that Ray Evernham had put the right chassis components under Jeff Gordon's DuPont Chevrolet. Gordon had immediately flashed to the front and established himself and his Monte Carlo as factors to be reckoned with. He seemingly built leads at will and at one point was so far ahead that he pitted for a green-flag, four-tire stop and still emerged from pit road with the lead.

While Gordon was flying at the front, the Kellogg's Chevrolet was purring along as well: It obviously

*(**Right**) Rick Mast (1) pulls alongside Kyle Petty, who was hoping to repeat the finish he had enjoyed the week before at Dover. It was not to be: Kyle's motor gave out early in the race. Mast fared a little better: He finished 21st, one lap down.*
*(**Below**) Mark Martin, who was in good spirits after qualifying on the front row, had a chance to relax with his wife, Arlene, prior to the race.*

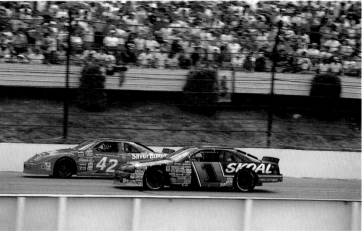

liked the chassis setup installed on Sunday morning. Despite a touch of the flu, the Chevrolet's driver moved it deftly through the field. With 10 laps remaining, he had made it all the way to second place and figured he was headed for a runner-up finish behind his Hendrick Motorsport teammate.

But then, Pancho Carter lost his engine, hit the wall and spun in the third turn. The incident brought out the final caution of the afternoon and set up a restart that featured all three Hendrick cars (Schrader was nipping at Labonte's heels) as well as Musgrave, who had been highly competitive throughout the event.

When the race restarted on lap 194, the unthinkable happened. Gordon missed a shift in his haste to get away from the field, and that single error was the only opportunity Labonte needed. Terry saw a puff of smoke, instantly recognized what had happened and dove for the inside. Terry passed Gordon for the lead as the field rumbled toward the first turn. All he had to do now was keep Musgrave and Schrader behind him, and he could add another trophy (his second of the season) to his display case.

Behind him, Schrader and Musgrave began battling for second place, and their side-by-side struggle allowed Terry to slip away to a 1.64-second victory. Musgrave beat Schrader to the line to claim his second-straight runner-up position. Sterling Marlin, on the strength of a late-race rush to the front, came home fourth, and Hut Stricklin put the finishing touches on another strong performance in Kenny Bernstein's Quaker State Ford to cross the line fifth.

Right behind the green Ford came a black one; Elliott brought the ThunderBat home sixth following a workman-like drive that had reminded many that the Redhead had not lost his desire to run at the front and win. Shepherd was seventh and Earnhardt came home eighth. Michael Waltrip posted his fourth-consecutive top-10 finish with a ninth place, and Brett Bodine beat Martin, who was forced to stop for a new battery when his alternator failed, for the final top-10 spot.

Gordon's mistake had bent the valves in the engine of

his DuPont Chevrolet, and by the conclusion of the race, he had fallen all the way from the lead to the final position on the lead lap, 16th. The error also cost him dearly in the point standings, where he dropped to 123 behind Earnhardt.

Jeff wasn't the only one to suffer from "pilot error." Wallace had been a contender throughout the day, but he spun away his chances for a good finish in the closing laps. The spin caused flat spots on his tires, and the subsequent stop for new Goodyears had dropped him a lap behind, to 17th place.

Darrell Waltrip didn't even make it to the finish. After just two laps, Waltrip was headed for the garage with engine failure. Saturday's inclement weather had caught up with him: Had the team been able to run at least three laps of practice, the engine problem would have been discovered and a new motor installed. Darrell was inconsolable.

So was Dale Jarrett. Early in the race, a bump from Marlin had sent the Texaco Ford into the wall. Larry McReynolds and the rest of the Robert Yates Racing team

For the second week in a row, Dale Jarrett was involved in an altercation in the opening laps of a race. This time, Robert Yates, Larry McReynolds and the rest of the crew went behind the wall at Pocono to repair the damage. Jarrett returned to the track and finished 38th.

had made hasty repairs and returned Jarrett to the track, but he could muster only 38th in the final rundown. To add insult to injury, following the Pocono event, he had fallen all the way to 17th in the point standings.

The day was also a frustrating one for Dover winner Petty. Kyle managed to move up from his 18th starting position, but his success was only temporary. Kyle's motor began overheating, and he completed only 118 laps before the engine went "bang!" He was classified 39th in the final rundown, and as he headed for the track's exit, he could only repeat what he had said the previous week: "Racing amazes me."

UAW-GM Teamwork 500

Race #13 — Final Race Results

Fin. Pos.	Str. Pos.	Car #	Driver	Team
1	27	5	Terry Labonte	Kellogg's Chevrolet
2	21	16	Ted Musgrave	The Family Channel Ford
3	1	25	Ken Schrader	Budweiser Chevrolet
4	15	4	Sterling Marlin	Kodak Film Chevrolet
5	17	26	Hut Stricklin	Quaker State Ford
6	25	94	Bill Elliott	McDonald's Ford
7	9	21	Morgan Shepherd	Citgo Ford
8	24	3	Dale Earnhardt	Goodwrench Service Chevrolet
9	23	30	Michael Waltrip	Pennzoil Pontiac
10	19	11	Brett Bodine	Lowe's Ford
11	2	6	Mark Martin	Valvoline Ford
12	16	87	Joe Nemechek	Burger King Chevrolet
13	4	10	Ricky Rudd	Tide Ford
14	6	7	Geoff Bodine	Exide Batteries Ford
15	3	43	Bobby Hamilton	STP Pontiac
16	5	24	Jeff Gordon	DuPont Auto Finishes Chevrolet
17	8	2	Rusty Wallace	Miller Genuine Draft Ford
18	39	29	Steve Grissom	Meineke Chevrolet
19	22	31	Ward Burton	Hardee's Chevrolet
20	11	12	Derrike Cope	Straight Arrow Ford
21	31	1	Rick Mast	Skoal Ford
22	26	15	Dick Trickle	Ford Quality Care Ford
23	20	77	Bobby Hillin	Jasper/USAir Ford
24	28	75	Todd Bodine	Factory Stores Ford
25	35	98	Jeremy Mayfield	RCA Ford
26	36	41	Ricky Craven	Kodiak Chevrolet
27	10	18	Bobby Labonte	Interstate Batteries Chevrolet
28	40	9	Lake Speed	Spam/Melling Ford
29	42	32	Chuck Bown	Active Trucking Chevrolet
30	29	37	John Andretti	Kmart/Little Caesars Ford
31	32	71	Dave Marcis	Olive Garden Chevrolet
32	38	90	Mike Wallace	Heilig-Meyers Ford
33	12	40	Greg Sacks	Kendall Pontiac
34	30	27	Jimmy Horton	Hooters Ford
35	33	78	Pancho Carter	Equipment Supply Company Ford
36	37	8	Jeff Burton	Raybestos Brakes Ford
37	34	33	Robert Pressley	Skoal Bandit Chevrolet
38	14	28	Dale Jarrett	Texaco Havoline Ford
39	18	42	Kyle Petty	Coors Light Pontiac
40	41	22	Randy LaJoie	MBNA America Pontiac
41	13	23	Jimmy Spencer	Smokin' Joe's Ford
42	7	17	Darrell Waltrip	Western Auto Chevrolet

MILLER GENUINE DRAFT 400

MICHIGAN INTERNATIONAL SPEEDWAY
JUNE 18, 1995
•••••

When the June Michigan race arrives, the typical parade of transporters heads up the interstate a day earlier than usual. Annually, transporters, race cars, crew chiefs, drivers and car owners of the Ford and Pontiac teams gather for an "employee day" at each make's corporate headquarters, giving workers a chance to see the cars and meet the drivers.

While Bill Elliott, Rusty Wallace and the rest of their teammates (18 strong!) were scribbling their John Hancocks in a Ford parking lot, Kyle Petty, Michael Waltrip and their teammates were hard at work at Pontiac, taking Sharpies to various items the General Motors workers wanted signed.

Chevrolet's teams were not part of the festivities this June, but Dale Earnhardt put the day off to good work. He competed in a charity fishing tournament held near the race track and celebrated his return to the lead in the point standings by whipping everyone in the tournament. One partici-

*Bobby Labonte (18) and Jeff Gordon (24) take their duel to the high side of Derrike Cope on Michigan's two-mile oval. In the end, Labonte would flex the muscles on the Interstate Chevrolet to grab the checkered flag. (**Right**) Virginians Jeff (left) and Ward Burton, two bright, young stars on the NASCAR Winston Cup tour, enjoyed a rare opportunity to relax together on race morning.*

pant, shaking his head in awe afterward, said, "It's unbelievable. The man fishes just like he drives on the track — wide open!" Earnhardt caught 34 pounds of fish for the winning total.

When the teams finally arrived at the pristine two-mile oval nestled in Michigan's serene Irish Hills, they immediately took note of the track's new, black blanket of asphalt. The entire track, previously worn and patched, had been repaved, and in typical Roger Penske style, no small strip had been left untouched. General manager Gene Haskett had

overseen the pavement of pit road, and new concrete pads had been poured for the working pit areas. The track simply sparkled. Not a piece of litter could be found in the vast exterior parking lots, and every trash can in the infield stood clean and at the ready. Haskett and track owner Penske had the place looking like a national park!

Due in part to the new pavement, everyone expected increased speeds at the track. From the first moment of practice, the only question was how many cars would blow past the old track record of 181 miles per hour, set by Geoff Bodine last year.

The answer was: nearly everyone!

The fastest of the fast — to no one's surprise — was the rainbow-hued Chevrolet featuring Jeff Gordon behind the wheel. The Michigan pole marked the seventh time this season he had posted the fastest lap in first-round qualifying. Gordon agreed that the new pavement was the primary catalyst for the increased speeds, but in addition, he pointed out that the cars were 100 pounds lighter than they had been last year, and Goodyear had brought a very good tire for the event. He also mentioned something about a

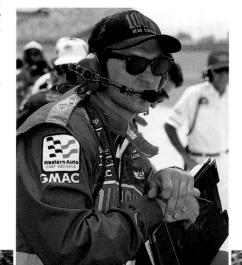

(Right) At Michigan, crew chief Ray Evernham engineered another pole for his driver, Jeff Gordon — the seventh in 14 attempts this year! (Below) Rusty Wallace uses the outside line to pass Derrike Cope (12), Todd Bodine (75) and Robert Pressley (33) in an attempt to lose Gordon, who is in hot pursuit. Wallace led early in the race and had a strong mount but was forced to settle for a third-place finish.

Monte Carlo being more aerodynamic than a Lumina.

Ricky Rudd's lap was more than 4.5 miles per hour faster than Bodine's record, but the Tide Ford driver felt like the final car on a subway train. Despite his outstanding lap — good enough for the outside of the front row — he had been a mile-and-a-half per hour slower than Gordon. In other words, if the two ran their qualifying speeds during the race, Gordon would be within a half-mile of lapping Ricky in an hour. The mere thought was enough to send Rudd walking back to his truck, shaking his head.

Sterling Marlin locked up the inside of the second row and was joined by Mark Martin, which made it Chevy/Ford on the first two rows. Wallace and Ted Musgrave claimed the third row in qualifying. Behind them were Earnhardt and Dick Trickle, who posted a strong run in the Bud Moore Quality Care Ford in front of many of his sponsor's executives. Talk about good timing — Trickle's eighth was his best starting position of the season. Jeremy Mayfield had a terrific run to grab the inside of the fifth row — the best start of his career — for Cale Yarborough's team, and Lake Speed "Spam-ed" his fellow competitors to claim the final slot in the top 10.

In all, 31 of the 38 cars that made the field on the basis of their speeds broke Bodine's old record. Morgan Shepherd, meanwhile, was the surprise head of the list of drivers who would need to take a provisional. Ken

(Above) Ted Musgrave had to sit on pit road while his crew fashioned a patch for the front air dam on the Roush Thunderbird. He did manage to maintain his position on the lead lap, however, and was able to salvage a top-10 finish. (Right) Ken Schrader was forced to pit when an oil leak was discovered on the Budweiser Chevrolet. The problem was fixed, but Ken lost several crucial laps in the process.

Schrader, the pole-winner at Pocono the week before, was right behind Morgan on the provisional list and followed by Kyle Petty, the winner of the Miller Genuine Draft 500 at Dover two weeks ago. Also forced to use a provisional was Dave Marcis. Gary Bradberry, who had begun the season with Jimmy Means' team, tried to qualify with his own Chevrolet, but he blew one engine in practice prior to the first qualifying session and then blew up his second motor in the final practice session before the second round of qualifying. It was an unsuccessful — and costly — trip to the Irish Hills for Gary.

The pilgrimage was even more costly for Greg Sacks. For the fourth time this year, Sacks failed to get the Kendall Oil Pontiac into the field, and on the Monday following the event, he found himself without a ride. Team co-owner Dick Brooks had released Sacks from the remainder of his contract for 1995.

Maybe Sacks should have inquired about Bobby Labonte's driving "secrets." Throughout the season, Labonte has raced with a couple of small, rubber soldiers taped inside his car. Yep. Little GI Joes. Hey, you know, whatever keeps the driver happy and psyched, crew chief Jimmy Makar reasoned when the idea first came up. Why not? One is taped on the front dash, so if the cars in front get too far away, the little guy can shoot them, get them

out of the way. Another is taped in the back, pointing out the rear window. Those other cars get too close, shoot 'em. It seemed to work at Charlotte a couple of races ago, so they cleaned 'em off real good — they didn't want those rifles to jam! — and put 'em back in at Michigan.

By quarter-distance at Michigan, the little guys had done their work. Bobby was at the point in the green and black Interstate Batteries Chevrolet. But he wasn't there for long, mind you, because Gordon and his Chevrolet buddies were working over everyone, and Jeff led seemingly at will.

Rudd, who had appeared able to keep pace with the Chevrolets, kissed the concrete on lap 71. After his Ford had come to a stop, Ricky took a quick helicopter ride to a nearby hospital, where he was diagnosed as having suffered a concussion. Rudd was later released and returned to his home near Charlotte Sunday night.

Earnhardt, who had also seemed capable of running with Gordon, found the wall after trying to pass Derrike Cope. The two cars had touched just enough to send the black Chevrolet into the concrete. The Goodwrench Chevrolet was too damaged to continue, so Dale, bruised leg and all, limped toward the airport. Rudd's and Earnhardt's difficulties left the battle at the front to Gordon and Labonte, and the two traded the lead often in the final 75 laps. This time, however, the green and black car held the upper hand, and Gordon was the driver giving chase.

Every time Jeff gathered enough steam to make a run at Bobby, Labonte would pull the trigger and sneak out another car-length. But all were familiar with the speed of the DuPont Chevrolet, and everyone expected Jeff simply to pick his spot and whip past Labonte for the victory.

Labonte's little soldiers, however, seemed to have an endless supply of bullets, and he continued to keep Gordon in his wake. He led the final 13 laps en route to his second victory of the season and his second in the last four weeks.

After the race, Gordon said he had just plain been out-

run by the Joe Gibbs-owned car. He had given it everything he could muster, but it wasn't enough this Sunday afternoon. He did, however, point out that the engine in Labonte's car came from Hendrick Motorsports.

Gibbs' team was built around an engine-leasing program with Hendrick right from the start. In fact, the winning motor had been pulled out of Terry Labonte's Kellogg's truck and installed in brother Bobby's Interstate car at the last minute. It prompted Terry — who finished ninth — to crack, "We'll see how many more motors he gets from us if he keeps running that good!"

The two young drivers' dramatic finish, measured at less than three car-lengths, overshadowed a scintillating late-race charge by Wallace. Following the final caution flag of the day, the race had restarted with 16 laps remaining. Wallace, who had lost a lap when he was trapped in the pits by a caution following a green-flag stop, made the lap up with the help of a later yellow.

He was seventh in line on the final restart, but he quickly ripped his way to third, flashing past a strong-running John Andretti with a lap left. Unfortunately for Wallace, by the time he found no one but Gordon and Labonte in front of him, the two Chevrolets had become just a couple of multi-colored blurs in the distance. Rusty was forced to settle for third place.

Andretti, who had led during the race and hoped crew chief Tim Brewer's mileage gamble would bring him his first victory, instead finished fourth. Morgan Shepherd,

(Left) Dale Earnhardt had a car capable of running with the leaders until he tangled with Cope and smacked the wall. The end result of the accident was a 35th-place finish and, more importantly, a drop in the points. Dale was now second behind Marlin.
(Below) Hut Stricklin (26) is anxiously looking for a hole to squeak through, but Bobby Hamilton (43), Joe Nemechek and Jimmy Spencer (23) are having none of it!

The entire Joe Gibbs Racing team joined a jubilant Bobby Labonte in the winner's circle to celebrate their second victory of the season. And they weren't shy about proclaiming themselves "Number One"!

who had fought his way to the front from his provisional starting position, finished a sparkling fifth. Dale Jarrett recorded a sixth, his best finish since April, in front of a group of delighted spectators. Ernie Irvan had invited some of the medical personnel who had worked with him last year in the Michigan hospital to attend the race. They were all pulling for the "28," and Jarrett had given them something to cheer about; he led at times and remained in contention throughout the event.

Marlin and Martin were seventh and eighth, ahead of Terry, and Musgrave posted another top-10 finish after he won his battle with Speed. Lake and Michael Waltrip captured 11th and 12th place, respectively, but not without a couple of altercations first. In the closing laps, Michael had forced Lake low on the frontstretch when Lake passed him for position. On the next lap, Lake moved Michael into the highest groove, preventing Michael from passing him and regaining his position. Michael was quick to express his

In front of a huge crowd on hand at Michigan International Speedway, Jeff Gordon leads the field under the green flag to begin the Miller Genuine Draft 400.

displeasure with the situation — and Lake. The following day, Michael's wallet was $10,000 lighter after NASCAR levied a fine on Waltrip for his actions.

Michael wasn't the only one to get hit where it hurts. Geoff Bodine had scraped the wall with five laps to go and drawn a black flag from NASCAR officials, but he had ignored the flag for the final five laps. Bodine was hit with a $5,000 fine.

Earnhardt's early exit, Marlin's eighth and Gordon's second gave the point race a whole new look as the teams headed for a weekend off — the first in two months. When the tour reassembled for the Pepsi 400, Marlin would take a six-point lead over Earnhardt into the fray. Gordon was now third, just 12 points behind Sterling and six behind Dale.

Miller Genuine Draft 400
Race #14 — Final Race Results

Fin. Pos.	Str. Pos.	Car #	Driver	Team
1	19	18	Bobby Labonte	Interstate Batteries Chevrolet
2	1	24	Jeff Gordon	DuPont Auto Finishes Chevrolet
3	5	2	Rusty Wallace	Miller Genuine Draft Ford
4	21	37	John Andretti	Kmart/Little Caesars Ford
5	39	21	Morgan Shepherd	Citgo Ford
6	29	28	Dale Jarrett	Texaco Havoline Ford
7	3	4	Sterling Marlin	Kodak Film Chevrolet
8	4	6	Mark Martin	Valvoline Ford
9	15	5	Terry Labonte	Kellogg's Chevrolet
10	6	16	Ted Musgrave	The Family Channel Ford
11	10	9	Lake Speed	Spam/Melling Ford
12	24	30	Michael Waltrip	Pennzoil Pontiac
13	14	77	Bobby Hillin	Jasper/USAir Ford
14	34	94	Bill Elliott	McDonald's Ford
15	42	71	Dave Marcis	Olive Garden Chevrolet
16	8	15	Dick Trickle	Ford Quality Care Ford
17	22	33	Robert Pressley	Skoal Bandit Chevrolet
18	20	31	Ward Burton	Hardee's Chevrolet
19	36	12	Derrike Cope	Straight Arrow Ford
20	37	29	Steve Grissom	Meineke Chevrolet
21	35	7	Geoff Bodine	Exide Batteries Ford
22	9	98	Jeremy Mayfield	RCA Ford
23	23	27	Elton Sawyer	Hooters Ford
24	32	32	Chuck Bown	Active Trucking Chevrolet
25	12	43	Bobby Hamilton	STP Pontiac
26	16	17	Darrell Waltrip	Western Auto Chevrolet
27	40	25	Ken Schrader	Budweiser Chevrolet
28	11	87	Joe Nemechek	Burger King Chevrolet
29	27	75	Todd Bodine	Factory Stores Ford
30	13	23	Jimmy Spencer	Smokin' Joe's Ford
31	26	8	Jeff Burton	Raybestos Brakes Ford
32	28	90	Mike Wallace	Heilig-Meyers Ford
33	30	41	Ricky Craven	Kodiak Chevrolet
34	18	1	Rick Mast	Skoal Ford
35	7	3	Dale Earnhardt	Goodwrench Service Chevrolet
36	33	81	Kenny Wallace	TIC Financial Ford
37	17	26	Hut Stricklin	Quaker State Ford
38	2	10	Ricky Rudd	Tide Ford
39	38	44	Jeff Purvis	Jackaroo Chevrolet
40	25	11	Brett Bodine	Lowe's Ford
41	31	22	Randy LaJoie	MBNA America Pontiac
42	41	42	Kyle Petty	Coors Light Pontiac

PEPSI 400

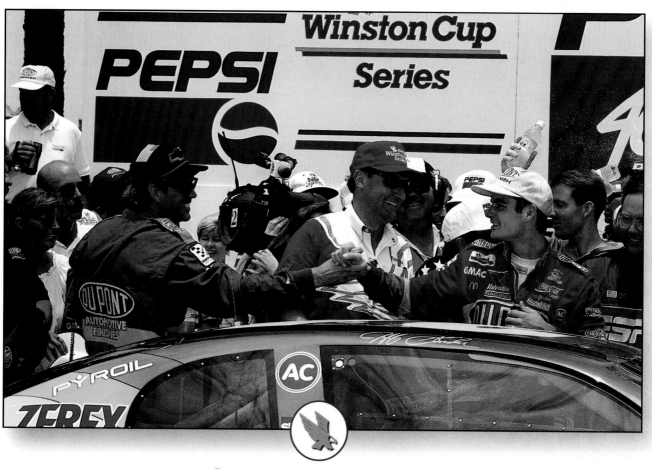

DAYTONA INTERNATIONAL SPEEDWAY

JULY 1, 1995

•••••

The drivers and crew members had varied plans for the weekend between the Michigan race and the upcoming Pepsi 400 at Daytona. Many spent some oft-postponed time with their families. Others, with their minivans and Suburbans packed to the headliners, headed for the beach for a few days of vacation.

Some, who simply can't get enough racing, headed for another track. Terry Labonte, getting a little practice for the upcoming Bud at The Glen, took his NASCAR Busch Series team to Watkins Glen and ripped off a stirring victory in the Lysol 300. Ken Schrader headed to Minnesota's lake country and won the pole before finishing seventh in Branierd's ASA race. Mark Martin traveled the farthest: He made a trip to Portland, Ore., to beat the regulars in a NASCAR Northwest Tour race on Portland's road course. And the drivers weren't the only ones making track moves!

Charlotte and Atlanta owner Bruton Smith and his Speedway Motorsports company had purchased 50 percent of the stock in North Wilkesboro Speedway and become a co-owner of the five-eighths-mile oval, along with the Staley family (former track president Enoch Staley had passed away just a few weeks earlier). It was the second track Smith had invested in this year; he had purchased a minority share in North Carolina Motor Speedway a few weeks

Amid the clamor of the victory lane celebration, the Dynamic Duo — Jeff Gordon and crew chief Ray Evernham — wordlessly congratulate one another on a job well done. Their collaboration in '95 had produced magical results — not the least of which were their four victories thus far.
***(Right)** Bill Elliott was unhappy, to say the least, about having to use his champion's provisional to make the field for the Pepsi 400. In the end, though, the former champion prevailed, clawing his way up to a solid 10th-place finish.*

by Sterling Marlin or the rainbow-painted Monte Carlo Jeff Gordon had put on the pole in seven of the season's first 14 races. Few paid any attention to a black Chevrolet driven by Dale Earnhardt during a few "shakedown" laps.

When we last saw Dale, he was limping through the Michigan garage area to his street car after losing an argument with the concrete wall. He had headed for the airport and climbed into his plane, which had jetted south. After a few days on his boat, "Sunday Money," Dale was ready to return to action. While he had been recuperating from the hard knock on his knee, the Richard Childress team had taken the Goodwrench Chevrolet to Daytona for a quick test to ensure the car was repaired correctly after the Talladega accident. Dave Marcis had shouldered the responsibility of testing the car, and

(Above) Jimmy Spencer was pensive prior to the Pepsi 400, but he put that nervous energy to good use once the race started; he gained five spots from his qualifying position to finish ninth, good enough to match his best finish of the season to date.
(Right) Despite his pit crew's quick work on the Factory Stores Ford, Todd Bodine was unable to capitalize on his sixth-place start: He wound up 23rd at the conclusion of the Pepsi 400.

prior to Staley's death. He was also in the process of preparing to move dirt for the new Texas Motor Speedway, which had been financed by the sale of Speedway Motorsports stock.

By the time the NASCAR Winston Cup teams arrived at Daytona for the famous track's second event of the season, some personnel changes had been made. Greg Sacks, released by Dick Brooks the day following the Michigan race, had been hired on a one-race basis to drive Junior Johnson's Hooters Ford. (Elton Sawyer, who had become Johnson's "regular" driver, was in Milwaukee with his Ford Credit team for the NASCAR Busch Series race and would be unable to make the trips back and forth from Wisconsin to Florida.)

Brooks had nominated ARCA Series point leader Andy Hillinburg to drive the Kendall Oil Pontiac at Daytona, and Andy hoped the one-race deal would evolve into at least several races in the black Poncho. Finally, car owner Bill Davis had released Randy LaJoie and named Jimmy Hensley to drive the MBNA-sponsored Grand Prix.

During qualifying, all eyes were on either the Kodak Chevrolet driven to back-to-back Daytona 500 victories when Dale climbed through the window for the first Pepsi 400 practice, he found that Marcis and the team had done their job.

Gordon had drawn the first number for qualifying, and he cranked off a 190.630-mile-per-hour lap in steamy temperatures. He didn't think it would last — and he was right. Sterling Marlin managed 190.718 mph, but he, too, said he didn't think it would stand up for the pole.

And like Gordon, Marlin was right, but it took longer for Marlin to be proven correct. In fact, after 27 other drivers had made their runs, the Kodak Chevrolet was still the fastest. Then Earnhardt rolled out. In his first competitive lap, he blistered the track with a circuit at 191.355 mph, nailing his second pole of the season and becoming the second driver this year to win more than one pole. He'd also earned his fourth-consecutive front-row start at Daytona.

It was a virtual Monte Carlo parade at the front after Bobby Labonte recorded the fourth-fastest lap and Robert Pressley grabbed the inside of the third row. Pressley had been just a tick faster than the best Ford, piloted by Todd Bodine. Dale Jarrett was seventh-fastest, and Michael and Darrell Waltrip grabbed the eighth and ninth positions. Michael's lap had revealed his as the fastest Pontiac. Martin captured the final spot in the top 10, barely beating Lake Speed and Dick Trickle.

Of the drivers involved in the personnel shuffle, Sacks fared the best: He made it into the field in the first round, turning the 20th-fastest lap. Hensley would start 31st, but Hillinburg had been forced to use a provisional to make the field. Other starters using standard provisionals were Bobby Hamilton, Ricky Craven and Ward Burton. Bill

(**Above**) Fine day for a Chevy parade, don't you think? Three members of this Monte Carlo quintet finished in the top three, and Robert Pressley brought the Skoal Bandit home in 11th. So who was the odd man out? Bobby Labonte, who completed only 48 laps before he was forced out when his Interstate Batteries machine burned a piston.
(**Left**) Dale Earnhardt (3) takes the inside lane to pass Dick Trickle's Quality Care Ford. Trickle performed steadily and finished 12th, but Earnhardt, though considerably less consistent, was on hand to battle for the victory. He eventually crossed the line third.

Elliott, meanwhile, used a champion's provisional and would start dead last with his McDonald's Ford. Steve Seligman, Kenny Wallace and Delma Cowart failed to make the field and were forced to watch the race on ESPN.

It was obvious that Jeff Burton was a little antsy, but he had a good rea-

son: He and wife Kim were awaiting the imminent birth of their first child. Jeff was only a phone call away; the cellular phone was with him everywhere he went. A plane was lined up, waiting outside Daytona's third turn, and if the cell phone rang, Jeff was gone. As it turned out, Kim didn't deliver daughter Kimberle Paige until daddy Jeff was back home on Monday, July 3.

(Above) The "Skoal Brothers" mix it up in the turn. In the Pepsi 400, Robert Pressley (33) was the stronger of the two; Pressley finished 11th, while Rick Mast finished 26th. (Right) Ricky Rudd prepares to do battle on Daytona's high banks. Apparently, he was more than ready for what the track had to dish out; he gained six spots from his 14th starting position and finished eighth. (Below) In front of a packed house, Sterling Marlin (4) lays a lap on John Andretti (37). John's Kmart/Little Caesars Ford was only one of many mounts that simply couldn't keep up the pace dictated by the Monte Carlos of Gordon, Marlin and Earnhardt.

Instead, it was Larry McReynolds, the popular crew chief for Robert Yates' Havoline Ford, who received a phone call, but it was not a welcome one. Dale Jarrett sent Larry back to North Carolina on his plane, and Larry arrived just an hour before his mother, Mary, succumbed after a long illness. Larry returned for the race, but the team went about its business with a heavy heart, and race day was made even darker by an engine failure in the Ford.

Everyone expected the Chevrolets to run away with the Pepsi 400, and the assembled throng of fans got just what they had anticipated. Earnhardt led, Marlin led, Gordon led, Marlin led, Gordon led, Marlin led, Gordon led — well, you get the picture.

Earnhardt's crew made an adjustment during the race that sent Dale backwards through the field, but they got a chance to correct the problem with a caution flag. He then whipped past six cars in 16 laps, and when Mike Wallace spun, bringing out the final yellow, the Chevrolets lined up for a one-lap sprint to the flag.

Gordon was at the point, with Earnhardt second and Marlin third. As they headed into the first turn, Sterling tried Dale on the low side. Dale countered and Marlin fell back, but Gordon gained a car-length. The three cars built up speed and rocketed into the third turn, where Sterling again tried Dale in an attempt to steal second place. With the black and yellow Monte Carlos dicing behind him, Gordon got away just enough — he flashed to the checkered flag

The DuPont Refinishes team donned its now-famous "Refuse to Lose" T-shirts in Daytona's victory lane after Jeff Gordon took the checkered just two car-lengths ahead of Sterling Marlin. Judging by the team's performance thus far, this would not be the last time those shirts appeared in a victory lane!

two car-lengths ahead. Behind him, Marlin managed to sneak his bumper in front of Earnhardt's at the finish line, claiming second.

Behind the three Chevrolets, Martin claimed the title of "best of the rest" by just acing teammate Ted Musgrave at the line for fourth place. Ken Schrader took sixth place ahead of Kyle Petty's Pontiac, the highest-finishing Tin Indian.

Ricky Rudd fought his way to eighth place, and Jimmy Spencer equaled his best finish of the season by coming home ninth. The "drive of the day" honor went to Elliott, however, who had scratched and clawed all the way from the last-place starting position to a fighting 10th place. Bill had run as far up as third during the race and felt his season was beginning to turn around. He beat Pressley for the final top-10 spot in the last lap.

After the race, Gordon was questioned about his nerves when he saw Earnhardt behind him for the one-lap restart. He was candid with his answer.

"Dale Earnhardt is the last person you want to see in your mirror in a situation like that. Dale likes to hang back on a restart and take a run at you, but I've learned about that. I checked up a bit, got him right on my bumper and used his air to help push me. He's done it to me the other way before, and it's cost me a race or two. Now, I've learned to do it my way, when I'm in front."

Hmm.

Sounds like "The Kid" is a quick learner!

Michael Waltrip had the second-highest finishing Pontiac (15th), but the "drive of the day" was unanimously awarded to Bill Elliott, who climbed 33 positions during the Pepsi 400 to finish in the top 10.

Pepsi 400

Race #15 — Final Race Results

Fin. Pos.	Str. Pos.	Car #	Driver	Team
1	3	24	Jeff Gordon	DuPont Auto Finishes Chevrolet
2	2	4	Sterling Marlin	Kodak Film Chevrolet
3	1	3	Dale Earnhardt	Goodwrench Service Chevrolet
4	10	6	Mark Martin	Valvoline Ford
5	21	16	Ted Musgrave	The Family Channel Ford
6	26	25	Ken Schrader	Budweiser Chevrolet
7	16	42	Kyle Petty	Coors Light Pontiac
8	14	10	Ricky Rudd	Tide Ford
9	15	23	Jimmy Spencer	Smokin' Joe's Ford
10	43	94	Bill Elliott	McDonald's Ford
11	5	33	Robert Pressley	Skoal Bandit Chevrolet
12	12	15	Dick Trickle	Ford Quality Care Ford
13	37	12	Derrike Cope	Straight Arrow Ford
14	25	7	Geoff Bodine	Exide Batteries Ford
15	8	30	Michael Waltrip	Pennzoil Pontiac
16	30	26	Hut Stricklin	Quaker State Ford
17	20	27	Greg Sacks	Hooters Ford
18	32	8	Jeff Burton	Raybestos Brakes Ford
19	33	5	Terry Labonte	Kellogg's Chevrolet
20	24	11	Brett Bodine	Lowe's Ford
21	11	9	Lake Speed	Spam/Melling Ford
22	40	41	Ricky Craven	Kodiak Chevrolet
23	6	75	Todd Bodine	Factory Stores Ford
24	13	21	Morgan Shepherd	Citgo Ford
25	27	71	Dave Marcis	Olive Garden Chevrolet
26	28	1	Rick Mast	Skoal Ford
27	22	2	Rusty Wallace	Miller Genuine Draft Ford
28	38	77	Bobby Hillin	Jasper/USAir Ford
29	29	32	Chuck Bown	Fina/Lance Chevrolet
30	31	22	Jimmy Hensley	MBNA America Pontiac
31	18	19	Loy Allen	Healthsource Health Plan Ford
32	35	98	Jeremy Mayfield	RCA Ford
33	36	37	John Andretti	Kmart/Little Caesars Ford
34	9	17	Darrell Waltrip	Western Auto Chevrolet
35	41	31	Ward Burton	Hardee's Chevrolet
36	42	40	Andy Hillenburg	Kendall Pontiac
37	23	90	Mike Wallace	Heilig-Meyers Ford
38	17	87	Joe Nemechek	Burger King Chevrolet
39	19	44	Jeff Purvis	Jackaroo Chevrolet
40	39	43	Bobby Hamilton	STP Pontiac
41	4	18	Bobby Labonte	Interstate Batteries Chevrolet
42	7	28	Dale Jarrett	Texaco Havoline Ford
43	34	29	Steve Grissom	Meineke Chevrolet

SLICK 50 300

NEW HAMPSHIRE INTERNATIONAL SPEEDWAY

JULY 9, 1995
•••••

In just three years, the NASCAR Winston Cup tour's visit to Dick and Bob Bahre's New Hampshire International Speedway has become one of the most popular stops on the circuit. That might be due to the beauty of New Hampshire in the summer, or it could be the warmth and friendliness of the residents of the neighboring communities who quickly dispel the long-standing myth of New England standoffishness.

Whatever the reason, the New England stop has quickly earned a well-deserved reputation as a most pleasant place to take the family for the weekend, and more and more drivers and crew members are doing just that.

Since the Bahres built the track — with their own money, no less, in these days of taxes going to build stadiums and arenas for other professional sports — the events at the one-mile superspeedway have played to sell-out crowds. Between last year's NASCAR Winston Cup race and this season's event, the Bahres added 4,000 seats — they were sold out before they were even built! With better access roads and an improved ability to move traffic before and after the events, there's no telling how many people the brothers could put on a show for.

Speaking of shows, the Bahres had a beauty heading their way. Jeff Gordon's "thinking-man's" victory at The Beach

Gordon may have looked like he was merely following along at New Hampshire — here he's close on the heels of Geoff Bodine (7), Hut Stricklin (26) and Ted Musgrave (16) — but in reality, he was lying in wait. Just ask Rusty Wallace and Dale Earnhardt!
***(Right)** Joe Nemechek had his Burger King Chevrolet "cooking" in qualifying for the Slick 50 300 — he qualified third fastest — but the sizzle fizzled during the race. By the finish, he had dropped to 19th.*

— his first trip to victory lane at the 2.5-mile oval in a point-paying race — had allowed him to close the gap between himself and point leader Sterling Marlin even more.

The closest point battle in the history of the modern era of the sport gave media members plenty to talk about as the teams unloaded in New Hampshire. Marlin was a mere seven points ahead of young Gordon and his rainbow-hued DuPont Chevrolet, and Dale Earnhardt had closed to within 16 points of the Kodak Chevrolet. Over

The Felix Sabates/Dick Brooks team, after trying Andy Hillinburg at Daytona, installed Rick Bickle in the Kendall Oil Pontiac for New Hampshire. Brooks was determined to "try out" several drivers before deciding who would be the man behind the wheel for the 1996 season. Over in Junior Johnson's camp, Elton Sawyer had returned to the Hooters Ford. Last week, Elton had competed in the NASCAR Busch Series race at Milwaukee, won by Dale Jarrett and his own Busch team.

Not surprisingly, Gordon and his DuPont Chevrolet

Nearly the entire field (is there anyone on the track?) took advantage of this caution, one of six during the race. As usual, it was a race in itself to get out of the pits, and as usual, Rusty Wallace's Brew Crew gave him a jump on the competition.

the course of the first half of the season, the three Monte Carlo drivers had been within a handful of top-five positions of each other.

NASCAR officials had issued an update on rear spoiler heights during the Daytona weekend, telling teams what would be permissible at New Hampshire. The sanctioning body continued to try to make the three makes of cars more competitive with each other, so for the Slick 50 race, Fords and Pontiacs would run spoilers of 6.375 inches high on the rear, while the more aerodynamic Chevrolets would feature a rear spoiler height of 5.750 inches for the 300-lap affair.

were the overwhelming choice for the Slick 50 300 pole. What was surprising was that Gordon skated up the slick track during his qualifying run and slapped the second-turn wall. The result was the slowest time of the session — not the fastest, as expected.

Gordon wasn't the only one to find the New Hampshire concrete unyielding. Jimmy Spencer and Eric Smith — who was piloting a car purchased from the Bill Davis team last year — each smacked the wall during practice. Travis Carter and his team rolled out the spare for Spencer, and Smith's team set about repairing its Ford (Smith's bare-bones effort had no spare car). Unfortunately, Smith's team couldn't complete the repairs in time for the first round of qualifying, and Carter's team couldn't get Spencer's Camel Ford ready in time, either.

Meanwhile, only the few crew members who had timed every car in practice had an idea of what Mark Martin and his Jack Roush-owned Valvoline Ford team had sitting in their garage area, waiting for qualifying. During practice, Mark had simulated a qualifying run and had turned the fastest time of the session. He knew the red, white and blue Ford was good, but he surprised even himself with his first-round qualifying effort on the slippery oval.

His actual qualifying lap was faster than the simulated one and set a new track record of more than 128.8 miles per hour. Even Mark, usually taciturn about his efforts, was impressed with the speed of a lap he originally had thought was not quite good enough.

On the outside of the front row was a green and black

Arches. Bill Elliott had turned in one of his best qualifying runs of the season to grab the outside of the second row.

Black and green were the colors of the third row: Bobby Labonte and Rick Mast had tied with their qualifying laps. Bobby claimed the fifth spot because his car owner ranked higher in the standings than Mast's.

Defending race champion Ricky Rudd cranked out the seventh-fastest lap to nail down the inside of the fourth row, barely ahead of Kyle Petty and Michael Waltrip. Ken Schrader slapped the Budweiser Chevrolet in the final top-10 position, just nipping Morgan Shepherd and Dick Trickle for the spot.

With thunderstorms threatening the proceedings, Gordon and 11 other drivers made second-round qualifying runs. Jeff claimed the fastest lap of the day, and although his speed was the 11th-fastest overall, it was good for only the 21st starting position, the worst the 23-year-old had posted this season to date.

Brett Bodine, Jimmy Spencer and Chuck Bown were all forced to take provisionals to make the New Hampshire field. Although Smith's team finally did complete repairs to his Ford, he recorded the slowest qualifying lap and didn't make the field.

If qualifying positions were any indication, NASCAR officials had been successful in their efforts to equalize the competition among the Fords, Pontiacs and Chevrolets. The top nine qualifying

(Left) Despite a promising eighth-place start, Coors Light Pontiac pilot Kyle Petty had a long and frustrating day at New Hampshire. After Petty had completed 194 laps, his engine failed, and he was relegated to a 37th-place finish.
(Below) Is this a speedway or an amusement park? Jeff Burton (8) and Jeremy Mayfield (98) play bumper cars while Hut Stricklin (26) watches over the proceedings. Dick Trickle (15) is probably just glad that he's in front of — rather than between — the two dueling drivers.

Chevrolet driven by none other than rookie contender Robert Pressley. He was pretty impressed, too!

The Leo Jackson team had entered a car for Pressley at New Hampshire last year, too — one of several events in which the team had provided cars for both Pressley and the retiring Harry Gant — but Robert had failed to make the field. This year, he more than made up for that disappointment by putting the Skoal-sponsored Monte Carlo on the front row.

Joe Nemechek continued his New Hampshire mastery by putting the Burger King Chevrolet solidly in the third-fastest position, but he barely beat out a red Ford carrying the Golden

(Above) Ricky Rudd did his best to keep his Tide Ford ahead of this hungry pack, but both the Valvoline Ford (third) and the Kellogg's Chevrolet (fourth) would overtake Rudd before he could reach the finish line. Rudd finished fifth. (Left) Ward Burton's "ride on the wild side" on lap 162 resulted in the fifth caution of the race. Ward's spin in the Slick 50 300 was only the latest setback in a season that had thus far been a disappointment to all parties involved.

positions were comprised of four Thunderbirds, three Monte Carlos and two Tin Indians.

Since the final "Happy Hour" practice had been rained out, competitors took the green flag with many unanswered questions about how their mounts would perform in the 300-lap race. One driver with a lot of questions was Gordon, whose team had made extensive repairs to the Chevrolet after his wall-banging episode on Friday. Ray Evernham and the DuPont crew had repaired a bent rear-end housing, a bent rear clip and bent tailpipes, and replaced both trailing arms as well as the right-front spindle and ball joint.

During the team's strategy session on Sunday morning, Evernham told Gordon to be prepared to make some two-tire stops because the crew chief thought it might be the best way to improve Jeff's track position early in the race.

Evernham turned out to be a prophet.

Martin immediately blasted to the lead from the start, but on the second caution, after 37 laps, Gordon hit pit road and headed back out with new right-side Goodyears — in the lead. Twice more during cautions, the combination of quick stops and two tires worked, keeping Jeff at or near the front of the field.

Halfway through the race, Gordon sat in third place, shaking his head in awe at what was unfolding in front of him. Rusty Wallace had propelled his Miller Ford up from its 20th starting spot to the front of the field, and Earnhardt had whipped the black Goodwrench Chevrolet to the point. Both had been helped by some outstanding work by their crews during pit stops.

The two black cars were beating and banging on each other in a side-by-side battle for the lead while Gordon

The future of NASCAR Winston Cup racing: (From left) Ted Musgrave, Jeff Gordon, Joe Nemechek and Ricky Craven clown around during driver introductions. Before the day was out, one of the four (Jeff Gordon) would sit atop the point standings.

watched, giving his helmeted head a shake now and then as he witnessed some of the moves between the two friends and rival competitors. "Every time I see Rusty and Dale go racing each other — especially for the lead — it amazes me," Gordon said after the race. "I wonder if they do it for the crowd or what they do it for, because they're just eating their tires up and rubbing fenders. It's actually pretty wild to watch it!"

Gordon waited for his chance. After 10 laps, he powered past both of the black cars. After that, the race was his to lose. Earnhardt ultimately had problems with loose lug nuts; he had to return to the pits to have them tightened. He then was forced to make another stop under green when a vibration developed in a new set of Goodyears. He finished 22nd, two laps behind. Marlin struggled all day with "a car that wouldn't drive and a motor that wouldn't pull." He finished ninth and subsequently lost the point lead.

Gordon's margin of victory was only 1.23 seconds over Shepherd, but the figure was not a true indication of his dominance in the final third of the race. Before the final caution had appeared, bunching the field for a 25-lap sprint, he had been more than nine seconds ahead.

The handling in Martin's Ford faded, and he was forced to settle for a third-place finish after dominating the first half of the event. Terry Labonte came home fourth, and Rudd was fifth. Wallace fell to sixth after a stop for repairs following a brush with Rudd. Derrike Cope, whose team was "going back to basics," brought the Straight Arrow Ford home seventh, beating Ted Musgrave and Marlin. Schrader claimed the final top-10 position, just ahead of Mast and Spencer.

Rick Mast leads the pack into the first turn at New Hampshire with Bill Elliott, Ted Musgrave, Derrike Cope and Dale Earnhardt close on his heels. Mast would hang tough until the end and post an 11th-place finish.

Slick 50 300

Race #16 — Final Race Results

Fin. Pos.	Str. Pos.	Car #	Driver	Team
1	21	24	Jeff Gordon	DuPont Auto Finishes Chevrolet
2	11	21	Morgan Shepherd	Citgo Ford
3	1	6	Mark Martin	Valvoline Ford
4	13	5	Terry Labonte	Kellogg's Chevrolet
5	7	10	Ricky Rudd	Tide Ford
6	20	2	Rusty Wallace	Miller Genuine Draft Ford
7	23	12	Derrike Cope	Straight Arrow Ford
8	17	16	Ted Musgrave	The Family Channel Ford
9	31	4	Sterling Marlin	Kodak Film Chevrolet
10	10	25	Ken Schrader	Budweiser Chevrolet
11	6	1	Rick Mast	Skoal Ford
12	40	23	Jimmy Spencer	Smokin' Joe's Ford
13	2	33	Robert Pressley	Skoal Bandit Chevrolet
14	9	30	Michael Waltrip	Pennzoil Pontiac
15	5	18	Bobby Labonte	Interstate Batteries Chevrolet
16	26	43	Bobby Hamilton	STP Pontiac
17	32	17	Darrell Waltrip	Western Auto Chevrolet
18	4	94	Bill Elliott	McDonald's Ford
19	3	87	Joe Nemechek	Burger King Chevrolet
20	37	77	Bobby Hillin	Jasper/USAir Ford
21	39	11	Brett Bodine	Lowe's Ford
22	18	3	Dale Earnhardt	Goodwrench Service Chevrolet
23	25	27	Elton Sawyer	Hooters Ford
24	36	9	Lake Speed	Spam/Melling Ford
25	30	8	Jeff Burton	Raybestos Brakes Ford
26	15	98	Jeremy Mayfield	RCA Ford
27	16	26	Hut Stricklin	Quaker State Ford
28	34	29	Steve Grissom	Meineke Chevrolet
29	24	71	Dave Marcis	Olive Garden Chevrolet
30	14	28	Dale Jarrett	Texaco Havoline Ford
31	19	41	Ricky Craven	Kodiak Chevrolet
32	35	90	Mike Wallace	Heilig-Meyers Ford
33	29	37	John Andretti	Kmart/Little Caesars Ford
34	12	15	Dick Trickle	Ford Quality Care Ford
35	22	7	Geoff Bodine	Exide Batteries Ford
36	28	75	Todd Bodine	Factory Stores Ford
37	8	42	Kyle Petty	Coors Light Pontiac
38	33	40	Rich Bickle	Kendall Pontiac
39	27	31	Ward Burton	Hardee's Chevrolet
40	41	32	Chuck Bown	Active Racing Chevrolet
41	38	22	Jimmy Hensley	MBNA America Pontiac

MILLER GENUINE DRAFT 500

POCONO RACEWAY
JULY 16, 1995
•••••

Just a week after the pleasant excursion in New Hampshire, the NASCAR Winston Cup tour was treated to another working holiday when the tour made its final stop of the season at Drs. Joe and Rose Mattioli's Pocono International Raceway.

The Pocono Mountain area is enjoying a resurgence as a popular vacation spot, and the festive atmosphere was infectious. Team members continued to enjoy the opportunity to share their sport with vacationers in the Northeast.

Jeff Gordon's New Hampshire victory, coupled with the finishes of Sterling Marlin and Dale Earnhardt, had changed the entire complexion of the point battle. Sterling was now 40 markers behind Gordon, and Earnhardt had fallen 92 points behind. The battle for fourth place was a weekly duel between teammates Mark Martin and Ted Musgrave. Ted had eased past Mark after New Hampshire and held a three-point margin heading into Pocono. Musgrave and Martin were trailing Gordon by 146 and 149 points, respectively, and both drivers realized that they needed to make a move — and soon — before the three Chevrolet drivers turned the point battle into their own private war.

Front-row mates Bill Elliott (94) and Mark Martin (6) peel away from the field to start the Miller Genuine Draft 500. Elliott had extended a lengthy streak by capturing the Pocono pole (he has won at least one pole in each of the last 12 seasons) and would do his home-grown effort proud with a top-five finish. (Right) The Texaco Havoline Ford team had struggled since Ernie Irvan's accident at Michigan the previous season, so Dale Jarrett's hard-fought, much-anticipated victory in the MGD 500 was particularly sweet.

For Ford fans, the season had become a nightmare. The Chevrolet Monte Carlo had turned out to be even better than expected, and the downforce built into the Chevrolet's body had clearly helped the car become the dominant player. At

the same time, the Ford teams themselves had struggled. Rusty Wallace had but a single victory to his credit — at Martinsville — and Martin had posted just one win, the Winston Select 500 at Talladega. Other Ford teams — the Wood Brothers, Bud Moore and Ricky Rudd's effort — had failed to win. Chevrolets had been on 12 of 16 poles and won 13 of 16 races.

For many Ford fans, the worst part of the season had been watching the Robert Yates team struggle. Expected by many to win right from the start with Dale Jarrett behind the wheel of the Texaco Thunderbirds, the team, instead, had been beset by problems. Dale had won the pole for the Daytona 500, and the team had posted four top-six finishes in the first six races, but beginning with the Winston Select 500 at Talladega, the black Ford's fortunes had taken a big hit. The team had plummeted as far

as 17th in the point standings following a succession of engine failures and accidents.

So, as the teams unloaded at Pocono, Jarrett, Yates and crew chief Larry McReynolds could only hope that the streak would reverse itself — and soon. The cars were well prepared, Jarrett was driving well and the motors were strong. All the team needed, McReynolds felt, was for Lady Luck to jump on board for a change. Larry wasn't entirely joking when he said he would happily install a special seat and safety harness for her in the Ford — she merely had to show up and be fitted!

The weekend was one of the steamiest in Pocono race history; when the cars were rolled out for the first round of qualifying, temperatures were pushing 100 degrees. But the sultry weather seemed to bring out the best in a Georgian — Bill Elliott claimed his first pole position for a NASCAR Winston Cup event since last year's spring Darlington race. It was the 47th pole of his career, the 41st on a superspeedway.

Since Mike Beam had left Junior Johnson's team and opened his own shop, concentrating on preparing Elliott's McDonald's Fords, the Elliott/Hardy team had begun to make progress. Bill had qualified fourth the week before at New Hampshire, but the Pocono pole was certainly the high-water point for the new team thus far this season. It

(Left) DuPont Refinishes crew chief Ray Evernham keeps close tabs on Jeff Gordon's fuel situation in the closing laps of the MGD 500. In the end, though, it made no difference: Dale Jarrett simply had Lady Luck on his side. (Below) By the time Todd Bodine (75) and Bobby Hamilton (43) flashed under the flagstand to take the checkered, their positions had been reversed; Bobby Hamilton brought the STP Pontiac home 19th, followed by Bodine in the Factory Stores Ford (23rd).

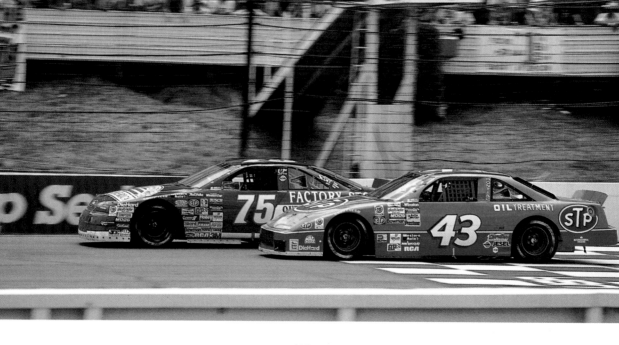

was hard for Bill to temper his delight and enthusiasm after his Pocono run continued his string of winning at least one pole position each year, a streak which had endured for 12 seasons.

"It's not a victory in a race, but we're making progress," the Redhead said, a familiar grin that had been long absent back on his face. "We've still got some work to do to be back at the front, race after race, but we're finally starting to feel like we're get-

top-10 position. Mast had barely beaten pole favorite Gordon and the Mane & Tail Ford driven by Derrike Cope, who was still on a roll following his seventh place at New Hampshire the previous weekend.

The Miller Genuine Draft Ford — a car many had expected to challenge for the pole at this event (especially since it was sponsored by the same brand of the Miller Brewing Company) — was absent from first-round qualifying.

(Top) It's hard to believe, but soon this trio — (from left) Dale Jarrett, Dale Earnhardt and Jeff Gordon — will be fighting each other tooth-and-nail for the victory. As for this kinder, gentler pre-race "meeting of the minds"? Well, it's only temporary! (Above) Rick Mast and Dale Jarrett (28) dice for position along the frontstretch at Pocono. Mast turned in a solid performance and finished 13th, but he just didn't have enough to keep up with Jarrett, who went on to claim the victory.

ting a handle on this whole situation with this new team."

Alongside Elliott on the starting grid was Martin, though he had qualified almost two-tenths of a second off the pace. Morgan Shepherd had grunted out his best starting position of the season, taking the inside of the second row and giving the Ford folks reason to hope with a 1-2-3 sweep in qualifying. Ken Schrader, who had nailed down the pole for the June Pocono race, had the Budweiser Chevrolet humming this time as well; he took the outside of the second row, just ahead of Earnhardt and Marlin.

Musgrave put the Family Channel Ford on the inside of the fourth row, and Bobby Hamilton continued his Pocono heroics by claiming the eighth-fastest lap with the Petty Enterprises STP Pontiac. Joe Nemechek made another strong qualifying run and slapped the Burger King Chevrolet in ninth place, and Rick Mast claimed the final

During an inspection, the roof flaps on Rusty Wallace's Thunderbird had been found to be of a different manufacture and material than the NASCAR-approved roof flap unit, and Wallace's car was not allowed on the track until the flaps had been replaced. The flaps on Wallace's car had been built by his team, and the error cost crew chief Robin Pemberton a fine of $20,000 and probation until August 30.

Despite the fact that the second day of time trials was even hotter than the first — temperatures reached 104 degrees — Wallace had no choice about whether or not he would run. A total of 14 other drivers had chosen to stand on their times rather than risk a slower lap because of the higher temperatures, but Rusty had to participate. His lap of 159.912 mph earned him the 22nd spot for the start of the Miller 500.

Ricky Craven, Todd Bodine and Elton Sawyer were forced to use provisionals to get into the field, but the only driver who went home was Randy McDonald. McDonald had failed to make the grid with a Pontiac fielded by the Hagan Racing Team.

Although Elliott had walked to his red Ford to start a race numerous times, this seemed to be a new and improved Elliott. As Bill sauntered down pit road, one couldn't help but notice that the confident spring was back in his step. Throughout the first half of this season, Bill and his team had fought the good fight and gone to the post every Sunday hoping for a finish that would propel the team to another level. Instead, the team had gotten the boost it needed from qualifying, and its confidence was contagious. For the first time all season, the Mac

the season; 13 drivers would trade the lead back and forth a total of 37 times before it ended. And as the event wound toward its three-quarter mark, it appeared that Wallace (now equipped with the right flaps) and Gordon would battle for the victory.

Then Jarrett looked over at the right side of his cockpit and found that, for the first time in a while, he had a passenger. She winked and smiled, and Dale headed for the front. He had caught the Wallace/Gordon duel by lap 156, and after racing those two down the frontstretch in a three-wide maneuver, Jarrett took the inside route into the first turn and captured the lead.

A collision involving Dave Marcis, Robert Pressley and Kenny Wallace resulted in the fifth caution of the race, and the leaders dove onto pit road for tires and fuel. Fully

Although he's leading at the moment, Darrell Waltrip would fare the worst of this trio: The engine in the Western Auto Chevrolet failed after 156 laps, relegating "DW" to 36th place. Bobby Hillin (77) and Lake Speed (9), meanwhile, turned in 12th- and 22nd-place performances, respectively.

Attack team was upbeat and ready to rumble.

For the first 14 laps of the race, the Golden Arches could be found at the front of the field, and Bill was beside himself. It was the first time he had led a single lap the entire season! Although he was surely concentrating on keeping the field behind him, one could almost see the grin creasing his face. It had been a long time! As the race progressed, Elliott and the red Ford remained a factor and a threat to win. There was plenty of rejoicing among long-suffering Elliott fans in the stands as well as those who had tuned in to the race via either radio or television.

The race developed into one of the most competitive of

aware of the history of the race track — 500-mile races have, at times, become mileage runs — McReynolds got on the radio and started putting information in Jarrett's ear.

"You know how this works, Dale," Larry said. "If this thing goes green the rest of the way, we're going to be really tight on fuel, and some of the others won't make it. Some will, and if we're going to be one of those, we have to start working the mileage deal right from the first turn of the first lap of this last part of the race. It's gonna be up to you. You're gonna have to roll in and out of the throttle like you've got an egg under your foot. You'll have to draft off everything that moves — even a deer! We have to start

A jubilant Dale Jarrett gives his team a champagne shower — the most refreshing kind — following his triumphant victory in the Miller Genuine Draft 500.

right now if we're gonna make it to the finish. If we get a yellow later, it all changes, but we've got to act like this thing is going to go green, and if we want to win it, we've got to do the mileage bit."

Jarrett kept nodding and nodding, his Texaco-emblazoned helmet bouncing up and down as he acknowledged McReynolds' advice.

Wallace led after the restart, but 10 laps later, Jarrett moved past him to the point. Then, on lap 178, Wallace, with Gordon in tow, whipped past to retake the lead, dropping Jarrett to third. With 14 laps to go, Gordon pulled Jarrett with him as he moved past Wallace. Then, on lap 188, Dale took the lead from Gordon.

The seriousness of the fuel situation became evident when, with just seven laps left, Wallace peeled off and headed for pit road — he was out of fuel. McReynolds took one look before borrowing a fuel dump can and a spray can of ether from a nearby team and sending a Yates crew member to the pit road entrance. McReynolds wanted to be ready in case Jarrett had to stop and couldn't make it all the way down pit road to his pit. It wasn't needed. Jarrett had just enough fuel to make it to the checkered flag — the engine stumbled in the third turn of the last lap but picked up just enough to get him across the line. He finished just a pair of car-lengths ahead of Gordon.

The demons had been banished: Jarrett and McReynolds hugged in Pocono's victory lane following their first victory together. Neither had forgotten that Larry's mother had passed away just a couple of weeks ago, and Larry honored her memory by dedicating the victory to her. It was a special win for the entire team. After struggling since the second Michigan race last year — when Ernie Irvan had been injured — the black-clad team had returned to the winner's circle.

Ricky Rudd and Musgrave fought their way to third and fourth, and Elliott was delighted with his fifth place. Geoff Bodine had galloped from 27th to sixth, and Martin, despite a stop for gas with just two laps remaining (and while he was running fourth), came home seventh. Jeremy Mayfield notched the best finish of his brief career and his first top 10 with an eighth place for Cale Yarborough's team, and Nemechek brought his homegrown effort a fine ninth place. Dick Trickle claimed his first top 10 of the season with Bud Moore's Quality Care Thunderbird.

For the second-straight race, Earnhardt and Marlin had struggled. Sterling was classified 18th and had the final car on the lead lap after suffering many problems with his shock absorbers. Dale had lost a lap during a pit stop, and since so many cars were on the lead lap, he had never been able to get his lap back. He was classified 20th at the end, and he walked away from Pocono a very disgusted driver.

Miller Genuine Draft 500

Race #17 — Final Race Results

Fin. Pos.	Str. Pos.	Car #	Driver	Team
1	15	28	Dale Jarrett	Texaco Havoline Ford
2	11	24	Jeff Gordon	DuPont Auto Finishes Chevrolet
3	13	10	Ricky Rudd	Tide Ford
4	7	16	Ted Musgrave	The Family Channel Ford
5	1	94	Bill Elliott	McDonald's Ford
6	27	7	Geoff Bodine	Exide Batteries Ford
7	2	6	Mark Martin	Valvoline Ford
8	38	98	Jeremy Mayfield	RCA Ford
9	9	87	Joe Nemechek	Burger King Chevrolet
10	25	15	Dick Trickle	Ford Quality Care Ford
11	14	31	Ward Burton	Hardee's Chevrolet
12	33	77	Bobby Hillin	Jasper/USAir Ford
13	10	1	Rick Mast	Skoal Ford
14	24	5	Terry Labonte	Kellogg's Chevrolet
15	16	11	Brett Bodine	Lowe's Ford
16	22	2	Rusty Wallace	Miller Genuine Draft Ford
17	31	23	Jimmy Spencer	Smokin' Joe's Ford
18	6	4	Sterling Marlin	Kodak Film Chevrolet
19	8	43	Bobby Hamilton	STP Pontiac
20	5	3	Dale Earnhardt	Goodwrench Service Chevrolet
21	21	30	Michael Waltrip	Pennzoil Pontiac
22	29	9	Lake Speed	Spam/Melling Ford
23	40	75	Todd Bodine	Factory Stores Ford
24	3	21	Morgan Shepherd	Citgo Ford
25	39	41	Ricky Craven	Kodiak Chevrolet
26	35	90	Mike Wallace	Heilig-Meyers Ford
27	23	8	Jeff Burton	Raybestos Brakes Ford
28	17	42	Kyle Petty	Coors Light Pontiac
29	41	27	Elton Sawyer	Hooters Ford
30	30	40	Rich Bickle	Kendall Pontiac
31	26	29	Steve Grissom	Meineke Chevrolet
32	20	22	Jimmy Hensley	MBNA America Pontiac
33	37	71	Dave Marcis	Prodigy Chevrolet
34	28	33	Robert Pressley	Skoal Bandit Chevrolet
35	32	18	Bobby Labonte	Interstate Batteries Chevrolet
36	12	17	Darrell Waltrip	Western Auto Chevrolet
37	34	81	Kenny Wallace	TIC Financial Ford
38	36	37	John Andretti	Kmart/Little Caesars Ford
39	19	12	Derrike Cope	Straight Arrow Ford
40	4	25	Ken Schrader	Budweiser Chevrolet
41	18	26	Hut Stricklin	Quaker State Ford

DieHard 500

TALLADEGA SUPERSPEEDWAY

JULY 23, 1995

•••••

There was no need for discussion. No reason to hold team meetings or call the manager out to the mound for a conference. No time outs were available. Everyone knew what needed to be done, and for the members of the Richard Childress team, there was no time like the present to get things turned around.

Just four races ago, the black-clad Goodwrench team had entered Michigan's gates 77 points ahead of Sterling Marlin and on course for driver Dale Earnhardt's much-sought-after eighth NASCAR Winston Cup title. Jeff Gordon had been 123 points behind, in third place, and the brilliance of the youngster's season had been blurred by the wily moves of the seven-time champion. Every Gordon thrust had seemingly been parried, and Earnhardt, crew chief Andy Petree and the other members of the crew had confidently been striding toward what they felt would be events in which they would shine and only increase their point lead.

Instead, the bottom had fallen out.

Mistakes had cost the team mightily, and rather than being the hunted, the team and driver were now the hunters. Now, following the second Pocono race, the Goodwrench team found itself in fourth place in the standings. The previ-

*Where there's smoke ... there's competition! These three drivers have some of the best of the best crews in the sport — Earnhardt's Flying Aces, Gordon's Rainbow Warriors and Marlin's Mighty-Mites — so it's probably no coincidence that they stood first through third in the point standings at the end of the DieHard 500. (**Right**) Talladega often offers three-wide racing, and the trio of Jeremy Mayfield (98), Morgan Shepherd (21) and Lake Speed (9) show fans how it's done. Of this flying formation, Shepherd fared best: He finished with a sparkling fourth place.*

ous four races had produced results of 35th, third, 22nd and 20th, and while the Childress team had been struggling, "The Kid" had taken advantage of every opportunity.

Gordon had finished second, first, first and second in those same four races, and now he held a 106-point lead over Marlin as the tour headed to Talladega. Ted

been the scourge of the short tracks, but in recent seasons, the fastest superspeedways had also become fair game for the black Chevrolets fielded from the Welcome, N.C., shop. So there was no question that the Monte Carlo selected from the stable to do battle at the mammoth oval was a good one.

Earnhardt had won the Busch Clash and then grabbed the outside of the front row before finishing second at the year's opener at Daytona. The second time around, the black Chevrolet had captured the pole for the Pepsi 400 and finished third. The car also had been super-competitive at Talladega in May in the Winston Select 500 before finishing 21st.

Everyone expected Dale to come out with his steely eyes glinting and guns blazing for the DieHard 500. At

(Left) "I can't be in trouble already — the race hasn't even started yet!" NASCAR Winston Cup official Jim Ball chats with Dale Earnhardt prior to the DieHard 500 at Talladega.
(Below) This is the stuff Talladega competition is made of: Derrike Cope (12) gets sandwiched between Rusty Wallace (2) and Bobby Hamilton as they vie for track position. In the end, however, the Straight Arrow Ford was stronger than either Wallace's or Hamilton's mounts, bringing Cope home 15th.

Musgrave had supplanted Earnhardt in third place, and Dale was now 164 behind the leader.

The point swing during those four races? A total of 287 between Gordon and Earnhardt.

Obviously, the Childress team needed a change of fortune if it hoped to challenge in the stretch run to the title.

For years, the Childress/Earnhardt combination had

this point of the season, he had little choice but to do just that. At the same time, everyone was waiting for Sterling and Jeff to wilt under the pressure of the point race.

Well, ladies and gentlemen, it could be a long wait.

While the media focused on the Childress team and Earnhardt, Tony Glover and the rest of his Kodak crew were busily stuffing Runt Pittman's latest creation into the

(Above) Front-row mates Sterling Marlin (4) and Bobby Labonte (18) lead the field down the frontstretch to start the DieHard 500. Marlin had a banner day at Talladega: He won from the pole (his first pole of the season) and claimed the Unocal bonus in the process. *(Right)* Kyle Petty's performance at Talladega was a bright spot in what had otherwise been a difficult season. Although he started 41st, he pulled himself up by his bootstraps to finish a scintillating sixth. Here, he dices for position with a pair of "30"s: Robert Pressley (33) and Michael Waltrip (30).

engine bay of the yellow Chevrolet. And it was a beauty.

Regardless, it took Sterling two days to win the pole for the DieHard 500. A rain shower interrupted the first day of qualifying and caused a three-and-a-half hour delay that eventually forced NASCAR officials to complete the session the following morning. Marlin had already run, rocketing around the track at 194.212 miles per hour, but he had to wait until qualifying was completed the following morning to see if his lap would stand for the pole. It did.

After he had won his first pole of the season, Marlin explained Pittman's absence from the last couple of events. Pittman, he said, had been back at the shop during the entire month of July, working on the restrictor plate engines. Runt had managed to squeeze a few more horsepower out of the engine thanks to his month of experimentation, and every one of those horses had paid off: Sterling had earned a berth in the upcoming February Busch Clash and also been put in position to capitalize on the huge Unocal Bonus. The money had rolled over for 16 races, and if he could take the victory from the pole, the $121,600 bonus would be his.

Bobby Labonte was on the outside of the front row, and Gordon, after making the decision to change motors (in practice, he'd felt the engine in his DuPont Chevrolet wasn't getting the job done), took the inside of the second row. It was the 11th time this season Gordon had claimed a top three starting position.

Continuing the trend of Chevrolet dominance was Ken Schrader, who plunked his Budweiser Chevrolet on the outside of the second row, making it three Hendrick Motorsports motors in the top four positions. (Labonte's car owner, Joe Gibbs, leases his engines from Hendrick for Bobby's Interstate Batteries Monte Carlos.)

Earnhardt was grinning at the end of the session. He was fifth in line for the start, inside the fastest Ford: Ricky Rudd's Tide Thunderbird. Michael Waltrip upheld the Tin Indian banner, putting his yellow Pennzoil Pontiac in seventh place for the start, and older brother Darrell had a super qualifying run to grab the eighth starting slot. John Andretti was equally impressive, claiming the inside of the fifth row, and Robert Pressley would start on Andretti's right.

Mark Martin, winner of the Winston Select 500 that had

Gordon tagged teammate Schrader, sending Ken on a wild ride that reduced his red Monte Carlo to rubble. Schrader suffered only a black eye, but Gordon was heartsick after seeing the aftermath of their collision in his rear-view mirror. Despite constant radio communications from Schrader, crew chief Ray Evernham and others on the Hendrick teams, Jeff could not rally himself to make a run at the leaders in

(Left) Clearly, Lady Luck was a passenger in Ken Schrader's Budweiser Chevrolet: He walked away from this with only a black eye. The accident occurred on lap 139 when teammate Jeff Gordon tagged Schrader and sent him spinning. (Below) Dale Jarrett "talks shop" with crew chief Larry McReynolds prior to the DieHard 500. The strategy they cooked up was good enough for second place — Dale J. just edged Dale E. at the line.

been held at Talladega in the spring, was disappointed with the lap that placed him 11th on the starting grid, ahead of Jeff Purvis (who had a strong performance) and Pocono winner Dale Jarrett.

There was little time for experimentation between qualifying sessions. Due to the rain delay, the second qualifying period began just a few hours after the first round had concluded, and only seven drivers tried to improve their times. One was Chad Little, whose team had bolted in a motor built by the Jack Roush shop. Chad used the motor to his advantage, clocking in at 192.116 mph. He was the fastest second-round qualifier, and as such, his name would be entered in the drawing for the wild-card spot in the Busch Clash.

Those running limited schedules who made the field during qualifying were Purvis, Loy Allen and Little. NASCAR Winston Cup regulars Bobby Hamilton, Derrike Cope, Kyle Petty and Ward Burton were forced to take provisionals. Bill Elliott, using a champion's provisional, became the 43rd starter for Sunday's 188-lap race. Jimmy Hensley, Delma Cowart and Steve Seligman were unable to qualify for the event.

Freight-train racing has always been a hallmark of the Talladega events, and the DieHard 500 was no exception. Clearly, the Chevrolets were in control of the race from the drop of the green flag; Fords led only three of the first 100 laps, and then only when the Monte Carlos at the front of the pack pitted under green-flag conditions.

It also was evident from the start that Marlin, Gordon and Earnhardt were the class of the lead pack. Others were able to hang on and battle for positions, even occasionally lead the race, but when it was time for show and tell, Jeff, Sterling and Dale appeared able to control the event.

The first caution of the event appeared on lap 113 for a piece of debris on the track. After that brief interruption, the field went right back to green. Then, on lap 139,

the closing laps.

Martin's Valvoline Ford was at the front on the restart, but Mark knew his minutes leading the string of Chevrolets were numbered. He was correct.

Two laps later, Marlin felt his time had come — he dropped the hammer on Pittman's motor, and the Chevrolet streaked to the point. Sterling felt his chances for victory were better at the front of the pack, where he could control his destiny. "I knew that it would take a real good run by the others to get the momentum to get by me because of how strong Runt's motor was," Sterling explained after the event. "I just felt that I could control things more by being in the front and making others catch me, rather than relying on someone working with me when I wanted to go and make a pass from behind. So I just got that Kodak Monte Carlo out in the front and let them chase me."

Chase him, they did.

But to no avail.

Of the nine drivers on the lead lap, Sterling felt the strongest challenger would be Earnhardt, and he was nearly correct. Also in the pack were Dale Jarrett, trying to make it two straight victories in the Havoline Ford, and Ford-driving Morgan Shepherd, Bill Elliott and Martin. Kyle Petty and Michael Waltrip, also on the lead lap, were in Pontiacs.

Jarrett fought his way through the pack, and with four laps remaining, whistled past Earnhardt into second place. Dale E. felt his best shot for victory would be to work with Dale J., but as it turned out, neither the black Ford nor the black Chevrolet had anything for Marlin in the closing laps.

Sterling's gamble had paid huge dividends. He streaked to the win, his third of the season, and claimed the Unocal bonus in the process. The victory pushed his race winnings to a total of $219,475 and allowed him to close slightly on Gordon in the points.

Jarrett finished second, just ahead of Earnhardt, and Shepherd came home fourth. Elliott was fifth, ahead of Kyle and Martin, and Gordon finished eighth. Ninth was Michael Waltrip, who had run solidly in the lead pack throughout the race. Of all the drivers, he had suffered most in the late-race shuffle, falling from fifth to ninth and coming home last on the lead lap. Jimmy Spencer claimed 10th and was the first driver a lap in arrears.

Schrader's accident had collected 11 other cars, including that of Rusty Wallace, whose big-track fortunes continued to be extremely frustrating to the Penske South team. He finished 30th.

Sterling Marlin was all smiles in Talladega's victory lane — and why shouldn't he be? First there was the pole, then there was the win, and then there was the $121,600 Unocal bonus. To top it all off, he had closed to within 78 points of Gordon in the standings.

For Earnhardt, his third place was nearly as good as a victory. He had stopped the bleeding, run extremely well and fronted the field regularly during the event. He had, in fact, even gained a few points on Gordon; Earnhardt had eased back into third place in the standings ahead of Martin and Musgrave.

With their backs to the wall, the Goodwrench team had, at least at one event, answered the challenge. But now, The Brickyard beckoned, and not a single member of the crew — least of all, the driver — had forgotten for a minute what had happened at Indianapolis Motor Speedway the previous year.

DieHard 500

Race #18 — Final Race Results

Fin. Pos.	Str. Pos.	Car #	Driver	Team
1	1	4	Sterling Marlin	Kodak Film Chevrolet
2	13	28	Dale Jarrett	Texaco Havoline Ford
3	5	3	Dale Earnhardt	Goodwrench Service Chevrolet
4	24	21	Morgan Shepherd	Citgo Ford
5	43	94	Bill Elliott	McDonald's Ford
6	41	42	Kyle Petty	Coors Light Pontiac
7	11	6	Mark Martin	Valvoline Ford
8	3	24	Jeff Gordon	DuPont Auto Finishes Chevrolet
9	7	30	Michael Waltrip	Pennzoil Pontiac
10	23	23	Jimmy Spencer	Smokin' Joe's Ford
11	33	16	Ted Musgrave	The Family Channel Ford
12	35	90	Mike Wallace	Heilig-Meyers Ford
13	21	98	Jeremy Mayfield	RCA Ford
14	28	27	Elton Sawyer	Hooters Ford
15	40	12	Derrike Cope	Straight Arrow Ford
16	30	77	Bobby Hillin	Jasper/USAir Ford
17	16	1	Rick Mast	Skoal Ford
18	22	97	Chad Little	Big B Drugs Ford
19	25	71	Dave Marcis	STG Chevrolet
20	42	31	Ward Burton	Hardee's Chevrolet
21	39	43	Bobby Hamilton	STP Pontiac
22	37	8	Jeff Burton	Raybestos Brakes Ford
23	32	87	Joe Nemechek	Burger King Chevrolet
24	19	7	Geoff Bodine	Exide Batteries Ford
25	31	29	Steve Grissom	Meineke Chevrolet
26	29	41	Ricky Craven	Kodiak Chevrolet
27	10	33	Robert Pressley	Skoal Bandit Chevrolet
28	34	11	Brett Bodine	Lowe's Ford
29	14	75	Todd Bodine	Factory Stores Ford
30	26	2	Rusty Wallace	Miller Genuine Draft Ford
31	2	18	Bobby Labonte	Interstate Batteries Chevrolet
32	4	25	Ken Schrader	Budweiser Chevrolet
33	38	5	Terry Labonte	Kellogg's Chevrolet
34	9	37	John Andretti	Kmart/Little Caesars Ford
35	20	9	Lake Speed	Spam/Melling Ford
36	27	26	Hut Stricklin	Quaker State Ford
37	36	32	Chuck Bown	Fina/Lance Chevrolet
38	17	15	Dick Trickle	Ford Quality Care Ford
39	15	19	Loy Allen	Healthsource Health Plan Ford
40	18	40	Randy LaJoie	Kendall Pontiac
41	6	10	Ricky Rudd	Tide Ford
42	12	44	Jeff Purvis	Jackaroo Chevrolet
43	8	17	Darrell Waltrip	Western Auto Chevrolet

BRICKYARD 400

INDIANAPOLIS MOTOR SPEEDWAY
AUGUST 5, 1995
•••••

Defending event champions are seldom treated like conquering heroes when they return to the site of their victory. But that was exactly what awaited Jeff Gordon when he stepped from an airplane in Indianapolis early in the week. His schedule was chockablock with personal appearances that ranged from civic block parties and corporate Coca-Cola meetings to a brief, 10-hole golf outing at the Brickyard Crossings sponsored by Chevrolet. Every minute of the week was accounted for, and Jeff found himself shuffled from one activity to another. Later in the week, he admitted that it had been fun but grueling at the same time. With wife Brooke at his side, Gordon worked his way through the week, signing autographs here, pressing the flesh there and fitting what seemed to be hundreds of interviews in between.

Part of the reason for all the hoopla was his superb victory the previous year in the inaugural event at The Brickyard. Part was the fact that he was the "hometown" hero, having resided many years in nearby Pittsboro before moving up to the NASCAR Busch Series level and then to NASCAR Winston Cup.

And part was the fact that he was the series point leader at the two-thirds mark of the season. If he still held the point lead at the conclusion of the Indiana weekend, he would also claim the $100,000 "leg" bonus posted by R.J. Reynolds (issued to the point leader two-thirds of the way through the season). Gordon had already claimed Reynolds' first

The traditional and visually spectacular balloon release signals the start of the second-annual Brickyard 400. The scoring pylon told the story: Could pole-sitter and defending champ Jeff Gordon repeat at The Brickyard? (Right) Dale Earnhardt responded with a resounding "no" and a three-car-length victory, which went a long way toward soothing the disquieting memories of his first-lap mishap in last year's race.

132

(Above) Two laps down, only 158 more to go! The race has just begun, but the leap-frogging has already started, and the fans are already on their feet. (Left) The No. 98 crew goes to work on Jeremy Mayfield's RCA Ford while the Quality Care team (foreground) waits anxiously for its driver, Dick Trickle. Unfortunately for Mayfield, quick work in the pits was simply not enough: He dropped from his eighth starting position to finish 29th.

$100,000 prize because he'd led the points after the one-third mark, and he also had grabbed the $50,000 from Gatorade (awarded halfway through the season to the current leader). Running at the front of the pack certainly had been rewarding for the youngster in 1995!

Gordon and every member of his Rainbow Warrior team knew that winning back-to-back Brickyard 400s would be a formidable task. The Brickyard 400 is one of two events every team focuses on during the season — the other is the Daytona 500 — so the best horses in the stable would be brought to the race, and nothing would be left to chance.

If capturing the PPG Trophy and the sterling silver brick wasn't enough inspiration, Speedway Chairman Tony George had made sure every driver, car owner and team member understood the importance of victory at The Brickyard. Teams understand dollars, so George had lit a propane torch under them when he announced the purse for the Brickyard 400: $4.5 million, the richest reward for competitors in the history of NASCAR Winston Cup stock car racing.

A lot can happen in 10 days, and in the 10 days since the DieHard 500 at Talladega, several events had unfolded. Hardee's had told team owner Alan Dillard that the company would not return the following season, but Ferguson Industries, a secondary sponsor on the blue and orange car, had increased its commitment to the team. Ferguson Industries now graced the flanks of the Chevrolet. Kendall Oil had decided to move its money for 1996, leaving car owners Dick Brooks and Felix Sabates to search for a new sponsor for the Pontiac, which would be driven by Rich Bickle at Indianapolis.

Geoff Bodine, who had struggled through the Talladega weekend with a kidney stone, was again at 100 percent following a surgical procedure to remove the stone. Lake Speed's Spam-mobile would carry Delta Faucets for the Brickyard 400, and Bryant Heating and Cooling had joined USAir and Jasper on Bobby Hillin's Thunderbird. Tide had announced it would continue its sponsorship of Ricky Rudd's team and be joined by Downy and Whirlpool appliances for the coming season.

Although the Robert Yates team had finished first and second in its last two outings, their joy had been tempered by recent events. Robert's mother, V.C. Yates, died the day before the action began at Indianapolis at the age of 93.

The race at The Brickyard had attracted more entries than positions in the field. Greg Sacks had been installed in the Active Motorsports Chevrolet, which would carry Fina's colors, after a test session in which he was a full second faster than Chuck Bown, the now-former pilot of Dean Meyers' cars. Kenny Wallace and Jeff Purvis were also on hand, and Loy Allen had been pressed into service with the Sadler Racing Ford after Scott Brayton was injured during a testing mishap. Billy Standridge, who had the Phillips 66 insignia painted on his Ford, was on hand, as was Pancho Carter. Steve Seligman and Joe Ruttman also had high hopes of making the field for the second-annual running of the event. One of the fans' favorites was A.J. Foyt, who had entered a Ford sponsored by Motorola in the days leading up to the event.

On Wednesday afternoon, a four-hour practice session was added, offering competitors a chance to shake down their equipment. Every car in the garage area — with the exception of Jeremy Mayfield and Cale Yarborough's RCA Ford — took advantage of the practice session. Jeremy and his teammates had so much confidence in their pre-event testing that they didn't run a single lap on Wednesday.

From the start, Gordon lived up to his advance notices. He rocketed around the track in the

(Right) This is where the story of the Brickyard 400 unfolded: in the pits. Green-flag stops were the order of the day, and nobody does them better than Dale Earnhardt's Flying Aces. He made his final green-flag stop without incident — more than can be said for Rusty Wallace — and once he got in front of Rusty and the others, there was no stopping him. (Below) Jeff Gordon may have been unable to repeat at Indy, but that $40,000 check for the Busch Pole Award still looks pretty good ... the Brickyard pole was Jeff's eighth of the season.

DuPont Monte Carlo, posting the times drivers would have to beat if they wanted the $90,000 in cash and prizes awarded to the pole-winner of the event.

On Thursday morning, it was more of the same — Gordon's rainbow-hued meteor was the car to beat. No one doubted he was the fastest, and Hendrick Motorsport teammate Terry Labonte as much as admitted it during a Busch Pole media luncheon held prior to the first round of qualifying. When Terry was asked what speed he thought would claim the pole, the Texan turned to Gordon, asking, "I don't know. What are you going to run, Jeff?"

Tens of thousands of fans had plenty of time to ponder that same question. Jeff had drawn a qualifying slot far down in the order, so everyone had to wait to see what number he put on the board.

First, however, Bobby Hamilton gave the fans reason to cheer when he put a 172.222-mph lap on the scoreboard. At first, Bobby didn't know if the fans were cheering for

his accomplishment or for his STP Pontiac. He didn't really care. He was delighted with the "whole package," as he called it; meaning the team, the car, the motor, the crew, the owner and himself.

Driver after driver tried to topple the Tennessean from the pole, but the time continued to stand. Finally, the line on pit road had dwindled to just Gordon and a handful of others. Jeff fired the Monte Carlo and, to the delight of the assemblage, worked his way through three quarters of his qualifying lap in fine style. Then, as he tried to get just that little bit more, he slid in the fourth turn and got nearly sideways. He instinctively made the correction and coaxed the Chevrolet back into a straight line; he had avoided what seemed a sure wreck and stood on the throttle the entire way. A roar followed him around the track on his cool-off lap: Despite the slip, he had turned a lap worth 172.536 mph — good enough to claim the pole. It was a great 24th birthday present for himself and his team.

The rains were the remnants of Hurricane Erin, and once the rain had curtailed qualifying, it threatened the race itself. NASCAR kept a wary eye on the radar, and finally, three hours after the scheduled start of the event, the rain abated, allowing the race officials to work on drying the track. The tens of thousands of fans who had thought the race would be rained out had already headed for their hotels, motels and homes. Then, on their car radios, they heard the message that the race was about to start. Cars made U-turns on the spot, and a mad dash for parking spaces began. Those same thousands of fans became a singular wave of people flooding back through the Speedway gates!

Sterling Marlin claimed the inside of the second row, and Bill Elliott continued his surge by qualifying fourth fastest. Bobby Labonte and Joe Nemechek slapped their Monte Carlos into the third row, and Michael Waltrip did his team proud, taking a spanking-new "yellow banana" to seventh place. He and Hamilton had a pair of Pontiacs in the first four rows! Mayfield confirmed that his decision not to practice on Wednesday had been the right one by grabbing the eighth starting position. Last year's pole-sitter, Rick Mast, and a Budweiser Chevrolet-driving Ken Schrader completed the top 10, just ahead of Dick Trickle and Brett Bodine. Earnhardt and Martin — who was sporting a new graphic package on his Valvoline Ford to celebrate the oil company's 100th year of racing activity — were 13th and 14th, respectively.

Friday's second qualifying session was expected to be crucial for many teams, particularly those regular runners far down the list. So when the second session was scrubbed due to rain, teams faced an unwelcome prospect: The field would be set with Thursday's times. Jimmy Spencer became the final qualifier based on times, and Steve Grissom, Mike Wallace and Elton Sawyer used provisionals to make the field. Jeff Purvis was only .002 of a second slower than Spencer, but since he had no provisionals, he was forced to the sidelines. Dave Marcis had already used all his provisionals, so he went home. Loy Allen, Billy Standridge, Pancho Carter, Steve Seligman and A.J. Foyt also missed the second running of the Brickyard 400. Joe Ruttman also suffered dearly because of the rain, but in a different way. His Ford had had engine problems on Thursday, which kept him from making a qualifying run. Obviously, he'd had no chance to qualify on Friday, so he became the only driver to practice and not attempt to qualify.

No one knew quite what to expect. The cars were basically untested in race form; only a brief "Happy Half-Hour" had been held late Friday afternoon. Crew chiefs guessed at chassis setups, and drivers planned on altering those setups during the first caution flag.

The only problem was that the first 132 laps of the 160-lap race ran under green-flag conditions. So, for those who had missed the handling package, it was a long afternoon.

For others, the race was a brilliant display of driver and crew talent. Rusty Wallace put on a show, rocketing up from his 24th starting position and taking "Midnight" all the way to the front just after half-distance. Earnhardt was at the top of his form, and with the help of the "Flying Aces" on pit road, he worked his way into contention. Dale Jarrett picked his spots, his crew adjusted the Havoline Ford, and though it took a little longer, Jarrett followed Wallace's tire tracks to the front of the pack. The outlook was not as rosy for Jeff Gordon: The handling on his DuPont Chevrolet was slowly going south.

During the final green-flag stops, the story of the race was written. Earnhardt came in, made his stop and headed back to the track without incident. Wallace stopped a lap later but was boxed in behind Rich Bickle and Joe Nemechek, who traded some sheet metal and bondo in front of the Miller Ford as Wallace was accelerating out of the pits. He was forced to slow almost to a stop as the two sorted things out, and by the time Wallace was back up to speed, Earnhardt had passed him for the lead.

When Jeff Burton spun just a couple of laps later, there was no reason to make another stop during the caution. Cars had tires and fuel to go the distance, since only 24 laps remained, and besides, a stop would mean a huge loss of track positions (19 cars were on the lead lap).

When the green flag fell, Earnhardt checked out.

Picture perfect: With the sun setting behind the grandstands, Dale Earnhardt flashes down the frontstretch to take the checkered flag. The victory was extra-special for the Goodwrench driver, who'd made the Brickyard 400 a priority at the start of the '95 season.

Wallace made a fine run at Earnhardt, but when he got up behind the Chevrolet, the nose of the Miller Ford washed out. Behind Wallace, Jarrett was blasting his way toward the front, and eventually, he caught the other two black cars. But he couldn't make a move to pass either one because his Ford's nose was doing the same thing Wallace's was. The Thunderbirds gave chase for all they were worth, but they looked like the neighborhood dogs yapping at a passing motorist. Earnhardt was in command.

He took the Goodwrench Chevrolet to a three-car-length victory, more than making up for his mistake of the previous year (he had smacked the fourth-turn wall on the first lap and eliminated himself from contention).

Elliott and Martin finished fourth and fifth, ahead of a struggling Gordon, and Marlin, Mast and Bobby Labonte claimed seventh, eighth and ninth, respectively. Morgan Shepherd grabbed the final top-10 spot, just beating Hamilton to the line.

For the second-straight week, Earnhardt had finished ahead of Gordon. He hadn't gained as many points as he had hoped, but still, he had gained.

And at the moment, more important than the point race was the fact that he had captured the Brickyard 400 and put the Earnhardt name in the record book at the most famous race track in the world. He felt a special warmth after the victory — he knew that his dad, Ralph, was proudly looking down at him.

A mishap on pit road negated the outstanding service Rusty Wallace had received throughout the race from his Miller Genuine Draft crew, and though he gave it all he had, he was forced to settle for second behind his good friend, Dale Earnhardt.

Brickyard 400

Race #19 — Final Race Results

Fin. Pos.	Str. Pos.	Car #	Driver	Team
1	13	3	Dale Earnhardt	Goodwrench Service Chevrolet
2	24	2	Rusty Wallace	Miller Genuine Draft Ford
3	26	28	Dale Jarrett	Texaco Havoline Ford
4	4	94	Bill Elliott	McDonald's Ford
5	14	6	Mark Martin	Valvoline Ford
6	1	24	Jeff Gordon	DuPont Auto Finishes Chevrolet
7	3	4	Sterling Marlin	Kodak Film Chevrolet
8	9	1	Rick Mast	Skoal Ford
9	5	18	Bobby Labonte	Interstate Batteries Chevrolet
10	33	21	Morgan Shepherd	Citgo Ford
11	2	43	Bobby Hamilton	STP Pontiac
12	23	37	John Andretti	Kmart/Little Caesars Ford
13	15	5	Terry Labonte	Kellogg's Chevrolet
14	7	30	Michael Waltrip	Pennzoil Pontiac
15	25	7	Geoff Bodine	Exide Batteries Ford
16	19	16	Ted Musgrave	The Family Channel Ford
17	20	17	Darrell Waltrip	Western Auto Chevrolet
18	11	15	Dick Trickle	Ford Quality Care Ford
19	10	25	Ken Schrader	Budweiser Chevrolet
20	22	10	Ricky Rudd	Tide Ford
21	34	75	Todd Bodine	Factory Stores Ford
22	29	26	Hut Stricklin	Quaker State Ford
23	38	23	Jimmy Spencer	Smokin' Joe's Ford
24	12	11	Brett Bodine	Lowe's Ford
25	32	42	Kyle Petty	Coors Light Pontiac
26	40	90	Mike Wallace	Heilig-Meyers Ford
27	6	87	Joe Nemechek	Burger King Chevrolet
28	21	33	Robert Pressley	Skoal Bandit Chevrolet
29	8	98	Jeremy Mayfield	RCA Ford
30	39	29	Steve Grissom	Meineke Chevrolet
31	28	41	Ricky Craven	Kodiak Chevrolet
32	35	22	Jimmy Hensley	MBNA America Pontiac
33	16	32	Greg Sacks	Fina/Lance Chevrolet
34	27	9	Lake Speed	Spam/Melling Ford
35	30	31	Ward Burton	Ferguson Chevrolet
36	31	81	Kenny Wallace	TIC Financial Ford
37	36	40	Rich Bickle	Kendall Pontiac
38	18	8	Jeff Burton	Raybestos Brakes Ford
39	17	77	Bobby Hillin	Jasper/USAir Ford
40	37	12	Derrike Cope	Straight Arrow Ford
41	41	27	Elton Sawyer	Hooters Ford

THE BUD AT THE GLEN

WATKINS GLEN INTERNATIONAL
AUGUST 13, 1995
•••••

Thus far, it had been a season any driver would consider one of the finest of his career. Of 19 starts, 15 had resulted in top nines. A win. A second. Three fighting third places. A pair of poles. Two other front-row starts. Well-prepared cars that were in the hunt week after week. An engine shop that provided great power race after race, and an over-the-wall crew that performed with great precision and prowess Sunday after Sunday. Team chemistry that was a model for others in the garage area. A brilliant strategist for a crew chief. And a car owner and driver dedicated to winning.

Sounds like a package that should be leading the point race, huh?

For Mark Martin and car owner Jack Roush, however, the season — great as it had been — had coincided with the introduction of the Chevrolet Monte Carlos, and there was little the team could do to make its Valvoline Thunderbirds any better than they were. As Mark had said earlier in the season, his team was "best in our class."

Darrell Waltrip (17) heads for the outside line in the short chute as he attempts to pass Bobby Labonte. Both drivers took home top-10 finishes: Bobby finished sixth, and Darrell fought his way to eighth after starting 27th. (Right) It was no surprise to find Mark Martin at the front of the field at Watkins Glen. He was gunning for his third-consecutive win from the pole at the picturesque road course in central New York state.

As the team headed for Watkins Glen and its famed road course — nestled high above majestic Seneca Lake in the Finger Lakes region of upstate New York — Mark, Jack and crew chief Steve Hmiel made big plans for the weekend. The effort was fourth in the point standings and trailed leader Jeff Gordon by 174 markers. The fifth place the team had recorded the weekend before at The Brickyard had helped their cause along, but The Glen was different. The team was

a proven winner at this track.

At the conclusion of each of the last two events at one of the most famous road courses in the world, Martin had taken the right-hand turn into victory lane. He had stood on the same podium that had welcomed the likes of Jimmy Clark, Graham Hill, Jackie Stewart and Emerson Fittipaldi following their victories in the Grand Prix of the United States.

Now Mark had a chance to three-peat.

If he could do it, he would join some very select company in The Glen's record books. Only World Champion Graham Hill (who claimed three consecutive Grand Prix of the

Wally Dallenbach got the call from Bill Davis to drive at Watkins Glen, only the second event in which he'd competed since he was released by Petty Enterprises one year ago following this very event. Wally jumped at the opportunity and nearly pulled off one of the biggest upsets in years.

United States wins in the early '60s) and the driver pairing of Al Holbert and Derek Bell (winners of three consecutive IMSA Camel Continental races, 1984-86) had emerged from the road course with three straight triumphs.

A pre-event testing session had featured the Roush team's potent road-course car as well as a spanking-new machine; Mark had his choice of the two mounts for The Glen. Despite the quality of the new car, he opted for the older

Elton Sawyer (left) takes advantage of an opportunity to gather a few pointers from road-course ace Ricky Rudd prior to The Bud at the Glen. Rudd, who won here in '88 and '90, consistently ran with the leaders and finished fourth. Sawyer's day was a little tougher: He finished 29th.

chassis; the new Thunderbird, which was stowed in the top of the transporter, would be a spare.

Mark wasn't the only driver approaching the race with confidence. Following their Brickyard victory, Dale Earnhardt and the Goodwrench crew arrived brim-full. And the Richard Childress team had yet another reason for the spring in their steps: They hadn't forgotten Dale's superb victory at Sears Point in May. Dale had stalked Mark, capitalized when the Ford driver had slipped in the Carousel and then whipped to the first road-course victory of his storied career. Also, Earnhardt had finished ahead of point leader Gordon in the last two races, and the team was ready to chop a few more points from Gordon's 121-point margin over the seven-time champion.

Sterling Marlin was merely going through his paces at The Glen. The Tennessean is the first to volunteer that he doesn't much care for road-course racing, and it was evident that he hoped to keep Gordon in sight, perhaps even narrow the 82-point gap between them, and then get on with the program.

A few new faces could be found among the cast assembled in The Glen's garage area. State College, Pa. (better-known as the home of Penn State's Nittany Lions), had contributed Butch Leitzinger to the entry list; he would drive Dick Brooks and Felix Sabates' Kendall Oil Pontiac. An accomplished road racer, Butch came into the sport naturally. His father, Bob, is a longtime championship-caliber sports car driver, and mother Sandra has for years been acknowledged as one of racing's finest watercolorists.

Leitzinger was joined in the garage area by another driver whose long background lies in the left- and right-hand turns associated with road courses. Wally Dallenbach had returned to the site of his last appearance with Richard

Martin was working on another string in addition to his back-to-back victories: He also had won the last two Bud at The Glen poles. So, it was no surprise that he was the No. 1 pick for this year's pole, or that his practice times backed up the choice. Once the first round of qualifying had gotten underway, however, even Mark began to have doubts about whether or not he could keep his string of poles alive.

When Terry Labonte, the second driver out in the first session, laid a 120.188-mile-per-hour lap on the field, Mark glanced over at Hmiel. They both raised their eyebrows. Terry's lap held up until Bill Elliott fired up the Mac Attack halfway through the session. When his speed of 120.332 mph was announced, the eyebrows went even

Petty's Pontiac (in 1994) to pilot a different Poncho at The Glen. He had signed with Bill Davis' MBNA-sponsored team for a one-race deal, and everyone hoped he could turn in a good performance with the black and green car. Canadian Ron Fellows hoped to do double duty and compete in both the Saturday Sports Car Club of America Trans-Am Championship event and Sunday's NASCAR Winston Cup race.

Leading up to the race was a week of "Race Fever Nights" in the surrounding communities. Tens of thousands of fans had had the chance to see show cars, collect autographs, purchase souvenirs and mingle with the racing crowd. It was a series of events that had, over the years, drawn other track officials to The Glen to learn how community involvement really works. Finally, though, it was time to see if Mark could find a way into the record book.

(**Right**) *Ted Musgrave finds a quiet moment for reflection inside The Glen's garage.* (**Below**) *Jeff Gordon (24) and Terry Labonte (5) team up to make a McDonald's sandwich out of Bill Elliott. Gordon and Labonte went on to claim top-five finishes, while Elliott fell to 11th.*

Saturday — he would start 27th. Marli lived up to his expectations with a 32nd-place start for Sunday's race. Bobby Hamilton, Steve Grissom, Dick Trickle and Ward Burton all used provisionals to make the race, but road racer David Murry, along with Mike Wallace and Eric Smith, failed to make the field and were forced to watch the race from the sidelines.

*(**Left**) Bill Elliott knows he had better hurry! He's being chased by three of the best road racers on the tour: Terry Labonte, Rusty Wallace and Ricky Rudd. (**Below**) Rusty Wallace was one of the few competitors who could run with Martin. He had positioned himself to mount a charge in the last third of the race, but a mishap on pit road — he ran into Geoff Bodine (who had slowed to wait for the pace car) — caused him to lose two laps while repairs were being made.*

higher. Both Mark and Steve gave a little shrug as if to say, "Well, guess we know what we've got to run now," and then headed for the red, white and blue Thunderbird to belt Mark into the seat.

It took Mark just over 73 seconds to decide the affair. After he'd pried his fingers from the steering wheel, he put another notch in his Glen belt. He had beaten Elliott by just .050 of a second, but it was enough to give him his third-straight pole on the 2.4-mile road course. He used it all, he told Steve after catching his breath. "There wasn't anything left. I used every inch of the track and every single corner. If I'd tried any harder, I would have gone through the guardrail somewhere."

Rusty Wallace underlined his competitiveness on the road courses by grabbing the fourth slot for the start. Behind him, Jeff Gordon and Michael Waltrip grabbed the third row. It was Michael's best qualifying performance since the Coca-Cola 600 at Charlotte. Ricky Rudd and Kyle Petty grabbed the seventh and eighth spots, and Jeremy Mayfield continued his strong qualifying performances by grabbing the inside of the fifth row, ahead of Morgan Shepherd. Dallenbach was the 12th-fastest driver in the session, an impressive showing, and Earnhardt locked up the 15th spot.

Leitzinger, trying too hard during the first session, looped the Pontiac at the end of the back straight. During the second qualifying session, however, he completed his circuit with ease, turning a lap of 118.738 mph and claiming a wild-card slot for the Busch drawing in the process (the drawing, held in December, determines the final qualifier for the Busch Clash). "It'd be interesting if I drew the wild card," Butch said with a grin. "Wonder if I could get a ride for Daytona!" Darrell Waltrip, who had broken the transmission during his first run, made it into the field on

With three poles already in hand, Sunday marked Martin's opportunity to extend his race-winning string. The largest throng in the history of the race track — a crowd of more than 100,000 — turned out to see if he could do it. Mark bolted from the pole and motored off, giving up the lead for only four laps during the first 56 circuits, and then only when the field was cycling through green-flag pit stops. It was clear, however, that Mark was not going to simply cruise to his third victory. He was busy fighting off Wallace, who was having a fabulous run at the front, as well as Dallenbach, who was threatening to score the greatest upset in NASCAR Winston Cup history since Greg Sacks won the Pepsi 400 at Daytona in 1985 with a pickup crew and a research-and-development Chevrolet.

A yellow came out on lap 61 after Robert Pressley's Skoal Chevrolet stopped on the track. Some of the leaders — including Mark and Rusty — didn't have enough fuel to go the remaining distance, so they opted for gas-and-go stops during the caution.

It was a serious case of déjà vu when Jack Roush and Steve Hmiel joined Mark Martin on the podium at The Glen. Mark had won the same event from the pole for three straight years, the first time that had been done in 11 years (Darrell Waltrip accomplished the feat at North Wilkesboro from 1982-84).

Mark, the first to finish his stop, slowed at the end of pit road and waited to fall in line behind the cars on the track that had chosen not to pit during the caution. Geoff Bodine, who had followed him down pit road, also slowed, but Wallace came down pit road full-tilt-boogie. He tried to avoid the other Fords, but he couldn't swerve far enough left. He hit Bodine and pushed Geoff's car into Mark's. The right front of the Miller Ford was junk, and his chance for victory was gone.

Dallenbach took the lead from Gordon on the restart and then went about building his margin to more than five seconds. He looked like a sure winner because, although Mark's Ford had not been damaged and he had managed to fight his way through the field to second, there was not enough time for Martin to catch the Pontiac. Wally was brilliant. Although he had been sick to his stomach earlier in the race — due to the fumes in the car — he was now ready to make a run to the flag. Amazing what being in the lead late in the race can do to make a driver feel better!

Mark was clipping a tenth here and a couple tenths there, but he had no hope of catching Wally at that rate. Then, a yellow — the final one of the race — waved, giving Mark a chance. He lined up behind his former Roush teammate, and the green reappeared with eight laps to go. A single lap later, Mark tucked his Ford underneath Wally's Pontiac in the first turn and began pulling away. Wally couldn't keep up the pace, and it was Martin who flashed under the flag first at the end of the 90th lap. Martin had won his third-consecutive race at The Glen and carved his name in the record book.

Behind Wally was Gordon, who had been in contention throughout the entire race and led twice as pit stops cycled through the field. Rudd was fourth, and Terry Labonte was fifth, barely ahead of younger brother Bobby. John Andretti had a sparkling run to seventh, and Darrell kept his Western Auto Chevrolet humming to an eighth place. Geoff was ninth, ahead of Ricky Craven. Elliott just missed a top-10 spot and was pressed hard for his 11th by Leitzinger, who acquitted himself admirably.

Following his Brickyard 400 win and a visit to Opryland, Earnhardt had expected a good finish at The Glen. Instead, he had struggled with transmission problems throughout the event and was classified 23rd at the finish. Sterling had found yet another reason to dislike road courses: His shifter broke, and he was ranked 21st at the conclusion of the race.

By leading the most laps and claiming the victory, Mark had sliced 15 points off Gordon's lead. However, Martin knew that if he was to have a chance of winning the championship, the Glen victory would have to be just the beginning.

The Bud at the Glen

Race #20 — Final Race Results

Fin. Pos.	Str. Pos.	Car #	Driver	Team
1	1	6	Mark Martin	Valvoline Ford
2	12	22	Wally Dallenbach	MBNA America Pontiac
3	5	24	Jeff Gordon	DuPont Auto Finishes Chevrolet
4	7	10	Ricky Rudd	Tide Ford
5	3	5	Terry Labonte	Kellogg's Chevrolet
6	11	18	Bobby Labonte	Interstate Batteries Chevrolet
7	17	37	John Andretti	Kmart/Little Caesars Ford
8	27	17	Darrell Waltrip	Western Auto Chevrolet
9	30	7	Geoff Bodine	Exide Batteries Ford
10	14	41	Ricky Craven	Kodiak Chevrolet
11	2	94	Bill Elliott	McDonald's Ford
12	21	40	Butch Leitzinger	Kendall Pontiac
13	26	16	Ted Musgrave	The Family Channel Ford
14	6	30	Michael Waltrip	Pennzoil Pontiac
15	31	12	Derrike Cope	Straight Arrow Ford
16	28	11	Brett Bodine	Lowe's Ford
17	13	28	Dale Jarrett	Texaco Havoline Ford
18	18	23	Jimmy Spencer	Smokin' Joe's Ford
19	40	31	Ward Burton	Hardee's Chevrolet
20	23	9	Lake Speed	Spam/Melling Ford
21	32	4	Sterling Marlin	Kodak Film Chevrolet
22	38	29	Steve Grissom	Meineke Chevrolet
23	15	3	Dale Earnhardt	Goodwrench Service Chevrolet
24	29	71	Dave Marcis	Olive Garden Chevrolet
25	9	98	Jeremy Mayfield	RCA Ford
26	4	2	Rusty Wallace	Miller Genuine Draft Ford
27	24	77	Bobby Hillin	Jasper/USAir Ford
28	39	15	Dick Trickle	Ford Quality Care Ford
29	34	27	Elton Sawyer	Hooters Ford
30	10	21	Morgan Shepherd	Citgo Ford
31	19	87	Joe Nemechek	Burger King Chevrolet
32	35	75	Todd Bodine	Factory Stores Ford
33	37	43	Bobby Hamilton	STP Pontiac
34	22	33	Robert Pressley	Skoal Bandit Chevrolet
35	36	68	Ron Fellows	Canaska Racing Chevrolet
36	16	25	Ken Schrader	Budweiser Chevrolet
37	33	1	Rick Mast	Skoal Ford
38	25	8	Jeff Burton	Raybestos Brakes Ford
39	8	42	Kyle Petty	Coors Light Pontiac
40	20	26	Hut Stricklin	Quaker State Ford

'95

GM Goodwrench Dealer 400

Michigan International Speedway
August 20, 1995
•••••

D ale Earnhardt's charge to regain the top slot in the NASCAR Winston Cup point standings had taken a solid hit at The Glen, and when the Goodwrench team arrived in Michigan's Irish Hills to do battle on its two-mile oval, the crew members remembered all too well what had happened to them during their last visit.

It was here that Earnhardt had clipped the concrete wall, and since the team had been unable to make repairs and get him running again, all Dale could do was limp away from the track. This time, the team had brought the Indianapolis-winning Monte Carlo in hopes that some of its Brickyard magic would rub off onto Roger Penske's spic-and-span track.

Dale had lost 76 points at The Glen and was now 197 behind leader Jeff Gordon — just when the stretch run to the title was gaining steam. Sterling Marlin was also gasping for air in the point battle. Obviously, the chase wasn't over yet, and everyone knew that anything could happen in the remaining races, but the 70 points Sterling had lost at The Glen with his shifter problems had put him a total of 152 points behind.

The only driver in the top four who looked like he had any momentum whatsoever — aside from the leader, of course — was Mark Martin. Mark's stirring victory at the Bud at The Glen had moved him into third place in the standings, ahead of Earnhardt, and he trailed Sterling by just seven

Bobby Hamilton, Steve Grissom and Geoff Bodine take advantage of Michigan's roomy layout to run three-wide in front of a capacity crowd. Of the three, Hamilton fared best: He finished eighth in the STP Pontiac. Bodine and Grissom ended up 27th and 29th, respectively. (Right) This family portrait may well become a common sight in NASCAR Winston Cup racing. Bobby Labonte is more than happy to pose for photographers in victory lane with wife Donna and son Tyler after his third win of the season.

The "Brew Crew" was instrumental in helping Rusty Wallace claw his way to the front of the field from his 24th-place starting spot. Rusty had one of the strongest cars in the race and was in contention for the win, but he was forced to make a late-race gas-and-go, which dropped him to a fifth-place finish.

points in their now-torrid battle for second place.

Jeff Gordon, meanwhile, had done exactly what he needed to do — consistently finish in the top 10 — and if he could maintain his pace, it would be extremely difficult to dislodge the youngster from the top rung of the point ladder. Since their second-place finish here in June, the Rainbow Warriors had won back-to-back events — the Pepsi 400 and the Slick 50 300 — "stumbled" to an eighth and sixth at Talladega and Indianapolis and recaptured their form with a third place at The Glen. Those kinds of finishes could put the team in position to deliver the knock-out punch in the point race later in the season.

As always, the August event at Michigan was of particular importance to the teams — it was the final time they would compete near the corporate headquarters of the manufacturers they represented. The race isn't nicknamed the "Backyard 400" for nothing. And since the event carried sponsorship from GM Goodwrench's Dealer group, it was easy to understand why Childress and Earnhardt had rolled out their Indianapolis winner. Better bring the best you've got for this one!

There was also plenty happening in the Pontiac camp. Rich Bickle was back in the Dick Brooks/Felix Sabates Kendall car, and Jimmy Hensley had returned to Bill Davis' MBNA-bankrolled effort. Davis was still glowing from Wally Dallenbach's great run to second at The Glen, and the team was juiced to make such finishes a habit. Kyle Petty and Felix Sabates had returned from their around-the-globe, world-record flight aboard a Concorde and were regaling anyone who would listen with their tales. Most stories involved the cramped quarters and the lack of showers, leading everyone to believe that the Concorde had unloaded its passengers and headed straight for the fumigation area of the airport. Thanks to Kyle's off-beat humor and one-line zingers, not to mention Felix's leftover Cuban accent, listeners were holding their sides with laughter.

At least one team — the Interstate Batteries team — was dead serious about the task at hand. Bobby Labonte had won the Coca-Cola 600 at Charlotte and followed it up with a victory here in June, but the team had struggled in the four races that followed. They finished 41st at Daytona, 15th at New Hampshire, 35th at Pocono and 31st at Talladega. The ship had been righted at Indianapolis with a ninth-place finish and then steered back on course with the rock-solid sixth place at The Glen. Afterwards, crew members, thinking that the little soldiers taped in the front and back of the green and black car needed some "R&R" from their patrols, removed them and put them in the air-conditioned lounge area of the Joe Gibbs-owned team's transporter. "Give them a nice, cool place to rest and restore some energy," one crew member said with a grin. Hey, why not?

Just before the cars rolled through the inspection line, the soldiers were brought back to the Interstate car and taped in place. The rest must have been just what the doctor ordered. Midway through the qualifying session, Bobby set the pace with a lap of 184.403 miles per hour. He had to wait, however, before he could claim his second pole of the season. Earnhardt made his qualifying run and

consecutive top-10 starting position, and Kenny had beaten Bobby Hamilton, in the fastest Pontiac, for the final top-10 slot.

Gordon led second-round qualifying, taking his backup car to a conservative 181.005 mph lap. After the field had been set, Kyle Petty, Todd Bodine, Jimmy Hensley and Dave Marcis used provisional starts to make the grid. Bickle, Tracy Leslie, Tim Steele and Loy Allen were forced to watch the race from an unwelcome vantage point: the stands.

The Kendall and MBNA teams were disconsolate. The previous week, Butch Leitzinger had given the Brooks/Sabates team a strong run, but now the car was being loaded onto the transporter. In the Bill Davis camp, everyone was scratching their heads, trying to find the answer

(**Left**) *Jeff Gordon (24) and John Andretti use the entire race track as they run down Michigan's frontstretch side by side. Gordon charged to the front from his 21st starting spot and led the most laps before finishing third. Andretti was strong in the early going but fell victim to engine failure in the first half of the event.* (**Below**) *Rookie contender Ricky Craven looks confident as he prepares to climb into his Kodiak Chevrolet. Ricky also drove confidently and put together an outstanding effort to finish a sparkling seventh.*

rolled onto pit road saying that raindrops were beginning to fall in the corners of the track.

Gordon, the pole favorite, decided to run despite the sprinkles. During his lap, he headed into the third turn carrying way too much speed — the DuPont Chevrolet was out of control. The blue car spun, drilling the concrete rear-end first, and then spun again, whacking the front. Before either Gordon or the car had returned to the garage area, Ray Evernham and the rest of the Rainbow Warriors were unloading the spare from the transporter.

After a 45-minute wait, qualifying resumed, but Bobby's lap just looked better and better with each successive qualifying attempt. Only Ricky Rudd, with a brand-new Tide Thunderbird, had anything for Bobby, but Ricky came up just a tick short. Labonte could officially add the Michigan pole award to the one he had claimed at Martinsville earlier this year.

Martin, determined to do his team proud since car owner Jack Roush's engineering company was located close by in Livonia, claimed the inside of the second row, and John Andretti matched his best starting position of the season with a strong, fourth-quick lap. Brett Bodine and Bill Elliott continued Ford's good fortunes, sharing the third row, and Dick Trickle grabbed the seventh spot with Bud Moore's Quality Care Ford. On his right — in the second-fastest Chevrolet in qualifying — was Earnhardt, who was just ahead of Jeremy Mayfield and Kenny Wallace. Mayfield's lap had earned him his third-to the puzzle. How could a team that had threatened to win and finished second the week before now need a provisional to get into the field?

As for Bobby Labonte's effort, well, it was no surprise to see the little soldiers being carried to the Interstate Batteries Chevrolet on Sunday morning. They had spent the night in the lounge in the team's transporter "getting a good night's sleep on that leather couch," grinned the crewman carrying the plastic figures. "Gave them a good, hearty breakfast ... in fact, took their order last night so we'd have exactly what they wanted. Tucked them in, turned on the stereo to the station they wanted and made sure they were comfy. Turned on the night-light so they wouldn't be nervous. This morning, they said they were ready for today's action." Who says racers aren't a wacky lot?

Throughout the first half of the Goodwrench Dealer

for long: They began working their way toward the front.

Lap after lap, it became more and more apparent that this race might turn into a mileage race — as Pocono had. For some teams, the realization came too late. For the Jimmy Makar-led Interstate Batteries crew, the window was perfect. The team could run 55 laps — no more — on a full load of fuel. They had made their stop on lap 145. This might work out!

Up ahead of the green and black Chevrolet, Rudd's engine gave up the ghost. Ward Burton headed for pit road for fuel. Martin and Wallace also were forced to pit for fuel. Geoff Bodine's engine faded. Now, with 19 laps remaining, the Interstate car was up to second. Only Gordon was between him and a sweep of the Michigan races.

With 15 to go, Gordon peeled off, headed for a 5.4-second stop for fuel. He could have stayed on the track and

Bill Elliott (94) and Bobby Labonte dropped to 11th and 13th, giving up their positions near the front of the field, after pitting for tires and fuel during the race's final caution. After the restart, the pair diced through traffic together as they charged toward the front.

400, it appeared that a Ford would end up in victory lane at the GM-sponsored race. There was no questioning the strength of Dale Jarrett — who rocketed from his 17th starting position to lead handily — but a lap past the halfway mark, Jarrett headed for the garage with a blown engine. The lead was handed to Elliott, and Rudd was not far behind.

Then Gordon established himself as a contender. The final caution appeared after Rick Mast hammered the concrete wall, and the leaders headed for pit road for tires and fuel. On the restart, Gordon, with a bevy of wannabes on his rear bumper, led the thundering herd under the flagstand. Elliott and Bobby Labonte, who had taken four new Goodyears on the stop, were 11th and 13th in line, but not

tried to stretch the fuel in his tank to the end, but he was the point leader, and the championship was much more important than a single victory. As many cars as there were on the lead lap, Gordon couldn't chance losing all those positions.

Just 12 laps remained, and Bobby Hamilton had moved up to second, but he, too, was forced to pit for fuel. Elliott then moved up to second and decided to gamble; he could only hope he had enough Unocal in the tank to get him home. He didn't. On the final lap, the red Ford ran dry. He fell all the way from second to ninth and was penalized a lap after he got a final-lap push from Ted Musgrave. Musgrave was just trying to give a fellow Ford driver a little help — problem is, last-lap pushes aren't allowed, so

The Jimmy Makar-led Interstate Batteries team kept Bobby Labonte near the front for most of the race, but it was Makar's decision to make the final pit stop for tires and fuel with 55 laps remaining that nailed down the team's third victory of the season.

NASCAR officials subtracted a lap from Bill's total.

After Elliott had begun to coast around the track, Terry Labonte had moved into his brother's tire tracks, although the difference between the two Chevrolets at the end was 6.8 seconds. Gordon recovered to finish third, just ahead of Marlin. Rusty Wallace came home fifth at his car owner's track, salvaging the best he could from his Miller Ford. Ward Burton was sixth, ahead of MAXX Rookie point leader Ricky Craven, and Hamilton rounded out the roster of lead-lap drivers in eighth place. Elliott was ninth, and Hut Stricklin brought the Quaker State Ford home in 10th place; both were a lap down.

Where were Earnhardt and Martin?

On their way home, by the time the race had ended. Mark's hopes had been crushed by a broken timing chain just 52 laps into the race; he was ranked 38th in the final results. Earnhardt had lasted 87 laps before his black Chevrolet was pushed behind the wall with a broken timing belt. He was 35th at the end of the race.

A total of 10 competitors had been eliminated by engine problems of one sort or another, an unusual occurrence in a season in which reliability had been noteworthy. And the problems had come at the worst possible time for Earnhardt and Martin. Gordon's calculating third place, combined with the finishes of the Goodwrench Chevrolet and the Valvoline Ford, had given the point standings an entirely new look.

The heart of the stretch run beckoned, and it was beginning to look like do-or-die for at least two of the title contenders.

On this day, the tale of the Dales did not have a happy ending. Both drivers were expected to be fast and didn't disappoint, but engine failures sent both Dales packing early. Dale Earnhardt took the Goodwrench Chevrolet to the garage on lap 87 with a broken timing belt. Dale Jarrett (28) lasted until lap 101 before his engine's crankshaft betrayed him.

GM Goodwrench Dealer

Race #21 — Final Race Results

Fin. Pos.	Str. Pos.	Car #	Driver	Team
1	1	18	Bobby Labonte	Interstate Batteries Chevrolet
2	13	5	Terry Labonte	Kellogg's Chevrolet
3	21	24	Jeff Gordon	DuPont Auto Finishes Chevrolet
4	14	4	Sterling Marlin	Kodak Film Chevrolet
5	24	2	Rusty Wallace	Miller Genuine Draft Ford
6	15	31	Ward Burton	Hardee's Chevrolet
7	16	41	Ricky Craven	Kodiak Chevrolet
8	11	43	Bobby Hamilton	STP Pontiac
9	6	94	Bill Elliott	McDonald's Ford
10	38	26	Hut Stricklin	Quaker State Ford
11	25	30	Michael Waltrip	Pennzoil Pontiac
12	9	98	Jeremy Mayfield	RCA Ford
13	7	15	Dick Trickle	Ford Quality Care Ford
14	36	23	Jimmy Spencer	Smokin' Joe's Ford
15	32	17	Darrell Waltrip	Western Auto Chevrolet
16	28	21	Morgan Shepherd	Citgo Ford
17	22	9	Lake Speed	Spam/Melling Ford
18	33	33	Robert Pressley	Skoal Bandit Chevrolet
19	40	75	Todd Bodine	Factory Stores Ford
20	27	90	Mike Wallace	Heilig-Meyers Ford
21	20	27	Elton Sawyer	Hooters Ford
22	41	22	Jimmy Hensley	MBNA America Pontiac
23	12	8	Jeff Burton	Raybestos Brakes Ford
24	10	81	Kenny Wallace	TIC Financial Ford
25	42	71	Dave Marcis	Tork Automotive Chevrolet
26	35	25	Ken Schrader	Budweiser Chevrolet
27	19	7	Geoff Bodine	Exide Batteries Ford
28	31	16	Ted Musgrave	The Family Channel Ford
29	30	29	Steve Grissom	Meineke Chevrolet
30	2	10	Ricky Rudd	Tide Ford
31	37	1	Rick Mast	Skoal Ford
32	18	87	Joe Nemechek	Burger King Chevrolet
33	17	28	Dale Jarrett	Texaco Havoline Ford
34	26	12	Derrike Cope	Straight Arrow Ford
35	8	3	Dale Earnhardt	Goodwrench Service Chevrolet
36	5	11	Brett Bodine	Lowe's Ford
37	4	37	John Andretti	Kmart/Little Caesars Ford
38	3	6	Mark Martin	Valvoline Ford
39	23	77	Bobby Hillin	Jasper/USAir Ford
40	34	32	Greg Sacks	Active Trucking Chevrolet
41	29	88	Gary Bradberry	Bradberry Racing Chevrolet
42	39	42	Kyle Petty	Coors Light Pontiac

GOODY'S 500

BRISTOL INTERNATIONAL RACEWAY

AUGUST 26, 1995

•••••

The Monday morning following Michigan's 400-mile event, the NASCAR Winston Cup tour was shocked by a pair of bombshells. First, Andy Petree, who had moved to the Richard Childress team from Leo Jackson's effort and then played a crucial role in Dale Earnhardt's last two championships, announced he would leave the team at the end of this season. He would return to Jackson's effort and work his way into a partial-ownership role.

It had always been his dream, he explained to a surprised group of media members, to become a car owner at the NASCAR Winston Cup level, and he had told Childress as much when he had gone to work for the Goodwrench Chevrolet owner two years ago. The opportunity had come sooner than anyone expected, but Childress surprised no one by encouraging Andy to fulfill his dream. Petree's departure would leave a big hole in the black-clad team from Welcome, N.C., but given the caliber of the personnel already on the team and the fact that, due to the team's success, there would be no shortage of qualified candidates anxious to apply, everyone expected Childress to be able to land a suitable replacement. To say that Childress' phone began ringing immediately — and off the hook — with calls about the position would be the understatement of the year.

Second, Ward Burton had been released from the Alan Dillard team. The message, which had come on the heels of his

Darrell Waltrip (17), Dale Earnhardt and Lake Speed (9) all took their turns at the front of the field. Earnhardt and Waltrip both went on to claim top-five finishes. Speed, however, got caught up in an accident and was eventually credited with 29th. **(Right)** *Terry Labonte's Monte Carlo displays the results of his last-lap dash to the checkered flag with Dale Earnhardt. Terry and the Kellogg's crew don't seem to mind the idea of the work which lies ahead, though. They thought Terry's third win of the season was well worth some overtime.*

planned to hire Ward when his contract with Dillard's team expired, was overjoyed by the chance to work with the young driver for the remainder of this season, calling it "Christmas in August."

To make room for Ward, Davis had released Jimmy Hensley, but it didn't take Jimmy long to find a ride, either. Dillard had hired Greg Sacks from the Active Motorsports team to fill the seat vacated by Ward, so Hensley immediately received a call from the Active team. He agreed to drive the Chevrolet on an "as-needed" basis.

At the head of the row of transporters at Bristol, Earnhardt and the remainder of the Childress team were taking Petree's announcement in stride. More important at the moment was finding a way to stop the point slide that threatened to eliminate Earnhardt from contention for his third-consecutive championship and the eighth Winston Cup of his career.

Despite Earnhardt's Indianapolis victory, the team's momentum had dissipated like wispy strands of early-morning fog in the mountains surrounding Thunder Valley. Rather than mounting the fullcourt press as they had planned, the Goodwrench team had stumbled after being hit by a sledgehammer in three consecutive races. They had fallen from 121 behind Jeff Gordon to 314 behind, a loss of 193 points. Faces in the Childress camp were understandably grim.

(Above) Rusty Wallace — the modern-day master of the short tracks — was confident about his chances of taking home the winner's trophy from "Thunder Valley." He qualified fifth and was fast in the opening laps, but little did he know what the race had in store for him.
(Right) Rusty's troubles were just beginning when Dale Earnhardt tagged him from behind on lap 32 and sent him spinning. While Rusty tries to recover, Earnhardt and Gordon slide by on the inside.

sixth place at Michigan, was somewhat of a surprise to the young Virginian. Because Hardee's had decided to end its sponsorship at the end of the season and given the limited success of the blue and orange Chevrolets in '95, Ward had been talking with several other teams regarding next season, but Dillard had given Ward the chance to start earlier than he had planned!

Less than 48 hours after the split, Burton had come to terms with Bill Davis to drive the MBNA Pontiacs for the remainder of this season — and the next. Davis, who had

Something good had to happen this weekend.

In those same three races, Sterling Marlin had also taken a beating, although his wasn't as severe as Earnhardt's. Although Sterling had lost 85 points since The Brickyard, he still remained second in the standings and was rapidly becoming the only driver with a chance of making a run at Gordon.

Mark Martin's victory at The Glen had given him

renewed hope, but an engine failure the following week at Michigan had sent the Valvoline team reeling. Like Earnhardt, Mark had lost a pile of points — 111 to be exact — and he was now 285 behind Gordon. It seemed that the nightmare simply wouldn't end.

Of course, they weren't the only drivers under a lot of pressure: Both Steve Grissom and Dave Marcis were out of provisionals, so qualifying at Bristol had become of particular importance to their teams. The two drivers now faced the unwelcome prospect of having to make the field on the basis of their qualifying times from now until Phoenix. With qualifying as tight as it was, both knew that one slip at Bristol, Darlington or anywhere else would send them packing.

Most drivers don't at all care to be the first one on the track in the opening moments of qualifying. They would prefer that someone else set the pace and put a number on the board. Helps them get rid of the jitters, they'll tell you.

But ask Terry Labonte about it, and he'll just look at you and shrug his shoulders. "Don't matter", he'll say. "One spot's as good as another, as long as the weather's the same all the way through the session."

He proved the authenticity of his nonchalance by taking to the track first on Friday night at Bristol and, after 15 seconds and change, laying a lap of 124.662 miles per hour on the timing lights. Driver after driver tried to beat the speed, but as the session ground toward its conclusion, the No. 5 was still atop the leader board.

Then Martin flipped the switch on the Jack Roush-owned Ford and proceeded to sweep the poles at Bristol for 1995. He ripped off a new track record of 15.339 seconds, an average speed of 125.093 mph on the high-banked concrete half-mile.

And since only four drivers remained in line behind him, Mark didn't have to wait long to ensure his lap would stand. He had claimed his fourth pole position of the season and the 28th of his career.

Michael Waltrip did the Pontiac folks proud by putting the Pennzoil Poncho on the inside of the second row, thereby giving each of the manufacturers a position in the top three. Jeff Gordon, the winner of the spring race here, plunked the DuPont Chevrolet on the outside of the second row. Rusty Wallace, who turned the fifth-fastest lap in "Midnight," was delighted because he knew the Miller Ford would be strong in the race.

Ricky Craven had a super qualifying run to claim the sixth-quick slot, ahead of Earnhardt and Ricky Rudd. Ted Musgrave and Derrike Cope put their Fords in the fifth row ahead of Hut Stricklin and Joe Nemechek. At the bottom of the list after first-day qualifying were Sterling and

Terry Labonte puts his Kellogg's Chevrolet under Darrell Waltrip
to gain another position en route to claiming the lead. On this night, the Western Auto Chevrolet pilot looked like the
Darrell of old, but not even he could handle Labonte, who had his Monte Carlo dialed in perfectly and went on to lead the final 69 laps.

Darrell Waltrip, who had earned identical times on the track. Sterling was given the final pit on the frontstretch because his car owner was higher in the standings than Darrell's. Waltrip would be forced to compete from the backstretch pit area.

The second day of qualifying posed a problem for many of the teams. It was held during the heat of the day, rather than in the evening, and everyone felt the times would be slower due to the warmer temperatures. Only 10 drivers decided to run again, and only two of those — Grissom and Marcis — made the lineup based on their speeds. Marcis had the last car in the field on the basis of qualifying laps. Two others who ran in the second session were forced to use provisionals. Those who used provisionals to make the field were Brett Bodine, John Andretti, Dick Trickle and Lake Speed. Kyle Petty, Joe Ruttman, Kenny Wallace, Jimmy Hensley, Bobby Hillin, Todd Bodine and Elton Sawyer all failed to make the field! It was the first time Kyle had missed a race because he had failed to qualify since he and Felix Sabates had begun their racing association in 1989.

One had only to look into Earnhardt's steely blues to know that Saturday's event under the Bristol lights would be worth every penny of the ticket price. Dale and his team were up against the wall and could be expected to run as hard as possible in search of the victory. What the fans would see was vintage Earnhardt: the awesome skill that the seven-time champion had honed to perfection through the years.

Although the race itself was slow to start — the rain-delayed event finally began at about 9 p.m. — the action was immediate. Dale bumped Rusty Wallace on lap 32 and was sent to the rear of the line for the restart once Wallace had recovered from the resulting spin. Dale wasted no time carving his way to the front, and by lap 185, he had moved into the top five. Four laps later, he was second behind Gordon. Just five more laps had passed before he

(Above) Michael Waltrip (30) was gunning for his first career win after starting third at a track that he admittedly dislikes. His bid for victory came abruptly to an end when he tangled with Rick Mast. (Left) Darrell Waltrip and his team were in need of an emotional boost, and Bristol was just the medicine Darrell had in mind. The driver of the Western Auto Chevrolet showed the form which had taken him to Bristol's victory lane 12 times in the past and was pleased with his fourth-place finish.

was leading. He then shuffled back and forth: After one caution, he dropped from the lead to 12th, and after the final yellow of the evening on lap 401, he dropped back to 16th. Once again, though, he charged through traffic, and with just 12 laps remaining, he passed Dale Jarrett for second.

Terry Labonte, meanwhile, had taken command of the race on lap 432. Although he would certainly be watching his mirror in the final 12 laps, he thought he had plenty of room to post his third triumph of the season. Earnhardt was coming hard, Terry knew. But there didn't seem to be enough laps left for Dale to catch — let alone pass — the red and yellow Kellogg's Monte Carlo.

Then Terry caught side-by-side lapped traffic and was balked slightly as he tried to find a way past. It was just the break Dale needed, and he dug the spurs into the sides of the Goodwrench machine. He closed on Terry's bumper, and as the cars exited

After drawing a qualifying slot fifth from the end, Mark Martin took his Jack Roush-owned Ford out on Bristol's concrete surface and logged a track-record, 125.093-mph lap to earn his fourth Busch Pole Award of the season.

the fourth turn on the final run to the checkers, there was little question what was coming. Terry knew it. Dale knew it. The crews along pit road knew. The 85,000-plus fans in Larry Carrier's fabulous half-mile knew it. Would he? Could he? Was this truly the Earnhardt of old, who'd let nothing stand in his way? Really?

Yep.

It wasn't the biggest bump in the history of the sport, but sure enough, Dale laid the right front of his Chevrolet on the left rear of Terry's. It was the only move he could make in a last-gasp attempt to win the race.

Terry had known what would happen, and he was ready: He pointed his Monte Carlo at the finish line and stood on the gas. He roared, sliding, out of the fourth turn, crossed the finish line and smashed the right-front corner of the Chevrolet into the concrete wall. It looked like something from "Days of Thunder."

The official margin of victory was a tenth of a second — about one car-length. When Labonte rolled, hissing, smoking and steaming, into the winner's circle, he could only shake his head and grin. That was some way to earn his third victory of the season!

Earnhardt had exited his Chevrolet at the Unocal pumps and was in the middle of talking with media members when a flying water bottle bounced off his black car. It had been tossed by a furious Wallace, who was venting his frustrations after an awful day: First, he'd been bumped and spun by Dale, and then he was later involved in another mishap that had sent his chances for a win down the tubes. Rusty had finished 21st. After an exchange of words, Dale told Wallace to call him Monday. "We need to talk," he told Wallace.

Behind Earnhardt, Jarrett completed a strong run to finish third, and Darrell Waltrip fought his way to fourth, despite the fact that he'd had to pit on the backstretch. Martin was fifth, and Gordon continued his roll toward a championship with a sixth place that included a long stretch at the front of the field. Marlin finished right behind Gordon, and Mike Wallace had a terrific run in Junie Donlavey's Ford to claim eighth place. Jeff Burton took the Stavola Brothers Ford, the final car on the lead lap, to ninth place, and Derrike Cope emerged with a top-10 finish despite fighting tire problems. Cope's car was strong — he had led twice during the race — but a set of mismatched tires and a nerf job by Earnhardt had cost him a chance at a lead-lap finish.

The race at the Tennessee half-mile had an appropriate sponsor for what turned out to be a slam-bang affair that included 15 caution flags. Once the body men got a look at their cars, post-Bristol, a lot of Goody's would be consumed!

Goody's 500
Race #22 — Final Race Results

Fin. Pos.	Str. Pos.	Car #	Driver	Team
1	2	5	Terry Labonte	Kellogg's Chevrolet
2	7	3	Dale Earnhardt	Goodwrench Service Chevrolet
3	16	28	Dale Jarrett	Texaco Havoline Ford
4	20	17	Darrell Waltrip	Western Auto Chevrolet
5	1	6	Mark Martin	Valvoline Ford
6	4	24	Jeff Gordon	DuPont Auto Finishes Chevrolet
7	19	4	Sterling Marlin	Kodak Film Chevrolet
8	27	90	Mike Wallace	Heilig-Meyers Ford
9	18	8	Jeff Burton	Raybestos Brakes Ford
10	10	12	Derrike Cope	Straight Arrow Ford
11	28	18	Bobby Labonte	Interstate Batteries Chevrolet
12	13	7	Geoff Bodine	Exide Batteries Ford
13	9	16	Ted Musgrave	The Family Channel Ford
14	25	25	Ken Schrader	Budweiser Chevrolet
15	3	30	Michael Waltrip	Pennzoil Pontiac
16	12	87	Joe Nemechek	Burger King Chevrolet
17	29	21	Morgan Shepherd	Citgo Ford
18	26	23	Jimmy Spencer	Smokin' Joe's Ford
19	34	37	John Andretti	Kmart/Little Caesars Ford
20	31	43	Bobby Hamilton	STP Pontiac
21	5	2	Rusty Wallace	Miller Genuine Draft Ford
22	23	29	Steve Grissom	Meineke Chevrolet
23	22	94	Bill Elliott	McDonald's Ford
24	14	33	Robert Pressley	Skoal Bandit Chevrolet
25	21	31	Greg Sacks	Hardee's Chevrolet
26	24	1	Rick Mast	Skoal Ford
27	32	71	Dave Marcis	Olive Garden Chevrolet
28	33	11	Brett Bodine	Lowe's Ford
29	36	9	Lake Speed	Spam/Melling Ford
30	30	98	Jeremy Mayfield	RCA Ford
31	15	40	Rich Bickle	Kendall Pontiac
32	6	41	Ricky Craven	Kodiak Chevrolet
33	11	26	Hut Stricklin	Quaker State Ford
34	17	22	Ward Burton	MBNA America Pontiac
35	35	15	Dick Trickle	Ford Quality Care Ford
36	8	10	Ricky Rudd	Tide Ford

MOUNTAIN DEW SOUTHERN 500

DARLINGTON RACEWAY
SEPTEMBER 3, 1995
•••••

B y the time the teams began unloading at Darlington Raceway for the annual running of the Mountain Dew Southern 500, NASCAR officials had met with both Dale Earnhardt and Rusty Wallace to help "clear the air" regarding their antics at the conclusion of the Goody's 500 the previous Saturday night. It appeared to work: Both drivers spoke in terms of the remainder of the season and the challenges facing each of them rather than retaliation for what had happened at Larry Carrier's half-mile.

There were, in fact, much more important items of business to which they needed to attend. Earnhardt and Wallace needed to be more concerned with what they had to accomplish in the final portion of the season rather than fuss about days gone by.

Wallace was seventh in the point standings and had but a single victory to show for the season. His goals for the remainder of the year were to find a way to win a few more, and more importantly, accumulate enough points to move into the top five at year's end. He needed to make up more than 260 points on fifth-place Ted Musgrave to accomplish the latter goal.

The decal on the side of Wallace's car was all the evidence needed to show that Rusty had not forgotten his gripe with Dale over the previous week's events (at Bristol). Inevitably, the two veterans — and friends — battled on the track, and they showed their professionalism by waging one of their classic duels without inflicting so much as a scratch. (Right) Jeff Gordon tightens the belts and flips down his visor as he prepares to tackle the track "too tough to tame." On this day, the young driver once again proved his talent with a stirring run to the front.

Earnhardt's brilliant second place at Bristol, for which he'd fought his way back through the field twice, had put the black-clad Goodwrench crew in the right frame of mind headed into Darlington. If there is any track on the circuit on

which Dale is considered the master, it is the balky, venerable 1.366-mile, egg-shaped pioneer superspeedway. He has posted nine career NASCAR Winston Cup victories there, including three Southern 500s. It looked like just the venue the Goodwrench team needed to continue the momentum they had produced at Bristol.

Dale's Bristol finish, combined with Jeff Gordon's sixth place, had allowed him to pick up 20 points on the youngster. It wasn't the huge chunk of points Earnhardt needed to tighten up the point chase, but after losing points in several races, gaining points was an accomplishment.

Sterling Marlin came to Darlington with a dual sense of purpose. He was second to Gordon in the point standings and trailed by 176. Sterling had won the TranSouth 400 in the spring and felt he had a real shot at sweeping the

year's events at the fabled track. And if he won the Southern 500, he also would win the $100,000 "consolation" bonus awarded by the Winston Select Million program. Bobby Labonte, by virtue of his Coca-Cola 600 victory, and Mark Martin, winner of the Winston Select 500 at Talladega, also were in contention for the R.J. Reynolds bonus money.

Heading into Darlington, Martin was third in the standings, trailing Marlin by 280 points but holding a 14-point margin over Earnhardt. Musgrave, Mark's teammate on the Roush Racing effort, was 391 behind and the only other driver with any type of chance to win the NASCAR Winston Cup championship.

When it comes to stretch runs and coming from behind to win championships, there is only one driver in the garage area with whom you should speak. Darrell Waltrip has both won and lost the Winston Cup in pressure-packed stretch runs, so he was the natural choice when it came to discussing whether or not the young DuPont team would be able to withstand the pressure of battling with a veteran group like Earnhardt and the Richard Childress team.

And "DeeDoubleYa" didn't disappoint the reporters gathered around the rear of his Western Auto Transporter who wanted an audience with the three-time champ. With his signature grin and wry humor in place, Darrell discussed the whys and wherefores of the title chase and

*(**Left**) John Andretti picked one of NASCAR's most prestigious events to capture the first pole of his brief NASCAR Winston Cup career. (**Below**) Sterling Marlin gets loose while battling Bobby Labonte (18) for sixth place on lap 285. Sterling and Ward Burton (22) would spin, while Labonte and Hut Stricklin (26) managed to continue without incident. All four remained on the lead lap and finished in the top 10.*

pointed out that traditionally, when the tour visits Darlington in September, there are usually several teams still in title contention — from a numerical standpoint. But he added that those who are still in the point battle aren't necessarily championship contenders.

"Darlington has a way of sorting things out," he mused. "What's probably going to happen here this weekend is that when teams come here, five drivers are in the point race. When they leave here Sunday night, more than likely, at least two of those teams will be out of it. And in a couple more weeks, another team will fall by the wayside. By the time we get to North Wilkesboro or Charlotte, it will be down to two. That's the way it seems to have worked over the years. So look for this event to change the complexion of the point race."

Not too long ago, DuPont crew chief Ray Evernham had been pooh-poohing talk of a championship. The team was just trying to do its best from race to race, he said. Just going from event to event, trying to win races. The team's just a young group, he kept pointing out, and needs time to work itself into a championship-caliber group. All they really want to do is run well each weekend, win five races, some poles and be in the top five or 10 at the end of the year. That would be a great accomplishment for the group, he reiterated.

Now, with the heat on the team erupting into a blue flame and with driver Gordon clearly in command of the point battle, Evernham and the remainder of the Rainbow Warriors were suddenly faced with harsh reality. Gone were the frolicking days when the team was viewed as the new group on the block. No longer could crewmen saunter, carefree, through the garage area; others were wondering when they were going to fall on their faces, or when their string of good luck would come to an end.

Nonetheless, the DuPont team had stuck to its guns and proven again and again that the blue Monte Carlos were extremely well-prepared and were pitted with skill and brio. As for Gordon, he had matured into a shrewd judge of when to push the car and when to ride. Truly, the team had championship potential, and if it could face down the challenge from Earnhardt and the Goodwrench crew, the team members felt they would win the championship.

Strangely enough, even though Marlin and Martin were closer in points to Gordon than Earnhardt, Evernham and the rest of the crew thought the biggest challenge would come from Dale and the Goodwrench

team. Few thought the Cup battle would come down to Gordon and either Sterling or Mark.

Throughout the practice session prior to the first round of qualifying, a pair of Fords were targeted by every stopwatch in the garage area. They weren't, however, the Thunderbirds of Wallace and Martin, as many would expect. Instead, Bill Elliott and Ricky Rudd's 'Birds were at the top of the practice times sheet. Elliott was continuing his team's progress, and Rudd and his Tide team were

Although Ricky Rudd (10) and Derrike Cope are running together, their days would end quite differently: Rudd started on the outside of the front row and ran with the leaders before losing a lap. He eventually was able to regain his lead-lap status and finished sixth. Cope, on the other hand, had to fight his way up from the 31st starting spot and eventually finished 15th.

out to prove that the upcoming loss of crew chief Bill Ingle, who had decided to leave the team at the end of the year in hopes of resuming his driving career, was something that could be overcome.

During qualifying, however, both Rudd and Elliott overdrove their Fords in search of the pole. Ricky's lap included an out-of-shape wiggle in the fourth corner, while Bill's run in the McDonald's machine included a near-spin as he had exited the second turn.

Rudd's bobble opened the door just a crack, but it was all John Andretti needed: He capitalized on the situation and claimed the very first pole of his young NASCAR Winston Cup career. He posted a lap of 167.379 miles per hour in the Blue Light Special, which sent his crew back to the garage area laughing and cheering. It also gained him entry into the most exclusive club in motor racing, the

Unocal/Darlington Record Club. In order to be inducted, a driver must post the fastest time of his make during qualifying for the Southern 500. Young John had accomplished the feat early in his career, and he had an entire year to look forward to his induction, which would take place at Darlington next Labor Day weekend.

Rudd's lap was good enough for the outside of the front row. Earnhardt ran what he called a "conservative" lap to grab the inside of the second row, where he found Dick Trickle alongside. Trickle's outstanding performance had given Bud Moore's Quality Care Ford its best starting position of the season.

Gordon and Marlin were side by side in the third row. Lake Speed and his Spam-mobile had a great run to seventh, and Ward Burton appeared on Speed's right in the MBNA Pontiac. Geoff Bodine and Hut Stricklin made up a Ford fifth row and captured the final positions in the top

the 46th-annual Southern 500. Early in the race, Gordon had spun and fallen backwards through the field, so many thought this would be Dale's perfect opportunity to pull back into contention for his eighth championship.

Gordon, however, had other ideas. After fighting back from the spin and barely avoiding another pair of on-track incidents, he worked his way to the front of the field. With just over 30 laps to go, he was in command and building a lead that would eventually measure more than five seconds.

But this was the Southern 500 — the race wasn't over quite yet! In the closing laps, a yellow flag appeared after Ted Musgrave's engine failed (Musgrave would drop to

Sterling Marlin was out to sweep Darlington's two events for 1995 and also lay claim to the $100,000 bonus made available through RJR's Winston Million program. His team was equally excited as they finished their work in the pits and directed Sterling back to the action.

10, barely ahead of Jimmy Spencer and Dale Jarrett. Burton, the fastest Pontiac driver, would also be inducted into the Record Club next September.

At the conclusion of second-round qualifying, Rick Mast, Kyle Petty, Rich Bickle (in the Kendall Pontiac) and Ed Berrier (the latest driver to take the wheel of the Active Motorsports Chevrolet) took the provisional starting positions. Billy Standridge, Brad Teague and Gary Bradberry failed to make the field.

Given his strong qualifying performance and his determination to cut into Gordon's point lead, everyone expected Earnhardt to arrive at the front of the pack early and stay there. He didn't disappoint. By the end of lap 20, he was at the point, and he went on to lead more than half of

22nd place in the final results), erasing Gordon's lead. Even worse, Earnhardt and Wallace were in his mirror when the green flew for the final time — just nine laps remained.

The large throng of fans expected some fireworks from the three leaders but had to be content with watching Gordon motor away to a victory of more than a half-second. Earnhardt, meanwhile, held off Wallace's every move to claim second place. Ward Burton gave Bill Davis' team something to cheer about by notching fourth, and Michael Waltrip piloted the Pennzoil Pontiac to fifth place, another fine finish for the Pontiac folks. Rudd had fought his way back from a lap behind to finish sixth ahead of Hut Stricklin, who had a heady race with the Quaker State

The damage to these tires is the result of Ricky Rudd's spin on lap 136. Note the inner liner inside the tire on the left, which did its job of supporting the weight of the car until Ricky could get back to his pit for fresh rubber.

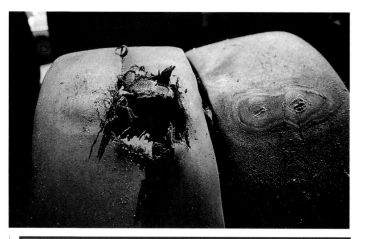

Ford. Bobby Labonte, Speed and Marlin claimed the final top-10 positions. Morgan Shepherd finished 11th despite having to work his way up from the rear of the field (he had missed driver introductions and been banished to the back of the lineup).

Some wondered if Gordon could fully appreciate the magnitude of his accomplishment: He was the second-youngest driver in history to win the storied Southern 500, an event many drivers feel is the capstone of a career. They needn't have worried.

After the race, Gordon was quick to acknowledge his crew's contribution to his victory, and then he talked about the importance of the event. "Everyone knows the history of this place and what it has meant to the sport," Jeff said. "To win here — especially to win the Southern 500 — is one of the greatest accomplishments of any driver's career. Some of the best have never been able to win this particular event, and I feel very honored to be able to take home the trophy. It's a very special race to everyone in the garage area, and it's a victory that everyone wants to have before they are finished with racing."

By leading the most laps, Earnhardt had gained the same number of points Gordon had. Therefore, the margin between the two in the standings was exactly the same as it had been when they entered the garage area for the first practice session on Friday.

When Darrell Waltrip decides to stop racing, he can begin a new career as a prognosticator. Musgrave's engine failure had dropped him to 474 behind and all but eliminated him from contention for the title. Martin, involved in a wreck early in the race that had sent him to the garage for repairs, finished 33rd. Although he was running at the finish, Mark had fallen to fourth in the standings, 396 points behind. The probability of him capturing his first Winston Cup had become a speck on the horizon.

PARSONS, PARKS INDUCTED INTO NATIONAL MOTORSPORTS PRESS HALL OF FAME

During the Southern 500 weekend at Darlington, a pair of champions became the 1995 inductees into the National Motorsports Press Association's Hall of Fame. Benny Parsons, who won the 1973 NASCAR Winston Cup title as a driver and now plies his trade as an award-winning commentator on ESPN's race telecasts, was honored for his on-track accomplishments during a career that spanned nearly 20 years. In 526 career starts, Parsons captured 21 NASCAR Winston Cup victories, one of which was the 1975 Daytona 500. Raymond Parks, an Atlanta-based businessman, won the first NASCAR title, awarded in 1949. At the time, Parks owned the cars driven to the championship by Red Byron. Others who drove for Parks and won in his cars include Bob and Fonty Flock and Bill France Sr. A former driver, Parks turned to car ownership following World War II. He left the sport in 1951.

Mountain Dew Southern 500

Race #23 — Final Race Results

Fin. Pos.	Str. Pos.	Car #	Driver	Team
1	5	24	Jeff Gordon	DuPont Auto Finishes Chevrolet
2	3	3	Dale Earnhardt	Goodwrench Service Chevrolet
3	21	2	Rusty Wallace	Miller Genuine Draft Ford
4	8	22	Ward Burton	MBNA America Pontiac
5	25	30	Michael Waltrip	Pennzoil Pontiac
6	2	10	Ricky Rudd	Tide Ford
7	10	26	Hut Stricklin	Quaker State Ford
8	13	18	Bobby Labonte	Interstate Batteries Chevrolet
9	7	9	Lake Speed	Spam/Melling Ford
10	6	4	Sterling Marlin	Kodak Film Chevrolet
11	30	21	Morgan Shepherd	Citgo Ford
12	1	37	John Andretti	Kmart/Little Caesars Ford
13	32	77	Bobby Hillin	Jasper/USAir Ford
14	22	43	Bobby Hamilton	STP Pontiac
15	31	12	Derrike Cope	Straight Arrow Ford
16	26	8	Jeff Burton	Raybestos Brakes Ford
17	15	33	Robert Pressley	Skoal Bandit Chevrolet
18	17	41	Ricky Craven	Kodiak Chevrolet
19	16	5	Terry Labonte	Kellogg's Chevrolet
20	42	32	Ed Berrier	ATS Wood Recycling Chevrolet
21	41	40	Rich Bickle	Kendall Pontiac
22	28	16	Ted Musgrave	The Family Channel Ford
23	38	25	Ken Schrader	Budweiser Chevrolet
24	40	42	Kyle Petty	Coors Light Pontiac
25	14	87	Joe Nemechek	Burger King Chevrolet
26	39	1	Rick Mast	Skoal Ford
27	34	29	Steve Grissom	Meineke Chevrolet
28	12	28	Dale Jarrett	Texaco Havoline Ford
29	11	23	Jimmy Spencer	Smokin' Joe's Ford
30	27	98	Jeremy Mayfield	RCA Ford
31	23	11	Brett Bodine	Lowe's Ford
32	35	27	Elton Sawyer	Hooters Ford
33	36	6	Mark Martin	Valvoline Ford
34	33	19	Loy Allen	Healthsource Health Plan Ford
35	9	7	Geoff Bodine	Exide Batteries Ford
36	4	15	Dick Trickle	Ford Quality Care Ford
37	19	71	Dave Marcis	Terramite Chevrolet
38	20	31	Greg Sacks	Hardee's Chevrolet
39	29	90	Mike Wallace	Heilig-Meyers Ford
40	18	17	Darrell Waltrip	Western Auto Chevrolet
41	24	94	Bill Elliott	McDonald's Ford
42	37	75	Todd Bodine	Factory Stores Ford

MILLER GENUINE DRAFT 400

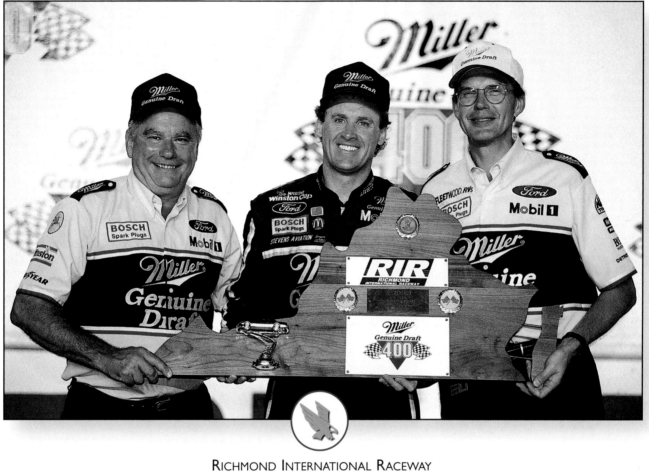

RICHMOND INTERNATIONAL RACEWAY
SEPTEMBER 9, 1995
•••••

Those who had predicted that the Rainbow Warriors would fold under the pressure of the stretch run for the championship were beginning to reconsider.

Dale Earnhardt had put together back-to-back second places at Bristol and Darlington, but Jeff Gordon had counter-punched his way off the ropes. His victory in the Mountain Dew Southern 500 at Darlington — a track at which Earnhardt is held with the same esteem as David Pearson and Cale Yarborough as masters of the pioneer superspeedway — had proven beyond a doubt that the DuPont team had reached down inside itself to answer Earnhardt's challenge.

Now the scene shifted to the Sawyer's mini-superspeedway in Richmond, where Paul and his sons had turned the old Fairgrounds half-mile into one of the most spectacular arenas on the entire NASCAR Winston Cup tour. With stands ringing the oval, the three-quarter-mile track looks much like a football stadium. Virginia's fans are among the most devout, and they turn out in droves for the annual affair under the lights in the Capital City. It's only fitting that the Sawyers have rewarded the fans' loyalty with one of the finest facilities in the sport.

*Rusty Wallace, winner of two of the last three night races at Richmond, made it three of the last four when he ran away with the victory in the final 100 laps. Assisting him in victory lane are Penske South's Don Miller (left) and Walter Czarnecki, executive vice president of the Penske Corporation. (**Right**) Dale Earnhardt and Jeff Gordon take a moment to chat prior to making their qualifying attempts at Richmond. Earnhardt, third in the qualifying order, would win the pole. Gordon was next in line in qualifying and would barely miss Dale's speed, securing the other front-row spot.*

As the drivers strode through the garage gate at Richmond, Sterling Marlin had reason to believe he could still win the title. He had lost 41 points to Gordon at Darlington and now trailed by 215, but he also knew that in the blink of an eye — or a flick of the wheel — anything could happen. He knew he could pull himself much closer to Gordon as the season wound down.

Rusty Wallace's third place, coupled with Ted Musgrave's 22nd-place finish at Darlington, had given Wallace renewed hope that he still could accomplish one of his team's goals during the final third of the season. Wallace had gained 73 points on Musgrave and was now only 155 points behind the Family Channel Ford driver in their battle for fifth place. Terry Labonte was also in the mix for that position, sandwiched between Musgrave and Wallace. Labonte was 37 points ahead of Rusty and 126 behind Ted.

Both Rusty and Terry had spring in their steps at Richmond. Labonte had won the last two outings on the oval, and he had beaten Geoff Bodine by a bumper in the Thursday night NASCAR SuperTruck Series by Craftsman event on the three-quarter-mile track. His last short-track outing had ended in Bristol's victory lane (despite Earnhardt's last-lap bid for victory), and he felt that his Hendrick Motorsport effort had shaken itself out of its mid-season slump.

Wallace, meanwhile, simply loves Richmond. He has always run like "Jack the Bear" at the track. Wallace had won two of the last three night races at Richmond, and there was nothing Rusty wanted more than to slap his black and gold Ford into victory lane in the event spon-

(Above) Gordon and Earnhardt swapped the lead throughout the first 100 laps, which included two cautions. During this yellow-flag stop, a crew member from Schrader's team (Ken qualified third) lends a hand to his Hendrick teammates on the DuPont crew.
*(**Right**) Ted Musgrave came to Richmond fifth in the point standings with Rusty Wallace and Terry Labonte nipping at his heels. Ted managed to hang onto the fifth spot with his 10th-place finish, but the gap had been closed even further by virtue of Rusty and Terry's one-two finish.*

sored by Miller, the same name on the flanks of his car. The Thunderbird he had chosen for Richmond, "Ronnie," had been named in memory of Ronnie Hopkins, who had built the car before losing a battle with an extended illness earlier in the season.

By the time Wallace had belted into his Ford for the first round of qualifying, Jack Roush had announced that Jeff Burton would leave the Stavola Brothers and join his team for the coming season. A third team, co-owned by Roush, Mark Martin and Musgrave, would be formed, and Buddy Parrott would act as the general manager. The new team would be based in the Charlotte area and would be separate from the two teams based south of Greensboro in Liberty, N.C. Also, Exide would leave the Geoff Bodine team and come on board with the new Roush effort as the primary sponsor. At the same time, Roush also confirmed that The Family Channel would return as the primary sponsor of Musgrave's Thunderbird for the coming season.

On the heels of the Roush/Burton announcement — and immediately after winning a brilliant duel with Mark Martin in Friday night's NASCAR Busch Series, Grand National Division race — Dale Jarrett was asked if his plans for the 1996 season were complete. For several weeks, Jarrett had been negotiating with sponsors to gauge the level of interest in expanding his Busch program to the NASCAR Winston Cup level. With Ernie Irvan slated to return to racing full-time as the driver of the Havoline Ford during the 1996 season, Jarrett had felt the need to explore his options regarding the coming season. He had had several offers to drive for other teams in addition to the option of campaigning with his own team.

But Jarrett announced that he and car owner Robert Yates had worked out a plan that would allow Jarrett to remain with Yates Racing. Robert Yates would field a second team for 1996, with sponsorship to be announced later in the season; both Dale and Ernie would be provided a car in which to compete. It was the best of both worlds. Jarrett would be able to remain with the team and drive competitive equipment, and Ernie would also receive quality cars and engines for his return to racing.

Yates' decision to field a pair of teams was a surprise to many because every indication until now had been that Jarrett would field his own effort for 1996. Now that the decision had cleared the air regarding his future, Jarrett and his Yates mates were determined to push the Havoline Ford from its current 12th place into the top 10 in points by year's end. They also were preparing to pro-vide a second car for Irvan in anticipation of his return to the sport.

The Roush and Yates teams may have stolen the spotlight during the early portion of the weekend, but when it came to qualifying, Earnhardt and the Richard Childress team once again proved that they were not about to roll over and let young Gordon win the championship without out a battle.

Earnhardt was the third driver on the track for qualifying. When the number had been drawn for him, he had not been the most delighted chauffeur on the property. Earnhardt had hoped for a high number, which would have put him on the oval late in the session, when the track is usually cooler and, therefore, faster. The third slot, however, turned out to be a great draw for Dale.

He rocketed around the track in just over 22 seconds and put a lap of 122.543 miles per hour in the book. He had given the other 43 drivers attempting to make the field the number they would have to beat. Gordon, the next driver up, is always a favorite for the pole position, but he failed to beat the lap. So did everyone else.

Earnhardt had taken the pole — his third of the season but his first on a short track. A check of the record book made his pole even more impressive. It was the first time since his rookie season in 1979 that the seven-time champion had earned the pole for a Richmond race. That first one had come in the Capital City 400 in September, on the

Greg Sacks (31) made his third start in the Hardee's Chevrolet at Richmond but was forced to retire before the race's midpoint after he was involved in an accident. Dale Jarrett had a much better night: He started 27th, steadily worked his way toward the front and finished fourth after a very solid performance in the Texaco Ford.

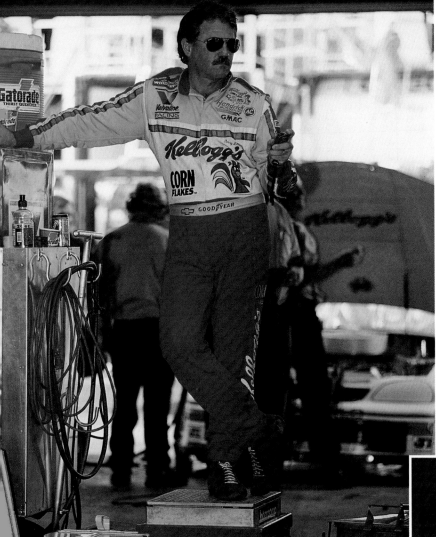

and Jeremy Mayfield. Those who went home included Ed Berrier (in the Active Motorsports Chevrolet), Jay Hedgecock, Shane Hall (in the Kendall Oil Pontiac), Steve Grissom (out of provisionals), Mike Wallace (at Junie Donlavey's home track, no less!) and Eric Smith.

When the Sawyers tore up the old half-mile and began building the three-quarter-mile track, one of the first things they did was install a lighting system to allow racing under the stars. That foresight was the reason the Miller Genuine Draft 400 ran on its scheduled day.

Rain delayed the start of the race from its scheduled 7:30 p.m. start, and while the huge crowd of more than 80,000 waited for the track to be dried,

(Left) During practice, Terry Labonte checks out his competition with the stopwatch. Terry himself was shooting for three straight wins at Richmond and was a strong contender during the race. In the end, however, he didn't have what he needed to catch a dominant Rusty Wallace; Labonte had to settle for second place. (Below) Richmond's smooth and wide surface invites two-abreast racing around the entire oval. Here, Dick Trickle (15) and Ted Musgrave demonstrate how it's done as their cars appear to glow under RIR's bright lights.

old half-mile corral that had existed before the Sawyers began their remarkable track renovations in 1988.

Alongside Earnhardt was Gordon, who missed beating Dale by just over .01 of a second. Ken Schrader and rookie contender Robert Pressley made up the second row, with Martin and Dave Marcis in fifth and sixth place. Marcis, who recently had been struggling to make races, benefited from a long conversation with Childress' crew chief, Andy Petree. Andy had told Dave the exact spring, shock and sway bar settings under Earnhardt's car, and when Dave went back to his Monte Carlo and installed the same handling package, his car went from struggling to top six!

Wallace took the inside of the fourth row with Sterling Marlin on his right, and Bobby Hamilton and Musgrave grabbed the final spots in the top 10. Brett Bodine and Ricky Rudd manned the sixth row.

The second round of qualifying was held during the daytime, and since the weather was warmer than it had been for the first session on Friday night, only six drivers chose to run to try to improve their times. Everyone else stood on their Friday night marks, which would prove to be a wise decision: None of those who ran in the second session made the field. The provisional starters were Lake Speed, rookie contender Ricky Craven, Jimmy Spencer

crew members mounted the pit wall and began inciting the crowd to do "The Wave" around the oval. The fans, eager for something to do, responded. As it caught on, television broadcasters who were trying to fill air time until the green flag dropped began keeping track of "wave-laps" by running a stopwatch to time the laps around the track.

Finally, with a weather window on the radar and with the track dry enough to begin competition, the green flag was dropped on the field at 9 p.m. It immediately became clear that a handful of cars were the class of the field. By half-distance, however, Wallace emerged from a tussle that had included himself, Gordon and Earnhardt. For the second half of the race, the only time Rusty fell from the point was when he gave up the lead during the last round

Rusty Wallace and his Penske South teammates proclaim themselves "Number One!" while Don Miller, keeping things in perspective, emphatically points out that it's the team's second win of the season.

of green-flag stops. When the field cycled through, he returned to the front and ran off to a five-second victory.

It was only his second win of the season (his first came in the spring at Martinsville), and the entire Miller team was jubilant. Richmond had once again rewarded the Missouri native; it was his fifth victory at the track and his fourth in the September night race.

Behind him, Terry Labonte barely edged Earnhardt for the runner-up slot after emerging in the second half of the race. Jarrett had fought his way through the field from his 27th starting position to claim fourth place. Bobby Hamilton had continued his string of strong performances and battled his way past Gordon with 12 laps remaining in the race to claim fifth place. John Andretti grabbed seventh, the first car a lap in arrears, and beat Rudd, Schrader and Musgrave in their own "lap-down" battle.

The lights had all but gone out on the title hopes of Martin and Marlin. Mark had lost a cylinder in the engine of the Valvoline Ford and was forced to struggle throughout the second half of the race with just seven cylinders. He had finished 15th, three laps behind — a very credible showing under the circumstances — and was now 433 points behind.

Sterling's Chevrolet had burned a gear during the morning practice session, and the team had borrowed a rear-end from another team for the race. After 268 laps, Sterling was behind the wall with rear-end problems from the borrowed part, but he did return to the fray after 38 laps. He was classified 33rd at the end of the race and lost another 91 points to Gordon. It also cost him second place in the standings, a position he had occupied since finishing ninth at New Hampshire in early July.

Dale Earnhardt leads the field through turns one and two as the Miller Genuine Draft 400 gets underway. Jeff Gordon, who started on the outside of the front row, would catch Dale on the second lap and lead the next 25.

Miller Genuine Draft 400

Race #24 — Final Race Results

Fin. Pos.	Str. Pos.	Car #	Driver	Team
1	7	2	Rusty Wallace	Miller Genuine Draft Ford
2	23	5	Terry Labonte	Kellogg's Chevrolet
3	1	3	Dale Earnhardt	Goodwrench Service Chevrolet
4	27	28	Dale Jarrett	Texaco Havoline Ford
5	9	43	Bobby Hamilton	STP Pontiac
6	2	24	Jeff Gordon	DuPont Auto Finishes Chevrolet
7	31	37	John Andretti	Kmart/Little Caesars Ford
8	12	10	Ricky Rudd	Tide Ford
9	3	25	Ken Schrader	Budweiser Chevrolet
10	10	16	Ted Musgrave	The Family Channel Ford
11	24	22	Ward Burton	MBNA America Pontiac
12	16	1	Rick Mast	Skoal Ford
13	20	8	Jeff Burton	Raybestos Brakes Ford
14	22	94	Bill Elliott	McDonald's Ford
15	5	6	Mark Martin	Valvoline Ford
16	11	11	Brett Bodine	Lowe's Ford
17	17	18	Bobby Labonte	Interstate Batteries Chevrolet
18	26	15	Dick Trickle	Ford Quality Care Ford
19	30	7	Geoff Bodine	Exide Batteries Ford
20	13	81	Kenny Wallace	TIC Financial Ford
21	35	9	Lake Speed	Spam/Melling Ford
22	15	17	Darrell Waltrip	Western Auto Chevrolet
23	38	98	Jeremy Mayfield	RCA Ford
24	29	75	Todd Bodine	Factory Stores Ford
25	21	42	Kyle Petty	Coors Light Pontiac
26	18	87	Joe Nemechek	Burger King Chevrolet
27	34	21	Morgan Shepherd	Citgo Ford
28	19	30	Michael Waltrip	Pennzoil Pontiac
29	36	41	Ricky Craven	Kodiak Chevrolet
30	4	33	Robert Pressley	Skoal Bandit Chevrolet
31	37	23	Jimmy Spencer	Smokin' Joe's Ford
32	25	26	Hut Stricklin	Quaker State Ford
33	8	4	Sterling Marlin	Kodak Film Chevrolet
34	14	12	Derrike Cope	Straight Arrow Ford
35	6	71	Dave Marcis	Olive Garden Chevrolet
36	28	77	Bobby Hillin	Jasper/USAir Ford
37	33	31	Greg Sacks	Hardee's Chevrolet
38	32	27	Elton Sawyer	Hooters Ford

MBNA America 500

Dover Downs International Speedway

September 17, 1995

•••••

A casual look at the Hendrick Motorsports DuPont team at work in the garage area at Denis McGlynn's Dover Downs International Speedway would never lead one to believe that these guys were in the middle of a point race for the most prestigious title in the world of stock car racing.

There was no muss, no fuss. Nor was there any strutting or gamesmanship. Instead, under the competent, level-headed leadership of crew chief Ray Evernham, each member of the team went about his job in workman-like fashion.

Dale Earnhardt had picked up 15 points at Richmond and closed the point gap between himself and Jeff Gordon slightly. But the black Chevrolet was still 279 points behind as the teams went about preparations for the newly named MBNA America 500 at the tricky Monster Mile in Delaware's capital city.

None of the crew members on either team had far to look to find their competition. They were within eight feet of each other in the garage area, and plenty of good-natured ribbing flowed back and forth between the two Chevrolet teams.

As Darrell Waltrip had predicted just two weeks before at the Mountain Dew Southern 500, the point battle had come down to just two teams. Sterling Marlin wasn't totally out of the race, but he was more than 300 points behind. In reality, the Kodak Chevrolet fielded by Morgan-McClure Racing was now battling Earnhardt and the Goodwrench car for second place.

*Ward Burton (dicing for position with Dave Marcis [71]) picked the right place and time to qualify fifth fastest: The MBNA 500 was sponsored by the same company that graces the flanks of his Bill Davis-owned Pontiac. And Burton wasn't the only one with good timing. Jeff Gordon's victory in the MBNA 500 (**right**) carried him a little closer to the NASCAR Winston Cup title and wowed the DuPont executives visiting from the company's headquarters in Wilmington, Del., less than an hour from the track.*

Just the sight of "Midnight" after Rusty Wallace had crunched the concrete wall during practice was enough to make the Miller Genuine Draft crew cringe. But from the "lemon" (Rusty's reserve car), the team made lemonade — a third-place finish.

Mark Martin's bad luck in the last two races had taken the championship fire out of the Valvoline team. Now, the effort had re-dedicated itself to winning as many races as possible during the remainder of the season to obtain the best point finish it could.

Tenuously holding onto fifth place in the standings, Ted Musgrave was staring intently in his rear-view mirror as Rusty Wallace and Terry Labonte made determined efforts to roust him from the final position in the top five. The two had chopped and hacked at Musgrave's margin, and their one-two finish at Richmond had moved Terry to within just 85 points of fifth place and Rusty to within 108.

By noon on Friday, as the teams worked their cars into qualifying trim, crew members were discussing recent events with raised eyebrows. Barry Dodson, the crew chief for the SABCO team fielding Coors Light Pontiacs for Kyle Petty, said he would be leaving the team at the end of the season. Also, Morgan Shepherd, who was winless for the season, would not be back with the Wood Brothers for the 1996 campaign. Dodson's decision made it three front-line teams — SABCO, Richard Childress Racing and Rudd Performance Motorsports — that would be searching for new crew chiefs for the coming season. In addition, Troy Selberg, the head wrench for Butch Mock's team, had indicated he also would be leaving at the end of the year, and no crew chief had been named for either the second Yates Racing team or the third Roush Racing team for the coming season!

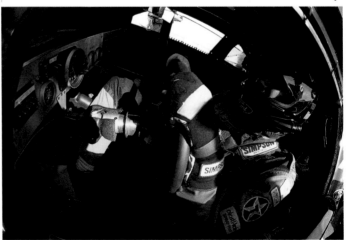

(Left) Jeff Gordon jumps away from the field on a restart — another indication of his dominance at Dover. Over the course of the afternoon, Jeff led 400 of the 500 laps en route to his seventh victory of the season. (Above) In qualifying, Rick Mast came up with a starting slot to match his car number after he notched the third pole of his career. It had been more than a year since he had posted his last pole position at the inaugural Brickyard 400 in Indianapolis.

The first qualifying session for the Dover field was filled with surprises. Perhaps no driver was more surprised than the pole-sitter! Rick Mast, whose Skoal Ford was fast off the truck, was on rails around the one-mile oval and notched the third pole of his career. It was barely .40 of a second faster than Gordon's mark, but it was enough to give Mast a reason to grin. His first pole, at Atlanta in November 1992, had been overshadowed by the hoopla surrounding the final race of Richard Petty's career, and the second had come at the inaugural Brickyard 400 just over a year ago.

Kyle Petty, the winner of Dover's May race, was back to form and claimed the inside of the second row. Bobby

The Wood Brothers' move to change drivers altered the complexion of the "Silly Season." With the seat of the Citgo Ford now open, the Woods would be besieged by calls and visits from drivers hoping to land the position with the first-rate effort.

One who would not be calling the Woods' shop in Stuart, Va., was Derrike Cope, who had signed an extension of his contract with Bobby Allison's team for the '96 season. After a strong start in '95, the team had experimented with chassis settings for several races and experienced poor results. But by mid-season, the team had gotten back on track by returning to the cars and settings from the beginning of the season and had run in the top 10 consistently in recent outings. Although small problems had hampered the team late in races, it was clearly on the right track. Everyone involved expected to begin locking down top finishes as the season headed for its end.

The Monster Mile was less than kind to Dale Jarrett. After starting 26th and working his way into the front pack, Jarrett cut a tire and kissed the concrete (not once, but twice!) less than 100 laps from the finish. He was eventually classified 30th.

*Jeff Gordon blew the field away at Dover, but Bobby Hamilton's performance in the STP Pontiac was equally impressive. Hamilton led for 83 laps midway through the race before finishing second, the highest finish for a Petty Enterprises car since 1987. Although he may not look it (**top left**), even The King was impressed with Hamilton's run!*

Labonte was right beside him. Ward Burton, carrying MBNA's colors on the flanks of his Bill Davis-owned Pontiac, did the race's sponsors proud and grabbed the inside of the third row, with Ricky Rudd on his right. Wallace was seventh-fastest in "Midnight," ahead of strong runs by Hut Stricklin, John Andretti and Jeremy Mayfield. Todd Bodine and Robert Pressley barely missed the top 10.

NASCAR officials had notified the teams that for the remainder of the 1995 races, the fastest 25 cars (rather than just the 20 quickest), would make the field in first-round qualifying, so Jeff Burton became the final qualifier during the first session. In the second qualifying period, Dale Jarrett turned a lap strong enough to be the sixth-fastest time overall. He would start from the 26th position on the grid.

Where was Earnhardt? Despite his pole at Richmond the week before, Dale was struggling this time. He would start 28th and have to fight his way through the field. Geoff Bodine and Michael Ritch, a part-time NASCAR Busch Series, Grand National Division competitor making his first NASCAR Winston Cup start in the Active Motorsports Chevrolet, were the provisional starters. Billy Standridge and Terry Fisher, who had spun and hit the wall during qualifying and damaged the RaDiUs team's only car, failed to make the field. The biggest surprise of qualifying was Greg Sacks' inability to get the Alan Dillard-owned Chevrolet into the field. Sacks had been the third-fastest driver during practice but couldn't get a qualifying lap fast enough to put the blue and orange Monte

Carlo into the field during the qualifying sessions.

Not too long ago, Dover's events were among the most sparsely attended races on the circuit. Over the last five years, however, McGlynn and his cohorts at the track have poured millions of dollars into facility improvements, including tens of thousands of additional grandstand seats, hospitality areas, walk-over bridges and camping and parking areas. The facility has been expanded each year, and the crowds have grown larger and larger.

On race day, a strange accident occurred between Kyle and Rusty during Saturday morning's practice session. Rusty's car, "Midnight," had an unfortunate meeting with the concrete wall. The Penske South team rolled the back-up off the transporter, so Wallace would start from the rear of the field for the Sunday event.

Since the start of the race was delayed for two hours while the track was dried from the morning's rain, there was ample time for the 96,000 fans to speculate on which black car would make it to the lead first and dispatch young Gordon from the point.

With DuPont's main honchos in attendance (their corporate headquarters are located less than an hour north in Wilmington), Gordon and his team had plenty of incentive to run well at the Monster Mile. No one, however, expected the team to make mincemeat of everyone in the field. The old-fashioned whipping began under gray skies, and by the time the sun peeped through, it was a done deal.

Part of Gordon's powerful victory came from the troubles of some teams that had been expected to challenge him. Part came from crew chief Evernham's gamble to put new, "sticker" Goodyears on the right side of the car and "scuffs" on the left during four-tire stops. Part came from the handling package under the blue Monte Carlo. And part came from Gordon's increasing maturity behind the wheel and his knowledge regarding when to push the car and when to take what it had.

It all added up to Jeff's seventh victory of the season. For the DuPont-sponsored team celebrating in front of the corporation's leading executives, it couldn't have come at a better track. If there had been any question of the company's commitment to the team, it would have been answered right on the spot.

Leading 400 of 500 laps is an overwhelming performance in any race, and Gordon may look back at the end of the season and point to the MBNA 500 as the key race on his way to a championship. Anyone who thought he and his team would be content to "stroke" their way to a championship needed merely to look at the Dover performance to understand the fire to win that burns in the bellies of every member of the blue-clad team.

Gordon's performance was brilliant, but equally impressive was Bobby Hamilton's run to the front. The STP Pontiac driver took the lead for a long stint (83 laps) midway through the race and was just over two seconds behind Gordon at the finish. It was the best finish for Richard Petty's car since 1987 and the highest Hamilton had ever finished in a NASCAR Winston Cup event.

To the delight of their fans, Wallace and Earnhardt both made great runs from the back of the field. Rusty took his reserve car to third, and Dale battled to fifth, finally subduing a persistent Marlin for the position with less than 30 laps to go. Joe Nemechek posted his best finish of the season with his Burger King Chevrolet, claiming fourth place.

Derrike Cope, after taking his Straight Arrow Ford to

the top five and staying there for most of the race, got tangled in a restart with Earnhardt and Wallace and lost the aerodynamic pressure on the nose of his Thunderbird. He was forced to settle for seventh place, a lap down. Martin, who had lost a lap with a mismatched set of tires during a green-flag run, finished eighth, ahead of Bobby Labonte (with an ill-handling car) and Rudd, who lost a lap when he was forced to return to the pits under green to have lug nuts tightened.

Dale Jarrett, who had taken his Havoline Ford all the way to the front pack, cut a tire just after the 400-lap mark and hammered the concrete wall. He then drifted across the track and bumped Mike Wallace. The two traveled up the track again, and both cars hit the wall. Mike emerged unscathed, but Jarrett suffered a broken left rib.

Rusty Wallace is not afraid to get down and dirty (figuratively speaking!) when it comes to turning wrenches and tuning engines. Besides, after smashing "Midnight" in a practice accident, Rusty probably figured the least he could do was lend a hand!

MBNA America 500
Race #25 — Final Race Results

Fin. Pos.	Str. Pos.	Car #	Driver	Team
1	2	24	Jeff Gordon	DuPont Auto Finishes Chevrolet
2	32	43	Bobby Hamilton	STP Pontiac
3	7	2	Rusty Wallace	Miller Genuine Draft Ford
4	24	87	Joe Nemechek	Burger King Chevrolet
5	28	3	Dale Earnhardt	Goodwrench Service Chevrolet
6	29	4	Sterling Marlin	Kodak Film Chevrolet
7	18	12	Derrike Cope	Straight Arrow Ford
8	16	6	Mark Martin	Valvoline Ford
9	4	18	Bobby Labonte	Interstate Batteries Chevrolet
10	6	10	Ricky Rudd	Tide Ford
11	13	16	Ted Musgrave	The Family Channel Ford
12	36	25	Ken Schrader	Budweiser Chevrolet
13	23	77	Bobby Hillin	Jasper/USAir Ford
14	12	33	Robert Pressley	Skoal Bandit Chevrolet
15	20	5	Terry Labonte	Kellogg's Chevrolet
16	34	23	Jimmy Spencer	Smokin' Joe's Ford
17	37	11	Brett Bodine	Lowe's Ford
18	17	94	Bill Elliott	McDonald's Ford
19	10	98	Jeremy Mayfield	RCA Ford
20	25	8	Jeff Burton	Raybestos Brakes Ford
21	5	22	Ward Burton	MBNA America Pontiac
22	22	41	Ricky Craven	Kodiak Chevrolet
23	15	15	Dick Trickle	Ford Quality Care Ford
24	39	7	Geoff Bodine	Exide Batteries Ford
25	14	29	Steve Grissom	Meineke Chevrolet
26	3	42	Kyle Petty	Coors Light Pontiac
27	35	71	Dave Marcis	Terramite Chevrolet
28	1	1	Rick Mast	Skoal Ford
29	30	30	Michael Waltrip	Pennzoil Pontiac
30	26	28	Dale Jarrett	Texaco Havoline Ford
31	38	90	Mike Wallace	Heilig-Meyers Ford
32	27	9	Lake Speed	Spam/Melling Ford
33	31	21	Morgan Shepherd	Citgo Ford
34	40	32	Michael Ritch	ATS Wood Recycling Chevrolet
35	21	40	Rich Bickle	Kendall Pontiac
36	19	17	Darrell Waltrip	Western Auto Chevrolet
37	11	75	Todd Bodine	Factory Stores Ford
38	8	26	Hut Stricklin	Quaker State Ford
39	9	37	John Andretti	Kmart/Little Caesars Ford
40	33	27	Elton Sawyer	Hooters Ford

GOODY'S 500

MARTINSVILLE SPEEDWAY

SEPTEMBER 24, 1995

•••••

L et's take a trip back a few years — say about 16 of them. A bright young challenger was driving a blue and yellow Chevrolet for a Californian named Rod Osterlund.

The team was only in its third year. It had a driver everyone expected to become a star and a 21-year-old crew chief in the final half of the season whose credentials merely read, "Wants to win more than anything else in the world."

That Osterlund Racing team had started the season hoping to win a few races and, if victory wasn't possible, wring the best possible finish from its Chevrolet.

During the first third of the year, the team had run at the front of the field with regularity, won here and there and put together top-10 finishes whenever it couldn't capture the victory. In the second third of the season, when everyone had expected the team's luck to take a turn for the worse, it simply kept chalking up top finishes. Soon, while the established stars of the sport were waiting for the inexperienced, young team to stumble, the sophomore driver made it to the head of the point standings.

Once again, the fans were treated to what has become a Martinsville tradition: "The Dale and Rusty Show." This time, it was Dale who came out on top; with just eight laps remaining in the race, Rusty's tires faded, allowing Earnhardt to take the lead and continue on for the win.

(Right) Martinsville's old master, Darrell Waltrip — he leads all active drivers with 11 wins here — takes rookies Robert Pressley and Ricky Craven (with Rudd in between) to school on Martinsville's inside line. Waltrip had a satisfying day, finishing eighth after steadily working his way into the top 10 from his 20th starting spot.

racing every event for a victory, rather than worry about points. Later, they all would admit that they were "young and dumb" and perhaps won the title in spite of several mistakes made during the course of the season.

Fast forward 16 years.

Now Earnhardt is the veteran driver, and it is the Richard Childress team that has no modern-day peer when it comes to winning titles. And just as before, it

(Left) Rusty Wallace was going for four straight wins at Martinsville, but it was not to be. First, his car was badly damaged in an early-race altercation with Ward Burton. Then, after working his way back to the front, Rusty was forced to stop on the track to avoid hitting Elton Sawyer (27) after Elton spun.
(Below) Although their teams are embroiled in battle at the top of the point standings, crew chiefs (left to right) Andy Petree, Ray Evernham and Tony Glover used the rain delay to engage in some friendly, casual conversation.

When the stretch run to the championship arrived, the two drivers closest to the point leader — Cale Yarborough and Richard Petty, together the winners of eight of the last nine championships — redoubled their efforts to make a run at the Osterlund team.

"Just watch this one," one veteran pit road observer had muttered as he nudged his companion. "It's time to fish or cut bait, and ol' Junior and Cale are gonna pull out the stops. The King and his guys from Level Cross aren't gonna run behind that new team, either.

"It won't be long before that California team has a change of luck, and then we'll see another race for the championship between Cale and Richard. That boy Earnhardt is good and he'll probably be a star some day, but he and that Osterlund bunch won't be able to match Cale and Richard when it comes to title time. Nobody knows more about winning championships than The King and Cale."

Dale Earnhardt, Doug Richert and the rest of "those boys down at that California team" obviously weren't listening. The pressure-packed stretch run came, and Osterlund's crew coolly stared down the superstars. Petty's challenge fizzled at North Wilkesboro and Martinsville. Earnhardt drilled Yarborough with a pair of wins at Martinsville and Charlotte. With their backs to the wall, Cale and car owner Junior Johnson clawed back with victories at Rockingham and Atlanta. But at the season finale in Ontario, Calif., Dale clinched his first championship by simply out-racing the three-time champion.

The new kids on the block had bucked the odds and won the NASCAR Winston Cup title. And they won it by

was beginning to look as though another group of upstart youngsters that had become tempered in the forge of the title chase would walk off with the championship. As race after race went into the record books, Jeff Gordon and his Rainbow Warriors, under the guidance of Ray Evernham, refused to bow to the pressure.

Instead, the team had won twice in the last three races and blunted every effort Earnhardt and Childress had made to close the gap in the points. Only once in the last 12 races had the team finished worse than sixth — and that was an eighth. Four victories were included in that string of 12 races, along with a pair of second-place finishes and two thirds.

Once again, youth and determination stared levelly at experience and motivation. This time, however, Earnhardt had found himself on the short end of the point table.

Things hadn't yet reached the desperate stage with the black-clad Goodwrench crew, but no one needed to remind the Childress team members that time was indeed ticking away with the passing of every race.

When the teams arrived at Clay Earles' lovely little half-mile in the Virginia highlands, everyone's eyes were focused on the battle between the two Chevrolet teams. Would this be the site of the "Great Turnaround"? Could Earnhardt make a run that would put him in the history books as the driver who had come from the furthest behind, the latest in the season, to wrest the championship from the point leader?

Gordon's lead was now 309 points over Earnhardt. The most points overcome by a NASCAR Winston Cup champion was 278 with six races remaining when Alan Kulwicki won the 1992 NASCAR Winston Cup Championship. There was no question Earnhardt's work was clearly cut out for him.

In addition to the championship chase, there were plenty of stories brewing to keep the media busy during the all-day rains on Friday and Saturday that kept the wheels from turning at Martinsville. Rusty Wallace had climbed to sixth place following Dover and now was just 73 points

behind Ted Musgrave, who currently occupied fifth place. Terry Labonte had fallen to seventh in the standings, but he was a mere 24 points behind Wallace in the three-way battle for the final position in the top five.

Bobby Labonte and crew chief Jimmy Makar had signed contract extensions with Joe Gibbs Racing, and both had committed to be with the team through the year 2000. Hut Stricklin was announced as the driver of the future for the Stavola Brothers after signing a three-year deal to take over the seat that would be vacated by Jeff Burton at the end of the season. Michael Waltrip and co-car owner Chuck Rider came to an agreement that would allow Michael to pursue his career with another team and leave the Pennzoil Pontiac team at the end of the season.

(Right) Although rain eventually washed out practice and qualifying at Martinsville, it provided Goodyear with an opportunity to test its new rain tire. Terry Labonte was the guinea pig, and after making several circuits around the half-mile speedway, he commented, "That's why the Formula One guys make so much money!"
(Below) Dale Earnhardt and his Goodwrench Chevrolet were superb at Martinsville: Dale started from the outside of the front row, led the most laps and captured his fourth win of the '95 season.

It didn't take long for Michael to become the leading candidate for the seat in the Wood Brothers Ford for the coming year! Finally, Barry Dodson and two other members of the SABCO team had packed their toolboxes and left the Coors Light team earlier in the week.

The biggest news, however, didn't involve the NASCAR Winston Cup teams. Instead, it was the NASCAR SuperTruck Series by Craftsman that was the focus of all the attention. Ernie Irvan would use the series to make his return to the sport. Just over a year after the accident (during an August Michigan practice session) that had nearly ended his life, Irvan had received medical clearance from all parties and planned to compete in the Saturday SuperTruck event. It was his first step toward resuming his career as a driver.

Unfortunately, the rains that swept the speedway meant that the starting fields for both the SuperTruck race

(rescheduled for Monday morning) and the NASCAR Winston Cup event would be determined according to owners' points. Because Ernie was a late entry and because he hadn't competed previously in the season, his truck didn't make the lineup. His return had to be postponed until the following weekend, when he would run in both the SuperTruck and NASCAR Winston Cup events at North Wilkesboro.

After the NASCAR rulebook had been consulted, Gordon and Earnhardt were placed on the front row for the start of the Goody's 500. Sterling Marlin and Mark Martin were lined up right behind them, and Ted Musgrave and Rusty Wallace made up the third row. The Brothers Labonte made up the fourth row with Terry on the inside, and Michael Waltrip and Morgan Shepherd, the future and present of the Wood Brothers team, were lined up side by side in the fifth row.

Because the starting lineup was determined by a combination of factors, including current car owner points,

winners from the previous year and entry-blank postmarks, Jeremy Mayfield, Todd Bodine, Hut Stricklin and Mike Wallace were forced to use provisionals to start the 500-lap event. Those who didn't make the field were Jimmy Hensley (back in the Alan Dillard Chevrolet), Greg Sacks (once again in the Active Motorsports Chevrolet), Rich Bickle (in the Felix Sabates/Dick Brooks Kendall Pontiac), Dave Marcis, Bobby Hillin and Kenny Wallace.

Sunday's weather was much cooler than Friday's and Saturday's — by as much as 20 degrees — but the rains had finally stopped. Teams that had tested at Martinsville earlier appeared to have a distinct advantage because of the lack of weekend practice time. One of the drivers expected to run at the front was Bobby Hamilton, who had driven the STP Pontiac at Martinsville in a test session that had produced some of the fastest lap times in the history of the flat half-mile. Bobby was given the 12th spot in the lineup based on points earned for car owner Richard Petty throughout the season.

(Left) The quarters on the half-mile short track are always tight, and this late-race restart is no exception. Jarrett, Elliott, Hamilton and Petty try to maintain their lead-lap status on the outside while Mike Wallace (90), Lake Speed (9), Jimmy Spencer (23) and Ward Burton (22) work the inside line to make up previously lost ground. (Below) The first days of autumn brought gray skies and cool temperatures to Martinsville, but that wasn't nearly enough to dampen the spirits of the capacity crowd on hand to witness the Cuppers on the beautiful half-mile oval.

Even in the early laps of the race, it was evident that Earnhardt had been dealt the best hand on this Sunday afternoon. He eased away from the field, led long stretches of the event and let Rusty Wallace and Terry Labonte wear out their cars, brakes and tires trying to catch him during the middle stages of the race. How good was Earnhardt's Chevrolet? For most of the race, he drove

using just his left hand, resting his right arm on part of the roll cage inside the Goodwrench Monte Carlo. Just your basic Sunday afternoon drive, right?

"Had the CD player on and listened to Brooks and Dunn," he said later. "Played a little Alabama, too."

The only time he got "up over the wheel" was in the final stages of the race, when a late-race caution led to a strategic move in the pits that eventually brought his fourth victory of the season. Earnhardt pitted on lap 464 for a pair of right-side tires, then lined up behind Wallace for the restart. Rusty hadn't made a stop for tires and was gambling that the Goodyears on the Miller Ford would be good enough to carry him to victory.

They weren't. Dale waited and waited while Rusty's tires (already 60 laps old) began giving a little in the corners. Finally, with eight laps remaining in the race, Wallace slipped in the corner. Earnhardt stuck his Monte Carlo in the low groove and eased past. He went on to pull away to a 1.3-second victory.

Behind him, Terry Labonte made his way past Wallace on the last corner of the last lap in a frantic run to the flag. Hamilton posted his third-straight top-five finish by fulfilling his team's expectations with a fourth place. Geoff Bodine returned to the front of the pack after an extended absence and finished fifth, while Bill Elliott claimed sixth place. Darrell Waltrip was eighth with a strong run, and Derrike Cope and Dale Jarrett rallied to finish ninth and 10th after bringing out the final caution of the race when they collided and spun while fighting for fifth place with less than 25 laps remaining.

Where was Gordon? Jeff had spent the day battling a brand-new car that didn't want to turn in the corners. He had been running 13th, but benefited from the Cope-Jarrett tussle and problems that befell others late in the race, including Sterling Marlin's ill-timed loss of the brakes on his Kodak Chevrolet (he had been running in the top five). Gordon finished seventh, and crew chief Evernham called the race "an embarrassment." Evernham vowed to leave all of the team's new cars in the shop for the remainder of the season and field nothing but the Monte Carlos the team had run earlier in the year for the rest of the races.

With his victory and the five bonus points for leading the most laps, Earnhardt had grabbed the maximum points available for the Martinsville weekend. He had gained 34 points on Gordon but still trailed by 275 with five races remaining on the schedule. Dale had made some headway but was still faced with having to gain an average of 55 points per race for the remainder of the season.

Everyone knew it wouldn't be an easy task, but no one was willing to count "The Intimidator" out just yet.

Goody's 500

Race #26 — Final Race Results

Fin. Pos.	Str. Pos.	Car #	Driver	Team
1	2	3	Dale Earnhardt	Goodwrench Service Chevrolet
2	7	5	Terry Labonte	Kellogg's Chevrolet
3	6	2	Rusty Wallace	Miller Genuine Draft Ford
4	12	43	Bobby Hamilton	STP Pontiac
5	17	7	Geoff Bodine	Exide Batteries Ford
6	11	94	Bill Elliott	McDonald's Ford
7	1	24	Jeff Gordon	DuPont Auto Finishes Chevrolet
8	20	17	Darrell Waltrip	Western Auto Chevrolet
9	16	12	Derrike Cope	Straight Arrow Ford
10	14	28	Dale Jarrett	Texaco Havoline Ford
11	28	42	Kyle Petty	Coors Light Pontiac
12	4	6	Mark Martin	Valvoline Ford
13	19	37	John Andretti	Kmart/Little Caesars Ford
14	8	18	Bobby Labonte	Interstate Batteries Chevrolet
15	25	15	Dick Trickle	Ford Quality Care Ford
16	33	98	Jeremy Mayfield	RCA Ford
17	36	90	Mike Wallace	Heilig-Meyers Ford
18	27	23	Jimmy Spencer	Smokin' Joe's Ford
19	10	21	Morgan Shepherd	Citgo Ford
20	22	9	Lake Speed	Spam/Melling Ford
21	32	22	Ward Burton	MBNA America Pontiac
22	21	11	Brett Bodine	Lowe's Ford
23	3	4	Sterling Marlin	Kodak Film Chevrolet
24	34	75	Todd Bodine	Factory Stores Ford
25	9	30	Michael Waltrip	Pennzoil Pontiac
26	23	29	Steve Grissom	Meineke Chevrolet
27	13	10	Ricky Rudd	Tide Ford
28	18	1	Rick Mast	Skoal Ford
29	5	16	Ted Musgrave	The Family Channel Ford
30	29	87	Joe Nemechek	Burger King Chevrolet
31	30	8	Jeff Burton	Raybestos Brakes Ford
32	15	25	Ken Schrader	Budweiser Chevrolet
33	31	27	Elton Sawyer	Hooters Ford
34	26	33	Robert Pressley	Skoal Bandit Chevrolet
35	24	41	Ricky Craven	Kodiak Chevrolet
36	35	26	Hut Stricklin	Quaker State Ford

TYSON HOLLY FARMS 400

NORTH WILKESBORO SPEEDWAY
OCTOBER 1, 1995
•••••

After Dale Earnhardt cruised to another grandfather clock at Martinsville (his sixth NASCAR Winston Cup victory at the track but his first in the fall race there since 1985!), a large group of media members should have been clustered around the rear of the black and silver GM Goodwrench Service transporter in North Wilkesboro's garage area.

Right next door, the rest of the media should have been standing around, waiting for Jeff Gordon to emerge, ready to ask questions about his 275-point lead and how he would approach the races remaining in the season. Would his team "bulletproof" his DuPont Chevrolet in hopes of giving him good finishes? Would the Hendrick Motorsport engine shop de-tune the power plants a touch, giving him more reliability as the chase for the Cup took on its final form? Could the young team withstand the charge that Earnhardt and the Richard Childress team would certainly make at the Rainbow Warriors in the last five races of the year?

Everyone should have been focused on the battle for the championship as the young challenger faced off against the wily veterans who together had won six championships in the last decade, including four of the last five.

The front row at North Wilkesboro was a family affair — the Roush family, that is! Teammates Ted Musgrave (16) and Mark Martin were more than a little delighted to capture the two most coveted spots on the starting grid. (Right) Ernie Irvan and wife Kim pose shortly before the start of the Tyson Holly Farms 400. For Ernie, the weekend had already been an "unqualified" success. After an absence of more than a year, Irvan had qualified second for Saturday's NASCAR SuperTruck race and seventh for the NASCAR Winston Cup event.

Members of Jack Roush's Valvoline team, en route to victory lane, congratulate Ernie Irvan on his fantastic return to the sport. Irvan did the Robert Yates team proud with a sixth-place finish in "88," a number reminiscent of Yates' earlier days with Bobby Allison and Darrell Waltrip.

This weekend, however, things were different.

The previous week's rains had played havoc with Martinsville's practice and qualifying sessions, and setting the fields via the rule book had postponed Ernie Irvan's return to the sport to this weekend. Ernie would try to qualify for both Saturday's NASCAR SuperTruck event and Sunday's Tyson Holly Farms 400. He would not return to the sport in stages, as originally set. Instead, he would try to run twice within 24 hours.

His NASCAR SuperTruck debut would be made in one of the Ford F-150s owned by himself and partner Mark Simo, which would carry the blue and yellow colors of NAPA. Joe Ruttman had been the team's driver throughout the season and was in contention for the year-long championship. Ernie's ride was a second entry from the team. Meanwhile, Robert Yates Racing crew chief Larry McReynolds had ridden herd on the Texaco Havoline team to prepare a second Ford Thunderbird for Ernie's return to the NASCAR Winston Cup level. The car was painted in the familiar black and tomato-red colors and carried the number "88" on its sides and roof.

"88"?

Robert Yates had chosen that number because it brought back pleasant memories of when he had built motors for DiGard and watched his power plants arrive in victory lane with both Robert Arthur Allison and Darrell Waltrip behind the wheel. The "88" will also be on the sides of his second team for 1996 — the effort fielded for driver Dale Jarrett, currently number "28."

It was easy to see that the focus of the weekend was on Irvan. Would he be competitive in his return to action? The sheer number of media members on hand stretched North Wilkesboro's meager press facilities to the bursting point, but Ernie did his best to accommodate the constant stream of reporters arriving at the rear of his transporters.

The questions began to be answered following qualifying sessions for both the NASCAR SuperTruck and Winston Cup events. Ernie qualified on the outside of the front row for the SuperTruck event, missing Mike Skinner's fastest lap by just a tick of the stopwatch. When he exited the blue and yellow Ford, his grin was a wide one, and if anyone had had any doubts about Ernie's passion, they were immediately erased. It was the Ernie of old — happy he had turned a lap good enough to start at the front of the field but disappointed that his time wasn't quite fast enough to claim the inside of the front row!

On the NASCAR Winston Cup side, his qualifying lap was just as impressive. He would start the race from the inside of the fourth row — seventh. Jarrett had been just a hair quicker and would start sixth. It had been quite a day for Irvan and for the entire Yates team, which had seen both its cars turn laps good enough for top-10 starting positions. The work done by McReynolds and his entire crew, providing first-rate equipment for both drivers, had been justified.

The Havoline team wasn't the only one delighted with its two-car effort during the first round of qualifying for the NASCAR Winston Cup event. Two drivers from another Ford team were grinning at each other over the roofs of their Thunderbirds.

Ted Musgrave and Mark Martin had the front row all to themselves for Sunday afternoon's 400-lapper. It was a great display of driver talent and team preparation. Musgrave had won his first pole of the season by bumping teammate Martin back to second fastest.

Bobby Hamilton continued his impressive performances with the Petty Enterprises entry, putting the STP Pontiac inside the second row. Hamilton's team members had received a scare Friday morning when they arrived at the track and found truck driver David Walker unconscious. Walker had been involved in a motorcycle accident earlier in the week and been treated for cuts and bruises, but he had driven the Petty transporter to North

with the Wood Brothers. He would change car makes — and motor oils! — and join longtime friends Eddie and Len Wood with the Stuart, Va., team.

Behind Jarrett and Irvan on the list of fast-timers were Ken Schrader and Morgan Shepherd, the driver Michael would replace in the red, white and blue Thunderbirds fielded by the Woods. Throughout the weekend, Morgan, when not belted behind the wheel of the Citgo Ford, was strolling through the garage area, talking with teams regarding a ride for the coming season.

Sterling Marlin, fighting to stay within reach of Gordon's point lead but at the same time battling with Earnhardt for the coveted runner-up position in the year-end point standings, took his Kodak Chevrolet to the final top-10 qualifying position, just ahead of Terry Labonte and Rich Bickle. Earnhardt and Gordon wouldn't have to look far to find each other on Sunday. They lined up, side by side, in the seventh row after Earnhardt turned the 13th-fastest lap, .2 miles per hour faster than Gordon. Jeff was disappointed with his effort — it was the team's worst qualifying session all season (other than a pair of times when Jeff had crashed).

(Left) Despite their crews' best efforts, neither Dale Earnhardt nor Bobby Hamilton would have a particularly good day. Earnhardt lost a lap during a green-flag stop en route to a ninth-place finish and consequently lost 27 points to Gordon in the title battle. Hamilton started a fine third but was relegated to 16th at the finish. (Below) Race fans might have thought they were seeing double on Sunday — they'd better get used to it. Robert Yates recently announced plans to field two cars for the remainder of the 1995 season: the No. 28 for Dale Jarrett and the No. 88 for Ernie Irvan.

Wilkesboro. During the night, though, he had become ill, and his team members hustled him to a hospital as soon as they had found him. Doctors performed surgery to remove Walker's damaged spleen.

Darrell Waltrip gave the garage denizens reason to blink when he cranked off the fourth-fastest lap of the first session. Michael Waltrip's fifth-fastest qualifying lap during the first session was a bittersweet one. It came with his current ride, the Bahari Racing Pennzoil Pontiac, on the heels of an announcement that Michael had signed a two-year contract (beginning in 1996)

With Rick Mast turning the fastest lap during the second round of qualifying, the final positions in the field were set. Kyle Petty, out of provisionals, made the field on his qualifying time — the Coors Light Pontiac was safely in the field in 27th place. Those using provisionals to make the field included Derrike Cope, John Andretti, Lake Speed and Robert Pressley. Others weren't so fortunate. Todd Bodine, Greg Sacks, Jeremy Mayfield, Ward and Jeff Burton, Mike Wallace and Jay Hedgecock all loaded their transporters at the end of the Saturday session.

The largest Saturday crowd in North Wilkesboro's history arrived to watch the NASCAR SuperTruck action. On the third lap, Irvan ripped past Skinner to take the lead. He ran in the top six throughout the first half of the race but was forced to retire when his team couldn't get a swaybar changed during the halfway break. Still, his return had thrilled the fans. He had been competitive and gone to the front like the Ernie of old. It was plenty to keep everyone talking until Sunday afternoon, when Ernie would be tried by fire behind the wheel of a NASCAR Winston Cup car — the first time in more than 13 months. Mike Bliss, with assistance from former SABCO crew chief Barry Dodson, won his first NASCAR SuperTruck race of the season, beating Butch Miller by just over a second.

(**Above**) *Nearly the entire field takes advantage of this caution to acquire some much-needed fuel and fresh rubber. This yellow was one of only two thrown during the race which combined accounted for only 10 laps.* (**Left / Inset**) *Ernie Irvan's fine performances in the NASCAR Winston Cup and SuperTruck events upstaged Mark Martin's impressive victory in the Tyson Holly Farms 400, but Martin didn't mind; he was delighted to again share the road with his longtime friend.*

A full house was on hand when the green flag dropped Sunday afternoon on the Tyson Holly Farms 400. At the start, Musgrave, Hamilton and Martin fought at the front of the field for the lead. Others came to the front following the event's first caution and, as the race ground on under green, Irvan became one of the leaders. It brought a roar of approval from the tens of thousands in attendance. Eventually, Ernie dropped off the point, but he ran steadily throughout the remainder of the event and was sixth at the finish, on the lead lap. It was an outstanding performance. Irvan, who had been given a 10 percent chance of survival

Jack Roush is double-fisting the stopwatches in practice for the Tyson Holly Farms 400. Any worries he may have had about his teams' preparations were put to rest when The Family Channel and Valvoline Fords snagged the first and second starting spots, respectively.

after his Michigan practice accident 13 months before, had beaten all the odds and made a triumphant return to the sport he loved.

At the front of the field, Martin began to assert himself with the Valvoline Ford. Since his Watkins Glen victory in August, Mark and the Roush team had struggled, finishing just once in the top five. At North Wilkesboro, Mark was patient, not abusing his tires, waiting to see what his mount wanted on this sunny Sunday afternoon. He kept waiting and waiting, but the Ford stayed perfect. Finally, he decided to let the Thunderbird have its head and began to cut into the eight seconds separating him from the race leaders.

With just over 50 laps to go, the red, white and blue Ford was back at the point and had the race in hand. Only Ricky Rudd's Tide Ford appeared to have enough mustard to run with the Roush car.

When Jarrett was tapped by Hut Stricklin on lap 368, sending the Ford into the first-turn wall, the second yellow flag of the race waved, and the leaders went to pit road. This set the stage for what many thought would be a late-race battle between Martin and Rudd. Mark's team did its work, turning the Valvoline Ford off pit road and back into the lead. Rudd's hopes were dashed, however. NASCAR officials brought the Tide Ford back onto pit road so a lug nut could be attached (only four were on the left-front wheel), and Ricky lined up seventh for the restart.

When the green flag flew, just 25 laps remained, and Martin set sail. Although Rusty Wallace did his best to catch the flying Ford with his own version of the car, he had nothing for the Roush machine at the end. Mark won his third race of the season and Wallace took second, less than a second behind. Rusty was delighted with his runner-up position. In his last five races, he had finished third, third, first, third and second, and he knew that all the pieces were finally in position.

Gordon fought his way to a "safe and sound" third place, barely ahead of teammate Terry Labonte, while Rudd passed Irvan in the final 10 laps to claim fifth place. Jarrett recovered from his late-race mishap to finish seventh, the final car on the lead lap. Schrader was eighth (his Budweiser Chevrolet was the first car a lap down), which gave Hendrick Motorsports three cars in the top eight positions at the end of the race.

Earnhardt failed in his quest to close the gap on Gordon. He fought a misfiring engine and lost a lap during a green-flag pit stop on his way to a ninth-place finish. The points he had gained the previous weekend at Martinsville had evaporated. He had lost 27 points to Gordon at North Wilkesboro and, as the teams packed up and headed out of the Brushy Mountains, was now 302 behind.

Tyson Holly Farms 400
Race #27 — Final Race Results

Fin. Pos.	Str. Pos.	Car #	Driver	Team
1	2	6	Mark Martin	Valvoline Ford
2	18	2	Rusty Wallace	Miller Genuine Draft Ford
3	14	24	Jeff Gordon	DuPont Auto Finishes Chevrolet
4	11	5	Terry Labonte	Kellogg's Chevrolet
5	24	10	Ricky Rudd	Tide Ford
6	7	88	Ernie Irvan	Texaco Havoline Ford
7	6	28	Dale Jarrett	Texaco Havoline Ford
8	8	25	Ken Schrader	Budweiser Chevrolet
9	13	3	Dale Earnhardt	Goodwrench Service Chevrolet
10	32	94	Bill Elliott	McDonald's Ford
11	16	7	Geoff Bodine	Exide Batteries Ford
12	5	30	Michael Waltrip	Pennzoil Pontiac
13	33	12	Derrike Cope	Straight Arrow Ford
14	4	17	Darrell Waltrip	Western Auto Chevrolet
15	10	4	Sterling Marlin	Kodak Film Chevrolet
16	3	43	Bobby Hamilton	STP Pontiac
17	34	37	John Andretti	Kmart/Little Caesars Ford
18	22	18	Bobby Labonte	Interstate Batteries Chevrolet
19	29	15	Dick Trickle	Ford Quality Care Ford
20	1	16	Ted Musgrave	The Family Channel Ford
21	17	41	Ricky Craven	Kodiak Chevrolet
22	23	11	Brett Bodine	Lowe's Ford
23	9	21	Morgan Shepherd	Citgo Ford
24	31	77	Bobby Hillin	Jasper/USAir Ford
25	25	26	Hut Stricklin	Quaker State Ford
26	26	1	Rick Mast	Skoal Ford
27	12	40	Rich Bickle	Kendall Pontiac
28	15	71	Dave Marcis	Olive Garden Chevrolet
29	19	31	Jimmy Hensley	Hardee's Chevrolet
30	27	42	Kyle Petty	Coors Light Pontiac
31	30	29	Steve Grissom	Meineke Chevrolet
32	28	87	Joe Nemechek	Burger King Chevrolet
33	36	33	Robert Pressley	Skoal Bandit Chevrolet
34	21	27	Elton Sawyer	Hooters Ford
35	35	9	Lake Speed	Spam/Melling Ford
36	20	23	Jimmy Spencer	Smokin' Joe's Ford

UAW-GM QUALITY 500

CHARLOTTE MOTOR SPEEDWAY
OCTOBER 8, 1995
• • • • •

The winds of change weren't the only ones blowing around Charlotte Motor Speedway when the teams assembled for the annual OctoberFast at Humpy Wheeler's 1.5-mile track. Hurricane Opal had whipped into the Southeast, blanketing Charlotte with clouds, rain and windy conditions.

As sheets of rain lashed the Speedway's grounds on opening day, NASCAR and Charlotte Motor Speedway officials scrambled to rearrange the practice and qualifying schedule.

The fall Charlotte race traditionally draws one of the largest media crowds of the second half of the season, and many teams use the weekend's activities to disclose their plans for the coming year. It's one of the best times to gain "ink" for a new sponsor or make changes within a team. Despite the threatening weather, this year was no different. The announcements this fall at Charlotte included Chuck Rider and Lowrance Harry naming Johnny Benson Jr., the current NASCAR Busch Series point leader, the new driver of the Bahari team's Pennzoil Pontiac; Johnny had signed a three-year contract. RCA signed on for another year with Cale Yarborough's team. Cale also announced that he had re-signed current driver Jeremy Mayfield and had locked up the youngster with options for the next seven years!

A rare sight! After failing to make a timed run fast enough to qualify for a starting spot, Dale Earnhardt was forced to exercise his former champion's provisional to gain entry to the field and rode shotgun for the start.

(Right) Mark Martin's Valvoline Thunderbird and Bobby Hamilton's STP Pontiac handled well throughout the race. Both drivers ran in the top 10 all day, but by the race's final stages, it was Martin and his Steve Hmiel-led team who had their machine dialed in perfectly. Mark set sail for the top spot, leaving Hamilton to finish 10th.

Jeff Gordon's hopes for a victory took a major hit (as did his lead in the points) when the driveline in the DuPont Chevrolet failed during a mid-race pit stop. The crew, forced to push the car behind the wall for repairs, returned Jeff to action 14 laps later. He eventually finished 30th and lost 97 points to Earnhardt in the process.

Ricky Craven, the leader in this year's MAXX Rookie of the Year competition, became a part owner of the Larry Hedrick team he drives for, giving the New Englander a much greater sense of security. D.K. Ulrich sold his interests in the No. 77 team to his partner, Doug Bawel, and others, including driver Bobby Hillin. Hooters President Bob Brooks disclosed that he had completed arrangements to purchase the remainder of the No. 27 team from Junior Johnson and then sell it to current crew chief Mike Hill and driver Elton Sawyer.

One of the headline-grabbers of the weekend was the news that Felix Sabates had hired three people from the Penske South organization: David Evans, who had been one of the keys to Rusty Wallace's engine program through the years, Billy Woodruff, who would become the new crew chief on the Coors Light Pontiac driven by Kyle Petty (former SABCO crew chief Barry Dodson had left just a couple of weeks before), and Ronnie Phillips, a cylinder-head specialist at Penske South who would assume that same role at SABCO.

On Friday, the weather cleared and practice began in earnest for the delayed first round of qualifying. Just a few hours before qualifying began, and while the garage area was still trying to absorb the news about the SABCO organization, word came that crew chief Jeff Hammond and car owner Dick Brooks had parted ways.

And there were still more surprises in store, at least for Ricky Rudd. Rudd arrived at his Tide Ford and found a "trophy" taped to the dash. It was a lug nut, accompanied by a note advising Rudd it was the "first-place North Wilkesboro trophy," a reminder of the previous Sunday's activities in the Brushy Mountains. It had been mounted by Dan Ford, known throughout the garage area as "Fossil" because, according to

Ward Burton, in the midst of another impressive run, is chased by Terry Labonte through Charlotte's fourth turn. Following the race's sixth caution, Ward rocketed to the point and opened a huge lead while fronting the field for 42 laps. His car developed a push, however, and he eventually finished seventh.

Rudd, "He's so old!" Ford had worked with Ricky during their days together with Hendrick Motorsports, where Ford is still employed.

Rudd got another surprise during the first round of qualifying; he became the only driver to turn a sub-30-second lap and claimed his second pole position of the season. Ricky had been the fastest qualifier earlier in the year at Sears Point and was quick to credit his crew for his success in winning the pole for the Charlotte race. Because Bill Ingle had announced a month previously that he would leave the team at the end of the season, Rudd said, "It would have been easy for our crew to start going off in three or four different directions. Instead, it's a credit to them that they have remained focused on the goals at hand — and that includes a victory before the end of the season."

In Friday's qualifying session, Rudd had had to use all there was in the Ford to keep a rookie off the pole. Ricky Craven, bolstered by his partial ownership role in the Hedrick team, nearly won a berth in the 1996 Busch Clash

strong qualifying run to claim the fourth slot for the Sunday race. Mark Martin and Morgan Shepherd made up the third row, just ahead of Todd Bodine and Terry Labonte; Bobby Hamilton and Ward Burton put their Pontiacs into the fifth row, just ahead of Jeremy Mayfield and Dick Trickle.

The biggest shock of the weekend came after the second round of qualifying had been completed. Dale Earnhardt's time during the second round (he had failed to make the top 15 during the first day) was not good enough to make the field! He used a former champion's provisional to get into the field and was the 43rd, or last, starter for Sunday's UAW-GM Quality 500. It was only the second time in his career that he had had to use a provisional to make a field — the only other time had been at Michigan in 1992!

(*Top right*) *This loyal fan came to Charlotte intent on wishing the popular redhead a happy 40th birthday. (**Above**) And for a while, it looked as though Bill would have more than his birthday to celebrate. After starting 28th, Bill threaded his way through the pack, and by the race's midpoint, he was in position to challenge the leaders. But a double celebration was not to be; Bill eventually faded to a 20th-place finish.*

at Daytona with his Charlotte qualifying run. He was just over seven-hundredths of a second slower than Rudd and put the Kodiak Monte Carlo on the outside of the front row.

Jeff Gordon, whom everyone expected to breeze through Charlotte and increase his point lead over Dale Earnhardt, had the third-fastest of the 48 cars that ran in the first qualifying session. Michael Waltrip turned in a

Others who used provisionals to climb into the starting field for the race were Derrike Cope, Mike Wallace, Elton Sawyer and Rich Bickle (in the crew chief-less Kendall Pontiac). Those forced to watch from the sidelines were Chad Little, Kenny Wallace, Jeff Purvis, Delma Cowart and Billy Standridge.

Earnhardt's failure to qualify was the hot item of con-

versation, particularly because Gordon had landed on the inside of the second row. Dale, however, seemed unconcerned and brushed aside the questions, saying that the GM Goodwrench Service Chevrolet would be plenty good enough to get to the front of the field.

When the green flag dropped on the 334-lap affair, it became clear that the seven-time champion's confidence was justified. Earnhardt, trailing by 302 points, knew exactly what he had to do — roll through the entire field to the front, as quickly as possible. He needed every available point and some poor luck for Gordon during the last four races to put any pressure on the DuPont driver.

Earnhardt's charge through the field alone was worth the price of admission. He blasted his way to 29th after the first caution flag flew on lap seven and was 20th when the second yellow came out for the field 16 laps later. At that point, the "Flying Aces" gave Earnhardt a two-tire stop, which vaulted him 14 positions toward the front of the field; after just 27 laps, the menacing black Chevrolet was sixth. From then on, he ran in the lead pack; he also went to the point for two circuits on lap 238, grabbing five bonus points.

Despite his team's constant adjustments during the race, however, Dale could not work himself into position to fight for the lead — mainly because a Valvoline Ford, for the second-straight week, held all the aces when it came to show-down time.

For the longest time, it looked like Terry Labonte was going to match younger brother Bobby's May victory at Charlotte, giving them a sweep of this year's events at the 1.5-mile oval. And, as the race wound toward its conclusion, it looked like Rudd, who had led handily during the race, would be but a distant challenger. Terry's gamble of taking right-side tires during his final stop gave him track position and eventually the lead but was also his undoing.

Martin's final pit stop included four fresh Goodyears, and the decision to take stickers on all four corners cost him time. He was fifth on lap 278 and worked hard to find a way past Rudd. He finally did, with 40 laps left in the race, and was grinning to himself, thinking that he was in the lead, when a voice crackled in his radio earpiece.

"Nice work, Mark," crew chief Steve Hmiel exclaimed, congratulating his driver. "Really good job. Now you're only six seconds behind Terry, and he's leading the race."

Martin's delight turned to chagrin. He couldn't even see Labonte on the race track.

"I figured that we were just racing for second at that point," Martin said after the event. "But then Steve started telling me that I was cutting into Terry's lead, and as lap after lap went by, pretty soon I could see Terry in the distance.

"It became pretty clear that Terry's tires were going away, and our car was stable on the four new tires. We just kept working and working, and Terry kept getting closer and closer."

With 22 laps to go, Mark had chopped the margin to 3.7 seconds, and 12 laps later, he was 1.6 seconds behind. The fans who had thought about leaving sat back down! With six laps to go, Mark was within six car-lengths; then, with just four laps remaining, he caught the Kellogg's Chevrolet and passed Labonte. There was nothing Terry could do. His car was slipping and sliding as he tried to complete 120 laps on left-side tires. And on the final lap, Earnhardt also moved past Labonte to claim second place at the conclusion of the 500-miler.

Labonte finished third, Rudd a fine fourth and Dale Jarrett fifth. Sterling Marlin was sixth, and Ward Burton posted a seventh-place finish with the Bill Davis Pontiac. Bobby Labonte, Rusty Wallace and Bobby Hamilton claimed the final positions in the top 10, with Hamilton barely nipping Derrike Cope, who had another strong run in Bobby Allison's Ford.

While Martin was celebrating his second-straight victory in the winner's circle, plenty of high-fiving was going on in the Goodwrench transporter. Earnhardt's brilliant run to second place had brought him 175 points in the battle for the championship, and this time, they were even more meaningful.

Gordon had snapped the rear end in his Chevrolet during a pit stop on lap 140 — the Rainbow Warriors had been frantic in their repairs of the DuPont machine. They replaced the broken parts in just 14 laps and returned Gordon to the track, where he made up one of his lost

Of Darrell Waltrip's six career victories at Charlotte Motor Speedway, only one has come in the fall 500-miler (in 1981). He would not fare much better this year: After starting from the 32nd position, Darrell was collected in an altercation with Ricky Craven on lap 165 and came to rest at the end of pit road. He was unable to continue and was credited with a 34th-place finish.

laps. His string of 15 consecutive top-10 finishes, however, had ended; he was classified 30th at the conclusion of the race. The track had punished the youngster and presented the seven-time champion with a big gain of 97 points.

As the teams headed home for a weekend off (the first one since the Brickyard 500 on August 5), Dale found himself a little higher in the standings but 205 points behind.

There was still a long way to go — and Gordon was still in command.

The question, as preparations began for Rockingham, was whether this new tension in the point battle was the Real Deal or just a tease.

Mark Martin is a happy camper in Charlotte's victory lane after claiming his second-consecutive victory and his fourth of the season. With this win, Mark Martin had "hit for the cycle" in 1995: He had won events at a restrictor-plate superspeedway (Talladega), a road course (Watkins Glen), a short track (North Wilkesboro) and now, the 1.5-mile Charlotte Motor Speedway.

UAW-GM Quality 500

Race #28 — Final Race Results

Fin. Pos.	Str. Pos.	Car #	Driver	Team
1	5	6	Mark Martin	Valvoline Ford
2	43	3	Dale Earnhardt	Goodwrench Service Chevrolet
3	8	5	Terry Labonte	Kellogg's Chevrolet
4	1	10	Ricky Rudd	Tide Ford
5	31	28	Dale Jarrett	Texaco Havoline Ford
6	14	4	Sterling Marlin	Kodak Film Chevrolet
7	10	22	Ward Burton	MBNA America Pontiac
8	24	18	Bobby Labonte	Interstate Batteries Chevrolet
9	20	2	Rusty Wallace	Miller Genuine Draft Ford
10	9	43	Bobby Hamilton	STP Pontiac
11	39	12	Derrike Cope	Straight Arrow Ford
12	36	23	Jimmy Spencer	Smokin' Joe's Ford
13	16	37	John Andretti	Kmart/Little Caesars Ford
14	6	21	Morgan Shepherd	Citgo Ford
15	18	42	Kyle Petty	Coors Light Pontiac
16	34	7	Geoff Bodine	Exide Batteries Ford
17	4	30	Michael Waltrip	Pennzoil Pontiac
18	21	26	Hut Stricklin	Quaker State Ford
19	17	16	Ted Musgrave	The Family Channel Ford
20	28	94	Bill Elliott	McDonald's Ford
21	26	9	Lake Speed	Spam/Melling Ford
22	15	87	Joe Nemechek	Burger King Chevrolet
23	40	90	Mike Wallace	Heilig-Meyers Ford
24	23	77	Bobby Hillin	Jasper/USAir Ford
25	2	41	Ricky Craven	Kodiak Chevrolet
26	7	75	Todd Bodine	Factory Stores Ford
27	22	11	Brett Bodine	Lowe's Ford
28	41	27	Elton Sawyer	Hooters Ford
29	11	98	Jeremy Mayfield	RCA Ford
30	3	24	Jeff Gordon	DuPont Auto Finishes Chevrolet
31	13	8	Jeff Burton	Raybestos Brakes Ford
32	12	15	Dick Trickle	Ford Quality Care Ford
33	33	32	Greg Sacks	Fina/Lance Chevrolet
34	32	17	Darrell Waltrip	Western Auto Chevrolet
35	29	25	Ken Schrader	Budweiser Chevrolet
36	35	1	Rick Mast	Skoal Ford
37	27	19	Loy Allen	Healthsource Health Plan Ford
38	42	40	Rich Bickle	Kendall Pontiac
39	38	31	Jimmy Hensley	Hardee's Ford
40	25	71	Dave Marcis	Olive Garden Chevrolet
41	37	29	Steve Grissom	Meineke Chevrolet
42	19	33	Robert Pressley	Skoal Bandit Chevrolet
43	30	93	Gary Bradberry	Bradberry Racing Chevrolet

ACDELCO 400

NORTH CAROLINA MOTOR SPEEDWAY

OCTOBER 22, 1995

•••••

The ACDelco 400 weekend had all the makings of a spectacular event and, true to its promise, the 400-miler in the North Carolina Sandhills was an event that will be talked about for years to come.

Much had been done at the track since the NASCAR Winston Cup teams had loaded their transporters following last February's event, the season's second race. Construction crews had razed the garage area, then built an entirely new one, as well as a new infield media center for participants and a new area for Goodyear's service crews to mount and dismount the racing Eagles. Suites, seats, concession and rest room facilities had also been renovated at the oval. During the opening days of the ACDelco 400 weekend, additional plans for more work on suites, the press box and spectator seats (to be completed by the February 1996 event) were unveiled. The track's management, led by President Jo Wilson and General Manager Chris Browning, had made great strides toward bringing the facility up to snuff and, with the additional plans, shown everyone that the one-mile oval would remain a player in the NASCAR Winston Cup world.

During the annual Unocal 76/Rockingham Pit Crew Championship, Junior Johnson's "11" team, led by Dean Combs, got driver Brett Bodine in and out of the pits in 23.692 seconds to capture the coveted title and pit road bragging rights for a year. In the process of acquiring a fourth pit crew title for Johnson (the others came in 1969, '72 and '79), the crew posted the only sub 24-second stop of the competition. (Right) Bill Davis' MBNA team leads a flurry of activity on pit road during an early-race caution period. Their fine work kept driver Ward Burton in the lead pack all afternoon, and Ward rewarded them with their first-ever trip to victory lane.

Many of the questions left unanswered at Charlotte were resolved at Rockingham. Ricky Rudd's Tide Ford team had announced that Richard Broome would be its leader for the 1996 season. He would head over to the RPM shop at the conclusion of the current season from his present position on the Kenny Bernstein team.

Troy Selberg, crew chief for the Butch Mock team and driver Todd Bodine, indicated he was leaving the Factory Stores-sponsored Ford team at the conclusion of the current season and would rejoin driver Lake Speed (with whom he had worked in the past) and the Melling Racing/Spam effort for the 1996 season. Todd Parrott had decided to accept the job offer from the

(Above) It was a day of "threes" for Mark Martin: He was shooting for his third-straight win, finished third in the race and, as a result, moved from fourth to third in the point standings. Trailing Mark is No. 3, Dale Earnhardt, who finished seventh. The trio of Darrell Waltrip (17), Ricky Rudd (10) and Steve Grissom (29) finished 12th, 13th and 14th, respectively — all were one lap down.

(Left) Jeff Gordon's story at the ACDelco 400 can be summed up in three words: pit road woes. Twice he was caught in the pits when the yellow flag flew, and once he was tagged and spun while trying to enter the pits. Here, Jeff's crew checks for damage after his spin. Jeff eventually finished 20th, two laps down, and lost 43 points to Dale Earnhardt in the chase for the championship.

Andy Petree, would leave to rejoin Leo Jackson for 1996, promoted longtime jackman David Smith to the role of crew chief and also moved Bobby Hutchens into the team manager's role. The pair would share decisions affecting research and development, and shop and at-track preparation and strategy.

The big news, however, was that Junior Johnson was negotiating to sell his famed "11" team to current driver Brett Bodine. Junior said the sale of the team carrying the number "27" (to Hooters' Bob Brooks, driver Elton Sawyer and crew chief Mike Hill) was expected to be completed following the Atlanta race and that his interests in the Travis Carter team (remaining intact for 1996 with Camel and driver Jimmy Spencer) had already been resolved — "a done deal," in Junior's words.

If Brett and Junior were able to come to terms and complete the sale of the "11" team, it would mean that for the first time in three decades, Junior would not have a team competing when the NASCAR Winston Cup tour unloaded at Daytona for the beginning of the season. Johnson said his reasons for selling his teams included his desire to spend more time with his family, which includes two young children. "I just think that this is a wise choice for me," Junior said when asked about his intentions.

newly formed second team from Robert Yates Racing. He would work with Ernie Irvan for the remainder of this year and then be the crew chief for Dale Jarrett and Yates' "88" Ford for the coming season. Parrott was yet another key player on the Penske South team who had decided to leave the Rusty Wallace effort and move to another team for the 1996 season.

Dick Brooks reached within his group and promoted Lance Hill to the crew chief's position after Jeff Hammond departed. And Brooks wasn't the only car owner to promote from within. Richard Childress, whose crew chief,

If that weren't enough to keep media members busy during a rain-soaked Friday at the track, there was another chapter to be chronicled in Ernie Irvan's return to the sport. Ernie had finished third in the NASCAR SuperTruck Series event during the "off" weekend between Charlotte and Rockingham and was back in the second Havoline Ford fielded by Yates at The Rock. An extensive test at the track had shown Ernie to be highly competitive, and everyone involved with the Yates effort expected to see the No. 88 near the front of the field following qualifying.

It didn't happen, however, thanks to a strange combination of circumstances that unfolded during the abbreviated Saturday morning practice session. Because rains had swept the track Friday, the Cup teams had only one hour of practice and a single qualifying session. The Unocal/Rockingham Pit Crew Championship also took place, with Brett Bodine and the Johnson team beating Kyle Petty and the SABCO effort in the annual pit crew battle.

Early in that one-hour practice session, Lake Speed had abruptly pulled up onto the racing surface after he finished warming up his Ford on the apron of the track. Todd Bodine, making practice laps, was surprised by Lake's move and got out of the gas to avoid a collision. Irvan, not expecting Bodine to lift, nailed the rear of the Factory Stores Thunderbird. Needless to say, the crews of the two teams had some early-morning work to do.

Todd's team took one look and decided to turn the "pit

Right-rear tire-changer Rick Viers makes his case to a NASCAR official; he is adamant that all five lug nuts are in place on the Goodwrench Chevrolet. He argued to no avail: Earnhardt was black-flagged seconds later.

stop" car into a race car. Ernie's team began making hasty repairs to the Havoline 'Bird. The Yates crew worked right up until qualifying time, but when the single round of time trials had been completed, Irvan's lap was only the 42nd-fastest on the list. The field contained just 38 spots, so Ernie, with no provisionals, was forced to wait until Phoenix to continue his Cup comeback.

Irvan's situation overshadowed the enormous amount of work done by Butch Mock's Factory Stores team, which turned what was essentially a "show car" into a race car in a very short amount of time. Todd put the Ford into the field with the 33rd-fastest lap and was effusive about his crew's accomplishments.

The shining moment of qualifying, however, was Hut Stricklin's capture of his first career NASCAR Winston Cup pole. The Calera, Ala., native was the 14th driver to hit the pavement, so he had been forced to wait while 33 drivers made their attempts to dislodge him from the pole. None could. It was Stricklin's first pole — the high mark of the season for a driver who had begun the year without a ride. It was also the first pole for the Kenny Bernstein-owned team since 1993.

Michael Waltrip rocketed the Pennzoil Pontiac to the second-fastest lap and claimed his best starting position of the season. Ward Burton slapped his MBNA Pontiac on the inside of the second row, with point leader Jeff Gordon alongside. Mark Martin, looking for a third-consecutive victory, was the fifth-fastest qualifier, and Dick Trickle made a statement about Bud Moore's Quality Care Thunderbird by putting it solidly on the outside of the third row, just a tick faster than Rudd's effort in the Tide Ford.

(Inset) In his 192nd NASCAR Winston Cup start, Hut Stricklin captured his first career Busch Pole Award. (Left) Hut led the first eight laps but would soon be overtaken by third-place starter Ward Burton. Michael Waltrip (30), who started from the other front-row spot, is being chased by fourth-place starter Jeff Gordon.

Darrell Waltrip was grinning after his lap. He was eighth-fastest and felt he had a real shot at victory at Rockingham. Joe Nemechek turned in a sterling qualifying effort with the Burger King Chevrolet and claimed the inside of the fifth row, while Derrike Cope had yet another good qualifying run with Bobby Allison's Ford, grabbing the final top-10 slot, just ahead of Morgan Shepherd. Gary Bradberry, driving the Alan Dillard Chevrolet on a one-shot basis, sparkled with a lap good enough for 12th!

Dale Earnhardt, who had hoped to maintain his momentum from Charlotte, was disappointed with his 20th-fastest lap. Lake Speed and Shane Hall, in the Dick Brooks Pontiac, used provisionals to get into the field. Dave Marcis, with no provisionals left, was unable to make the field after crashing during his qualifying lap. Loy Allen, Jay Hedgecock, Norm Benning and Allen Russell also failed to make the field.

Richard Brickhouse, a longtime NASCAR Winston Cup competitor who last competed in 1982, attempted to make a comeback at Rockingham. The Rock had been the site of his NASCAR Winston Cup debut in 1968 (he finished fourth), but things had changed considerably since then, as the 56-year-old driver soon discovered. Brickhouse, in a Chevrolet owned by Dr. Dick Skillen (of Chapel Hill, N.C.), was more than 10 miles per hour too slow to make the field. He would have to wait for another day to attempt his comeback to the sport.

On Sunday afternoon, when the green flag fell on the first 400-miler in the history of the track, Rick Mast found himself behind the wheel of a green and black rocketship. He worked his way to the front from his 16th starting position and dominated the first half of the race. No one had anything for the Skoal driver during those first 250 laps, and it appeared that Mast was headed for his first NASCAR Winston Cup victory. The dream ended abruptly, however, after Rick slowed on the track — engine failure had put him out of the event.

Earnhardt then went to the lead, and it appeared as though the seven-time champion was in the catbird's seat to chop a pile of points from Gordon's lead. Jeff was in trouble. He had been clipped and spun by Greg Sacks and twice had been caught by yellow flags immediately after his green-flag stops. Despite the fact that his DuPont Chevrolet was one of the fastest cars in the field, the incidents had cost him laps to the leaders. Luck appeared to have abandoned the rainbow-hued team.

The event entered its final 100 laps with Earnhardt clearly a contender for victory and Ward Burton rocketing along in a contending position in his black Pontiac. But any fans who wondered if it would be a "boring" finish would shortly be answered with a resounding "No"!

The drama began on lap 327 when Earnhardt hit pit road under green while running sixth. One of the orange-painted lug nuts on a replacement tire fell off, so the tire-changer slapped a black replacement on with a healthy "brraaap" of the air wrench. Because it was the same color as the black wheel well, a NASCAR inspector, eye-balling the tire to make sure all the lug nuts were on, saw only four orange-colored lug nuts. After Earnhardt was back on the track, he was shown the black flag to return to have the lug nuts inspected. Dale headed back to pit road. When he stopped, it was clear that all five lug nuts were on the wheel. He was waved back into action, but the stop had cost him a lap and dropped him from his contending sixth position to 14th.

NASCAR immediately began searching for a way to remedy the situation with equity and made the decision to display the caution flag. It was an unprecedented move: NASCAR would allow Earnhardt to make up the lost lap. During the caution, however, Dale and three other drivers pitted for fresh tires, willing to go to the end of the longest line of cars on the track for violating the "closed pits" flag displayed during the initial laps of the yellow. NASCAR then allowed all teams who desired to change tires to do so, so all would be on equal footing for the upcoming green flag. Officials lined the cars up in the order they were in before the caution flag and made preparations to restart the race with nine laps to go.

Earnhardt lined up eighth for the restart and was able to pick up a single spot in the remaining laps. Gordon finished 20th, two laps behind. Earnhardt had gained another 43 points in his desperate chase of the young point leader.

At the front of the field for the restart was Ward Burton. Within the young Virginian's grasp was not only his first

Kyle Petty celebrated Halloween with this special paint job, featuring a jack-o'-lantern designed by his daughter, Montgomery Lee. But Kyle's car turned into a pumpkin late in the race, relegating him to a disappointing 32nd-place finish.

NASCAR Winston Cup victory, but also the first for the Bill Davis team he had joined just a few races ago. In Burton's mirror, however, were two of the hardest chargers in the business — Rusty Wallace and Mark Martin — and Burton knew that both Ford drivers would make every effort to dislodge his Pontiac from the point.

Ward eyed the green flag and mashed the pedal to the mat. He jumped to an early lead on the restart and found that neither Martin, looking for his third-consecutive Cup victory, nor Wallace, hoping to win his third race of the season, could catch the green and black Poncho. Ward kept his wits about himself and drove off to a popular 1.9-second victory. Wallace took second place, ahead of Martin and Terry Labonte, while Ward's younger brother, Jeff, took his Stavola Brothers Ford to a fine fifth place. Sterling Marlin was sixth, just ahead of Earnhardt, while Ricky Craven survived a brush with Darrell Waltrip on the final lap to place eighth. In the last corner, Waltrip and Craven had come together, with Darrell collecting Gordon in the aftermath. The mishap dropped Darrell to 12th place when Nemechek and Bill Elliott flashed past to claim the final positions in the top 10.

Ward Burton took the lead in the ACDelco 400 with 60 laps remaining and never relinquished his point position, nailing down his first career NASCAR Winston Cup victory. It was also the first for the team and its owner, Bill Davis.

ACDelco 400
Race #29 — Final Race Results

Fin. Pos.	Str. Pos.	Car #	Driver	Team
1	3	22	Ward Burton	MBNA America Pontiac
2	18	2	Rusty Wallace	Miller Genuine Draft Ford
3	5	6	Mark Martin	Valvoline Ford
4	13	5	Terry Labonte	Kellogg's Chevrolet
5	32	8	Jeff Burton	Raybestos Brakes Ford
6	28	4	Sterling Marlin	Kodak Film Chevrolet
7	20	3	Dale Earnhardt	Goodwrench Service Chevrolet
8	21	41	Ricky Craven	Kodiak Chevrolet
9	9	87	Joe Nemechek	Burger King Chevrolet
10	23	94	Bill Elliott	McDonald's Ford
11	19	98	Jeremy Mayfield	RCA Ford
12	8	17	Darrell Waltrip	Western Auto Chevrolet
13	7	10	Ricky Rudd	Tide Ford
14	31	29	Steve Grissom	Meineke Chevrolet
15	22	7	Geoff Bodine	Exide Batteries Ford
16	6	15	Dick Trickle	Ford Quality Care Ford
17	33	75	Todd Bodine	Factory Stores Ford
18	11	21	Morgan Shepherd	Citgo Ford
19	10	12	Derrike Cope	Straight Arrow Ford
20	4	24	Jeff Gordon	DuPont Auto Finishes Chevrolet
21	26	77	Bobby Hillin	Jasper/USAir Ford
22	37	16	Ted Musgrave	The Family Channel Ford
23	27	28	Dale Jarrett	Texaco Havoline Ford
24	39	9	Lake Speed	Spam/Melling Ford
25	14	37	John Andretti	Kmart/Little Caesars Ford
26	34	23	Jimmy Spencer	Smokin' Joe's Ford
27	36	11	Brett Bodine	Lowe's Ford
28	1	26	Hut Stricklin	Quaker State Ford
29	25	33	Robert Pressley	Skoal Bandit Chevrolet
30	17	43	Bobby Hamilton	STP Pontiac
31	35	27	Elton Sawyer	Hooters Ford
32	15	42	Kyle Petty	Coors Light Pontiac
33	24	25	Ken Schrader	Budweiser Chevrolet
34	16	1	Rick Mast	Skoal Ford
35	12	31	Gary Bradberry	Hardee's Chevrolet
36	40	40	Shane Hall	Kendall Pontiac
37	38	32	Greg Sacks	ATS Wood Products Chevrolet
38	2	30	Michael Waltrip	Pennzoil Pontiac
39	30	90	Mike Wallace	Heilig-Meyers Ford
40	29	18	Bobby Labonte	Interstate Batteries Chevrolet

DURA-LUBE 500

PHOENIX INTERNATIONAL RACEWAY

OCTOBER 29, 1995

•••••

When the NASCAR Winston Cup circuit first came to Buddy Jobe's Phoenix International Raceway in 1988 (Alan Kulwicki broke through in that race to post his first career victory and complete his self-titled "Polish Victory Lap"), a huge question mark hung over the event. Would Phoenix really be a place where fans would turn out to see the NASCAR Winston Cuppers compete? Well, since that first full-fledged race, the event in the Valley of the Sun has given competitors, officials and fans plenty of reasons to visit the one-mile track.

Spectators have come to love the saguaro cactus-dotted Sonoran Desert, the red rocks of Sedona's artsy area and the indescribable beauty of the Grand Canyon, located just a couple of hours north. A shuttle plane ride away is the glitter of Las Vegas, and the Phoenix/Scottsdale area boasts some of the finest golf courses in the country — emerald islands surrounded by the desert wasteland.

More importantly, the fans at the one-mile track have created a special atmosphere in which the NASCAR Winston Cup drivers and officials enjoy plying their trade. The tens of thousands of fans who pile into the expanded grandstands are among the most knowledgeable of any stop on the tour.

Any questions concerning the viability of Phoenix International Raceway in 1988 could readily be answered with this photograph, taken at the 1995 Dura-Lube 500. This year, well over 100,000 spectators packed into the stands and onto the hillside to watch Ricky Rudd (right) capture his first win of the season. Rudd was clearly delighted to visit victory lane once again, and with good reason. With the victory, Rudd extended his streak of consecutive winning seasons to 13.

The gamble by Jobe and NASCAR in 1988 has resulted in the largest crowds in the history of the state of Arizona ever to attend a sporting event. Jobe's ongoing improvements of the modified oval continue to make the track one of the best in the sport. This year, well over 100,000 packed into the stands and the terraced hillside outside the fourth turn to see the newly named Dura-Lube 500.

Two drivers, however, paid no attention to the golf courses, the desert, the dog track or any of the other attractions in the Valley of the Sun. It was all business in the Dale Earnhardt and Jeff Gordon camps; both viewed the Dura-Lube 500 as the pivotal event in the final stages of the battle for the NASCAR Winston Cup championship.

Earnhardt had gobbled huge chunks of Gordon's seemingly unassailable point lead in the last two events at Charlotte and Rockingham and strode into the Sonoran Desert trailing by 162. To have any chance of winning a record eighth championship and becoming only the second driver in the history of the sport to win three consecutive titles, he needed another big gain in points at Phoenix and a big helping at Atlanta in the season finale. True, it would be an uphill battle, but he had gained 140 in the last two races, and if he could add just a few more in each of the last two events, he would be able to complete the most historic come-from-behind victory in NASCAR's storied history.

(Above) All eyes were glued to these two particular machines. Jeff Gordon (24) desperately needed a good finish to end a two-race slide in the point standings, and Dale Earnhardt just as badly needed a strong run to sustain his championship hopes. Earnhardt also needed Jeff to have some problems, but it was not to be; Gordon finished fifth, only two slots behind Earnhardt. (Left) Ernie Irvan (88) was back in the saddle at Phoenix, and did he ever let Dale Earnhardt know it! Apparently, Irvan's pre-race huddle with interim crew chief Todd Parrott (inset) was a resounding success; his Havoline Ford was dialed in perfectly for the first two-thirds of the race. Visions of a Phoenix victory lane visit, however, literally went up in smoke when his engine blew after 197 laps.

Young Gordon and his equally youthful DuPont team came to Phoenix needing a solid race to stop a two-race skid during which their point lead had dwindled from 302 (after North Wilkesboro) to 162. The rainbow-hued team was still in command of the point race, however, and a strong finish in the desert would all but lock up the championship. Gordon and the DuPont team could also cement the championship right here, with one race remaining on the schedule, if Earnhardt and his Goodwrench team had problems.

The two teams' strategies were clear from the minute they unloaded in the garage area. Earnhardt would go to the front and chase every available point. Gordon would be just as determined and run the race with the goal of keeping the black No. 3 in sight. Gordon's object was to finish. If, late in the race, he got a chance to win, fine. If not, he would take the best finish he could. It was too late in the game for the DuPont team to employ kamikaze tactics.

Although the fans focused on the black and blue teams

stopped by Junie Donlavey's transporter to congratulate Mike Wallace. Two days after the Rockingham event, Mike and wife Carla had welcomed little Matthew Ryan to the family, which already includes Lindsey and Christina.

Elton Sawyer and crew chief Mike Hill were wearing smiles almost as big as the one on Mike's face. The pair had put together a package with Batesville, Ark., attorney David Blair and his wife, Suzanne, to purchase the "27" team from Junior Johnson and Hooters' Bob Brooks. The sale would become final on November 15. Junior said he was still negotiating with Brett Bodine, who wanted to purchase the "11" team from Johnson's company. Further up the aisle in the newly named Dick Beaty Garage (in honor of NASCAR's former "Top Cop," who had been enormously respected as one of the fairest and firmest NASCAR Winston Cup Directors in NASCAR history prior to his recent retirement), Terry Labonte and crew chief Gary DeHart had their own reasons to smile. Both

When Ernie Irvan's domination ended with a blown engine, Derrike Cope (12) was among those who forged to the front. Worn left-side tires were Cope's downfall, however; he had to fend off Dale Earnhardt for second while Ricky Rudd surged to the win. Rusty Wallace, in the Miller Genuine Draft Ford, followed Dale across in fourth place, and Ted Musgrave (16) finished sixth.

in practice, another black car commanded its share of attention. Ernie Irvan was back for his second NASCAR Winston Cup race (he had skipped Charlotte and failed to make the Rockingham field due to circumstances that included weather and a practice mishap).

Ernie's finishes in the NASCAR SuperTruck Series events since the North Wilkesboro race had proven he was on form, and everyone expected him to make the race at Phoenix and run to the front.

As teams made their chassis changes from practice to qualifying trim, drivers, crew members and car owners

had extended their contracts with Hendrick Motorsports for five more years.

With 50 cars on hand, it was clear that many teams would be happy simply to make the field and that several would be extremely disappointed when qualifying was completed. When the final field was determined, Bill Elliott and A.J. Foyt illustrated the extremes.

With a lap that he later said "wasn't a very good one," Elliott won his second pole position of the season. When he faced reporters after qualifying, the Redhead said he was pleased for his team and for sponsor McDonald's but

that his heart was really in Houston, where his nephew Casey (older brother Ernie's son) was receiving treatment for an extended illness.

The Georgian's lap barely beat Earnhardt's mark on the track. Gordon, meanwhile, proved his team had not taken the conservative route by recording the third-fastest lap in qualifying and plunking the Rainbow Machine on the inside of the second row. Rick Mast would start alongside Gordon. Mark Martin and Rusty Wallace made up the third row in their Fords, and Brett Bodine barely bested Bobby Hamilton for the inside of the fourth row. Morgan Shepherd and Kyle Petty (whose Pontiac featured the pumpkin designed by his daughter, Montgomery Lee) were the last of the top-10 qualifiers, just a tick better than Robert Pressley and Ted Musgrave.

When the field was set based on time trials, Geoff Bodine and Ricky Craven, along with Todd Bodine and new daddy Mike Wallace, used provisionals to make the field, as did NASCAR Winston West competitors Doug George and Ernie Cope (Derrike's cousin).

For the second time this year, Foyt carried Motorola sponsorship but failed to make the field. His time was the 40th-fastest, but he had no provisionals at his disposal. The 61-year-old driver was disappointed but indicated he would try again at future events.

Others who failed to make the field were Chad Little, Mike Bliss, Shane Hall (in Dick Brooks' Pontiac), Scott Gaylord, Wayne Jacks, L.J. Pryor and Rich Woodland Jr.

For the first two-thirds of the race, it seemed to onlookers that they had been transported back in time. Irvan, whose Havoline Ford was dialed in perfectly, fought hammer and tongs with Earnhardt at the front of the field and established the Ford as the dominant car in the event. Equally stunning was the fact that he was performing these deeds with his backup car — the same one he had driven at North Wilkesboro — he had damaged his primary machine in a practice accident. Irvan simply was sensational at the front of the field, especially when one considered that he was running at the point with two tires much less fresh than those on the cars chasing him.

Dreams of a Phoenix victory, however, went up in a cloud of smoke when the engine in the Thunderbird let go. Although Ernie had led the most laps in the race and grabbed the Gatorade Front-Runner Award, his race was over. He coasted into the garage after 197 laps, the engine in the black Ford silent.

Bill Elliott (94) did his first-year team proud by snagging the pole for the Dura-Lube 500. Although Mark Martin (6) was behind Elliott at the start (he qualified fifth), he had passed him by the finish. Martin came home eighth, six places ahead of 14th-place finisher Elliott.

Boys will be boys! Forget the race, forget the title, forget everything that's at stake — when it comes right down to it, there's always time for a little leg-pulling! Veteran Dale Earnhardt lays his best line on Jeff Gordon while DuPont crew chief Ray Evernham looks on warily. Newcomer Gordon proves he learns fast off the track, too — by keeping his mouth shut!

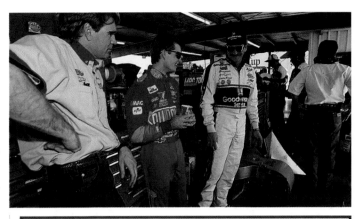

At that point, the race took on a totally different look — Ricky Rudd and Derrike Cope forged to the lead. As the last 100 laps wound down, it became clear that the Phoenix track would welcome a new winner to its victory lane when the 312 laps had been completed. The question was, would it be Rudd, trying to capture his first win this year, or Cope, hoping to bring Bobby Allison's team its first victory in its six years of existence?

The fans in the stands were torn: Who should they pull for in the closing laps? Rudd was trying to extend a string of 12 consecutive winning years, second only to Earnhardt's 14-year mark. Cope hadn't won since 1991, and a win for the Straight Arrow-sponsored Thunderbirds would be just the tonic the team needed.

In the end, it came down to left-side tires, and Cope found himself on left-sides that were much more worn than Rudd's. Ricky pulled away to a half-second victory to extend his streak to 13 consecutive seasons. Derrike, who found himself in a dogfight with Earnhardt for second place in the final three laps, managed to hold off the Goodwrench Chevrolet by a half-car-length to claim the runner-up position behind Rudd.

Earnhardt had done as much as he could in the desert. He had led the race and taken third place (his ninth-consecutive top-10 finish, all but three of which were top threes). Yet, as he flashed across the line, he merely had to look in his mirror to watch his hopes for an eighth championship evaporate.

Finishing two positions behind him was the rainbow-painted DuPont car. Gordon had done exactly what he had needed to do. He had raced with Earnhardt throughout the day and several times had viewed the black No. 3 in his mirror, rather than out his windshield. In the closing laps, he had carried what his team had considered a 15th-place car to fifth place, and by doing so, he had all but locked up the championship. True, Earnhardt had gained 15 points on Gordon at Phoenix, but Jeff would now go to Atlanta with a 147-point lead, a virtually unassailable margin.

After running at the front of the field throughout the afternoon, Rusty Wallace finished a strong fourth. Musgrave brought his Family Channel Ford home in sixth place, ahead of Morgan Shepherd, who posted his first top-10 finish since the Brickyard 400.

Martin came home eighth, ahead of Mast and Ken Schrader, who just beat Dale Jarrett and Sterling Marlin to the line to claim the final position in the top 10.

Gordon and his team, led by crew chief Ray Evernham, weren't celebrating yet. One event remained, and anything could happen. The corks weren't popped, but the scent of victory champagne was heavy in the desert air.

Dura-Lube 500
Race #30 — Final Race Results

Fin. Pos.	Str. Pos.	Car #	Driver	Team
1	29	10	Ricky Rudd	Tide Ford
2	18	12	Derrike Cope	Straight Arrow Ford
3	2	3	Dale Earnhardt	Goodwrench Service Chevrolet
4	6	2	Rusty Wallace	Miller Genuine Draft Ford
5	3	24	Jeff Gordon	DuPont Auto Finishes Chevrolet
6	12	16	Ted Musgrave	The Family Channel Ford
7	9	21	Morgan Shepherd	Citgo Ford
8	5	6	Mark Martin	Valvoline Ford
9	4	1	Rick Mast	Skoal Ford
10	15	25	Ken Schrader	Budweiser Chevrolet
11	26	28	Dale Jarrett	Texaco Havoline Ford
12	20	4	Sterling Marlin	Kodak Film Chevrolet
13	16	5	Terry Labonte	Kellogg's Chevrolet
14	1	94	Bill Elliott	McDonald's Ford
15	13	37	John Andretti	Kmart/Little Caesars Ford
16	39	7	Geoff Bodine	Exide Batteries Ford
17	7	11	Brett Bodine	Lowe's Ford
18	35	87	Joe Nemechek	Burger King Chevrolet
19	11	33	Robert Pressley	Skoal Bandit Chevrolet
20	17	98	Jeremy Mayfield	RCA Ford
21	38	77	Bobby Hillin	Jasper/USAir Ford
22	31	9	Lake Speed	Spam/Melling Ford
23	25	8	Jeff Burton	Raybestos Brakes Ford
24	40	41	Ricky Craven	Kodiak Chevrolet
25	41	75	Todd Bodine	Factory Stores Ford
26	27	81	Kenny Wallace	TIC Financial Ford
27	36	45	Ron Hornaday Jr.	TootsieToy Chevrolet
28	30	71	Dave Marcis	Prodigy Chevrolet
29	32	15	Dick Trickle	Ford Quality Care Ford
30	24	27	Elton Sawyer	Hooters Ford
31	8	43	Bobby Hamilton	STP Pontiac
32	33	29	Steve Grissom	Meineke Chevrolet
33	28	23	Jimmy Spencer	Smokin' Joe's Ford
34	37	30	Michael Waltrip	Pennzoil Pontiac
35	19	26	Hut Stricklin	Quaker State Ford
36	42	90	Mike Wallace	Heilig-Meyers Ford
37	23	18	Bobby Labonte	Interstate Batteries Chevrolet
38	21	17	Darrell Waltrip	Western Auto Chevrolet
39	10	42	Kyle Petty	Coors Light Pontiac
40	14	88	Ernie Irvan	Texaco Havoline Ford
41	43	07	Doug George	RaceStuff/Olson Technology Ford
42	34	22	Ward Burton	MBNA America Pontiac
43	22	32	Greg Sacks	Dura Lube Chevrolet
44	44	19	Ernie Cope	Straight Arrow Chevrolet

NAPA 500

ATLANTA MOTOR SPEEDWAY
NOVEMBER 12, 1995
•••••

With two weeks between the Phoenix race and the season-ending NAPA 500 at Atlanta Motor Speedway, there would be no excuses regarding preparation for the final race of the year. There was plenty of time for the crews to fine-tune machinery and for the engine development shops to put the finishing touches on the qualifying and race engines for the contending teams.

Jeff Gordon's DuPont team, nearing the first NASCAR Winston Cup championship in the history of Hendrick Motorsports — which started in 1985 with a similarly named driver, Geoff Bodine — left nothing to chance. On its way home from Phoenix, the team unloaded no fewer than three Chevrolet Monte Carlos for a rain-abbreviated test session at Atlanta. When the cars were loaded back onto the transporters, Gordon and crew chief Ray Evernham said they were ready for the NAPA 500 weekend.

Missing from the Atlanta garage during the testing sessions was the black Goodwrench Chevrolet and driver Dale Earnhardt. Dale and car owner Richard Childress were confident the car they planned to bring to the 1.5-mile oval would be ready to race. No testing was needed.

For Earnhardt and Childress, the battle was all but concluded. They had put together a brilliant stretch run that included nine consecutive top-10 finishes and posted an average finishing position of 3.77 during those nine races (Gordon's

*Dale Earnhardt captured the gold with an Olympic effort in the NAPA 500. Marlin's sterling performance earned him the silver medal and moved him into third place in the final point standings, and Wallace showed no signs of being rusty as he continued his late-season surge to take the bronze. But the day belonged to a jubilant Jeff Gordon **(right)**. He may have been disappointed with his 32nd-place finish in the race, but it was more than enough to lock up the 1995 NASCAR Winston Cup Championship.*

Dale Earnhardt slips his Goodwrench Chevrolet past Ricky Rudd's Tide Ford on lap 17 to take the lead for the first time in the race as pole-winner Darrell Waltrip runs solidly in third. Dale would relinquish the lead only during rounds of green-flag pit stops and lead 268 of the race's 328 laps while averaging a track-record 163.633 mph. Dale may have fallen short in his bid for the championship, but his dominating performance in the NAPA 500 served notice of his intentions in '96!

average finishing position during that same time frame was 8.77). Dale had chopped 155 points off Gordon's lead of 302 during the string of events, but it had not been enough to pull the seven-time champion into the position he wanted — close enough to really apply the heat to Gordon and his young and relatively inexperienced team.

Instead, Earnhardt now headed for Bruton Smith's Atlanta track knowing exactly what he had to do. Earnhardt had to win the race and lead the most laps — gaining every single point he could for the event. At the same time, he had to hope that something untoward would happen to Gordon so that Jeff would finish dead last in the maximum 42-car field. If Gordon finished 41st or if he led a single lap, the title would go to the DuPont team.

It was a combination of circumstances that was remote, at best. And it became even more remote in the days prior to the race, when team owner Rick Hendrick filed entries for another pair of cars — one to be driven by Jimmy Horton and one by Jack Sprague. If either or both made the field, they could be ordered to the garage on the first lap of the race by the team owner, thus ensuring Gordon the championship.

Like nearly every other track on the tour, the face of Atlanta Motor Speedway continues to change and improve. The first steps toward "flopping" the track were evident when the teams unloaded at the track. A new, 20,000-seat grandstand, topped by a row of corporate hos-

pitality suites, stared down at teams from the beginning of the current backstretch. Once the Centennial Olympics in Atlanta are finished in the summer of '96, construction crews will become more readily available to track General Manager Ed Clark. He will then oversee the completion of construction of a new garage area, pit road, seats, suites, control tower and other buildings, and the current backstretch will become the frontstretch. It is a large task, but the number of improvements made to Atlanta during the past two years indicates that Clark is more than capable of turning the oval into one of the premier facilities in the country.

Usually, the "Silly Season" peaks at Charlotte Motor Speedway, but this year, the site of several sponsor announcements regarding the coming season was Atlanta. Healthsource will step up to the plate next season for a full year of action as the primary sponsor of Tri-Star Motorsports and driver Loy Allen. Jeff Hammond, with the Dick Brooks team earlier this year, will become the new crew chief for the Tri-Star effort.

Robert Yates' second team, led by driver Dale Jarrett and crew chief Todd Parrott, will carry Ford's Quality Care and Red Carpet Lease colors for 1996 and beyond. While Jarrett and his teammates were celebrating the new red, white and blue colors on the "88" Thunderbird, Steve Grissom and his Diamond Ridge mates were delighted to show off their new yellow Chevrolet, complete with Hanna-Barbera cartoon characters. Diamond Ridge's

NASCAR Busch Series effort would also be backed by a Ted Turner-owned company; Grissom would pilot machinery carrying World Championship Wrestling colors in 1996.

Butch Mock's Factory Stores of America team made it official: Morgan Shepherd would drive for the Ford effort in 1996 (Todd Bodine would be released from his duties after the Atlanta race). Shepherd and Mock would join together with new primary sponsor Remington Arms Company for the coming season. Factory Stores would remain with Mock's team, but in an associate sponsor's role.

Needless to say, the media members present for the weekend had plenty to write about. There was the young team about to claim its first championship. There was the veteran team (favored to win the title at the beginning of the season) in a back-to-the-wall position and with a very slim chance of claiming a third-consecutive championship. There were new sponsors to welcome into the fold.

And when the first round of qualifying had been completed, there was yet another story to be told. An old favorite was back at the head of the list — a position from which he had been missing for two years. There are few better stories to write than when Darrell Waltrip sneaks up on the field and springs one of his surprises, and that's exactly what happened.

Morgan Shepherd's Citgo Ford (right) caught the fans' attention with this promotional paint scheme for the new James Bond movie, "Goldeneye." Rusty Wallace (below) used the season-capper to premiere the '96 colors for the Miller Ford — sans Genuine Draft.

clear that, despite his time away from the pole-winner's microphone, Darrell had not lost his touch. He was full of quips and quotes. "Just didn't want people to think that I was too old to get down there to the interview room fast," he grinned before popping through the door.

The second row was made up of Bobby Hamilton and Dick Trickle, who was starting perhaps his final race in a Bud Moore Ford. Jeremy Mayfield surprised many by claiming the inside of the third row, with Rusty Wallace alongside. Michael Waltrip prepared for his final race in the Pennzoil Pontiac by notching the seventh-fastest lap, and Gordon grabbed the eighth-fastest lap in the session in his DuPont Chevrolet. Mark Martin and Ricky Craven claimed the final spots in the top 10, with Craven beating Earnhardt for 10th place by .012 of a second.

For yet another weekend, rain played a role in the starting grid for a NASCAR Winston Cup race: Saturday's second round of qualifying was weathered out. The final portion of the field was determined by Friday's times, forcing Grissom, Robert Pressley, Todd Bodine and Kyle Petty to use provisionals to make the field. It also meant that several drivers, including Shane Hall and Mike Wallace, were forced to watch the final race of the season from the sidelines. Although Sprague did not make the field with his qualifying lap, Horton did, giving the Hendrick forces the single "extra" car in the field they needed, should push come to shove. Later on Saturday afternoon, however, Horton was injured in an accident in the year-ending ARCA race, so Jeff Purvis started Sunday's race in the white Chevrolet.

Then, after 10 months of criss-crossing the country and with more than 11,000 racing miles behind them, drivers belted into their cars Sunday afternoon to determine the outcome of the NAPA 500.

In the first round, Darrell claimed the 17th pole position of the season for the Monte Carlos! His lap was just .020 of a second faster than Ricky Rudd's, but it might as well have been two minutes quicker. Darrell was delighted and wasted no time whipping from the garage area to the infield media center for his interview. It was immediately

Darrell Waltrip sat on the pole, literally, for the first time since April 1992 after turning a qualifying lap of 185.046 mph in his Western Auto Monte Carlo. It was the lift he and his team needed to vault them into the '96 season after a disappointing 1995: Darrell finished 19th in the final point standings with four top-five and eight top-10 finishes.

The issues were settled early in the race. Clearly, Earnhardt was ready to do what he needed to do. He rocketed through the field after the drop of the green flag and headed for the point. Like every other driver in the field, Gordon could only watch as the black Chevrolet reached the front.

During the first round of green-flag pit stops, Gordon stayed out longer than the others in the front pack and led the single lap he needed to clinch the championship. With a banner raised behind his crew on pit road, Evernham called on the radio to his driver: "Okay, let's pit next time by for tires and fuel, Champ." Dutifully, Gordon headed for pit road. The NASCAR Winston Cup title was his no matter how he finished in the race.

Further down pit road, Earnhardt was determined to end the season in winning form, title or not. It was a bittersweet race for Dale and his team. Crew chief Andy Petree would leave the team the Monday morning following the race, headed back to Leo Jackson's team to become a part-owner of the Skoal-sponsored car driven by Robert Pressley. In his three years with Earnhardt and Childress, Petree had quarterbacked a pair of NASCAR Winston Cup titles as well as this year's second place. It would be a difficult parting for all, so this Sunday afternoon, everyone was determined to end their association with a victory.

The seven-time champion put the black Chevrolet on cruise control — much as he had in September at Martinsville — and simply drove away from the field. No one had anything for Earnhardt at Atlanta; he went on to lead 268 of the 328 laps. It was vintage Earnhardt; when the old-fashioned whipping was over (just a pair of caution flags had slowed the race for 11 laps), only six cars remained on the lead lap. It was Dale's seventh win at the track — tying him with Cale Yarborough for the all-time lead — and the 68th win of his career.

After leading the lap he needed to clinch the crown, Gordon struggled throughout the race. Finally, his team decided to just enjoy the last race of the year and, during one of the last stops of the day, Evernham and Hendrick, among others behind the pit wall, did something they had always wanted to do. Evernham became the tire-changer and Hendrick the windshield cleaner. Other non-regular crew members manned the jack and carried the tires. It was fantasy time and, when the stop was completed (some 39-plus seconds), Gordon was laughing so hard he could hardly contain himself. He headed back to the track to complete the event and, when the final run-down was handed out, he was classified 32nd, 14 laps behind Earnhardt. It hardly mattered.

The point margin at the end of the year stood at 34 points; once again, the championship had been decided by bonus points. Gordon had led early and often in races throughout the season and compiled 64 more bonus points than Earnhardt, more than enough to wrest the title

from the proud champion. It would be a factor Dale would mull over continuously in the weeks before the 1996 season began at Daytona Beach.

Sterling Marlin had a superb run to second place at Atlanta which, when combined with Mark Martin's problems with his Valvoline Thunderbird, allowed him to move into third place in the final point standings. Mark's problems turned out to be very costly. The difference between third and fourth place in the final point standings was $110,000.

Rusty Wallace charged to third place at Atlanta, cementing his fifth place in the final standings, while Bill Elliott moved to eighth place in the final points with the help of his fourth-place finish in the race. Ward Burton was fifth at Atlanta, underscoring the growing competitiveness of Bill Davis' MBNA Pontiac team, and Jimmy Spencer, with the last car on the lead lap, claimed his best finish of the season by taking sixth place.

Ernie Irvan, who had a brilliant run going in the second Yates car (he had climbed all the way to second place before fading to fourth in the final laps), ran out of gas with six laps to go and was forced to pit for a splash of fuel. He finished seventh, ahead of Bobby Labonte and Bobby Hillin, who posted his best finish of the season. Ricky Rudd held on for 10th place after a late-race battle with Geoff Bodine.

In the final point standings, Terry Labonte finished sixth ahead of Ted Musgrave. Rudd grabbed ninth place behind Elliott. Bobby Labonte was 10th in the final standings for the season, claiming the final position on the stage at the Waldorf-Astoria. Robert Pressley fell out of the race early, handing the MAXX Rookie of the Year title to Ricky Craven after a year-long battle that had come down to the final event of the year.

Earnhardt had done all that he could. He had dominated the race and scored the maximum number of points, but the cagey veteran could not prevent Gordon from claiming the title. As Dale stood in the garage area, facing the cameras and notepads, Gordon, Hendrick and Evernham climbed aboard the red and white-decorated flatbed truck at the start/finish line. They were about to take the traditional lap of honor.

At the beginning of the year, they were the longest of long-shots to win the crown.

Now, 10 months later, they were the 1995 NASCAR Winston Cup Champions.

Dreams really do come true.

NAPA 500

Race #31 — Final Race Results

Fin. Pos.	Str. Pos.	Car #	Driver	Team
1	11	3	Dale Earnhardt	Goodwrench Service Chevrolet
2	18	4	Sterling Marlin	Kodak Film Chevrolet
3	6	2	Rusty Wallace	Miller Ford
4	15	94	Bill Elliott	McDonald's Ford
5	31	22	Ward Burton	MBNA America Pontiac
6	37	23	Jimmy Spencer	Smokin' Joe's Ford
7	26	88	Ernie Irvan	Texaco Havoline Ford
8	21	18	Bobby Labonte	Interstate Batteries Chevrolet
9	35	77	Bobby Hillin	Jasper/USAir Ford
10	2	10	Ricky Rudd	Tide Ford
11	16	7	Geoff Bodine	Exide Batteries Ford
12	7	30	Michael Waltrip	Pennzoil Pontiac
13	12	5	Terry Labonte	Kellogg's Chevrolet
14	28	87	Joe Nemechek	Burger King Chevrolet
15	22	37	John Andretti	Kmart/Little Caesars Ford
16	1	17	Darrell Waltrip	Western Auto Chevrolet
17	9	6	Mark Martin	Valvoline Ford
18	5	98	Jeremy Mayfield	RCA Ford
19	36	9	Lake Speed	Spam/Melling Ford
20	20	11	Brett Bodine	Lowe's Ford
21	13	1	Rick Mast	Skoal Ford
22	33	21	Morgan Shepherd	Citgo Ford
23	4	15	Dick Trickle	Ford Quality Care Ford
24	25	19	Loy Allen	Healthsource Health Plan Ford
25	3	43	Bobby Hamilton	STP Pontiac
26	34	58	Jeff Purvis	Leukemia Society Chevrolet
27	17	16	Ted Musgrave	The Family Channel Ford
28	27	27	Elton Sawyer	Hooters Ford
29	23	31	Gary Bradberry	Hardee's Chevrolet
30	10	41	Ricky Craven	Kodiak Chevrolet
31	38	28	Dale Jarrett	Texaco Havoline Ford
32	8	24	Jeff Gordon	DuPont Auto Finishes Chevrolet
33	41	42	Kyle Petty	Coors Light Pontiac
34	30	32	Greg Sacks	Active Motorsports Chevrolet
35	24	12	Derrike Cope	Straight Arrow Ford
36	19	8	Jeff Burton	Raybestos Brakes Ford
37	29	71	Dave Marcis	Olive Garden Chevrolet
38	14	26	Hut Stricklin	Quaker State Ford
39	39	29	Steve Grissom	Meineke Chevrolet
40	42	75	Todd Bodine	Factory Stores Ford
41	40	33	Robert Pressley	Skoal Bandit Chevrolet
42	32	25	Ken Schrader	Budweiser Chevrolet

REFLECTIONS

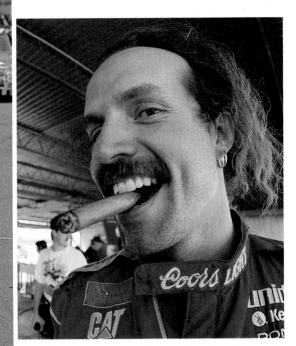

(Above) Kyle Petty celebrates his win at Dover with a big grin and a big stogie. During the year, Kyle recorded one top five and five top 10s. Kyle will again drive for SABCO in '96, but he'll be surrounded by an all-new supporting cast, many of whom are former Penske South crew members.

(Opposite Page) Is the sun rising on a new NASCAR Winston Cup era? Just ask Dale Earnhardt. Fifteen years ago, he had been the upstart driver who stole a championship, but the tables were turned on him this year when newcomer Jeff Gordon captured his first Winston Cup at Earnhardt's expense. And Gordon is just one of a slew of talented young drivers beginning to emerge on the stock car racing scene.

(Above) Here, Geoff Bodine (7) is leading the pack at New Hampshire, but it was not to be his day: He was eliminated from the race by an accident less than 40 laps from the finish. Those trailing him, however, were destined for glory: Mark Martin (6) finished third, and Jeff Gordon (24) finished first and stole the point lead from Sterling Marlin.

(Right) A welcome sight for thousands of Ernie Irvan fans: Ernie back in uniform. Completing his comeback from a devastating practice accident at Michigan, Irvan competed in both the NASCAR Winston Cup and SuperTruck events at North Wilkesboro in October. Next year, Irvan will resume his role as Yates' primary driver, and Dale Jarrett, thanks to his great performance in Ernie's absence, will drive the team's second car.

(Above) Former NASCAR Winston Cup champion and current television announcer Benny Parsons had, without a doubt, the best seat in the house for the September Darlington event. Heilig-Meyers was gracious enough to provide Benny with a throne fit for a king so he could continue his color commentary in comfort.

(Left) Rookie Ricky Craven splashed onto the NASCAR Winston Cup scene in February with backing from Kodiak and immediately became embroiled in a heated battle for the Rookie of the Year title with fellow freshman Robert Pressley (who drove the Skoal Bandit). On the strength of four top-10 finishes, Craven clinched the crown. He hopes to carry that momentum into the '96 season.

(Above) NASCAR Winston Cup fans were quick to criticize the government for meddling with the tobacco industry and just as quick to defend both Winston and NASCAR. In a show of support for their much-loved sport, fans wearing T-shirts such as these cropped up in garage areas and grandstands around the country.

(Right) Jimmy Hensley was more than happy to don this driver's suit at the June Dover event after Western Auto's regular, Darrell Waltrip, bowed out less than six laps into the race. Darrell, who had been injured in The Winston Select, had had to use a provisional to get into the Dover field, but his replacement made the best of it. Hensley climbed 19 positions during the race and finished 20th.

(Inset) Like father, like son ... Matthew Martin looks like an old pro behind the wheel, but he clearly is not content with just any ride — only a Monster Truck will do! Although Dad (below) had only a stock car at his disposal, he managed to notch the victory — his second win of the season — at Watkins Glen.

(Above) Honeymooners Michael and Buffy Waltrip have good reason to look forward to their second year together. Michael will take over Morgan Shepherd's ride in the Citgo Ford in 1996 and is anxious to work with the famed Wood Brothers.

(Left) Lake Speed recorded two top-10 finishes in 1995 for his first-year team. Speed will return to his dual role of team manager and driver in 1996 and has high hopes for the upcoming season now that the "learning year" is behind him.

(Below) With his Phoenix victory, Ricky Rudd extended his streak of winning at least once every year to 13 seasons (he is topped only by Dale Earnhardt, who boasts 14 winning seasons in a row). The Phoenix win was also memorable because it was Rudd's last with crew chief Bill Ingle, who left the team at the conclusion of the '95 season.

(Above) Elton Sawyer, who's already made a name for himself in the Busch Series (he finished ninth in 1995 with two top fives and nine top 10s), hopes to do the same in the NASCAR Winston Cup Series. Sawyer was named to drive the Hooters Ford at the spring Martinsville race and will continue to drive the machine next year for new owners David and Suzanne Blair.

214

AUTOGRAPHS

UMI publishes the Official NASCAR Preview and Press Guide.
For subscription information phone 1-704-374-0420.